THE
HISTORY OF
FRANCE

THE
HISTORY OF
FRANCE

W. Scott Haine

The Greenwood Histories of the Modern Nations
Frank W. Thackeray and John E. Findling, Series Editors

Greenwood Press
Westport, Connecticut • London

Library of Congress Cataloging-in-Publication Data

Haine, W. Scott.
  The history of France / W. Scott Haine.
      p. cm.—(Greenwood histories of the modern nations, ISSN 1096–2905)
    Includes bibliographical references and index.
    ISBN 0–313–30328–2 (alk. paper)
    1. France—History. 2. France—History—Chronology. I. Title. II. Series.
  DC35.H35 2000
  944—dc21   99–055229

British Library Cataloguing in Publication Data is available.

Library of Congress Catalog Card Number: 99–055229
ISBN: 0–313–30328–2
ISSN: 1096–2905

First published in 2000

Greenwood Press, 88 Post Road West, Westport, CT 06881
An imprint of Greenwood Publishing Group, Inc.
www.greenwood.com

Printed in the United States of America

The paper used in this book complies with the
Permanent Paper Standard issued by the National
Information Standards Organization (Z39.48–1984).

10 9 8 7 6 5 4 3 2 1

Contents

Series Foreword

The Greenwood Histories of the Modern Nations series is intended to provide students and interested laypeople with up-to-date, concise, and analytical histories of many of the nations of the contemporary world. Not since the 1960s has there been a systematic attempt to publish a series of national histories, and, as series editors, we believe that this series will prove to be a valuable contribution to our understanding of other countries in our increasingly interdependent world.

Over thirty years ago, at the end of the 1960s, the Cold War was an accepted reality of global politics, the process of decolonization was still in progress, the idea of a unified Europe with a single currency was unheard of, the United States was mired in a war in Vietnam, and the economic boom of Asia was still years in the future. Richard Nixon was president of the United States, Mao Tse-tung (not yet Mao Zedong) ruled China, Leonid Brezhnev guided the Soviet Union, and Harold Wilson was prime minister of the United Kingdom. Authoritarian dictators still ruled most of Latin America, the Middle East was reeling in the wake of the Six-Day War, and Shah Reza Pahlavi was at the height of his power in Iran. Clearly, the past thirty years have been witness to a great deal of historical change, and it is to this change that this series is primarily addressed.

With the help of a distinguished advisory board, we have selected nations whose political, economic, and social affairs mark them as among the most important in the waning years of the twentieth century, and for each nation we have found an author who is recognized as a specialist in the history of that nation. These authors have worked most cooperatively with us and with Greenwood Press to produce volumes that reflect current research on their nation and that are interesting and informative to their prospective readers.

The importance of a series such as this cannot be underestimated. As a superpower whose influence is felt all over the world, the United States can claim a "special" relationship with almost every other nation. Yet many Americans know very little about the histories of the nations with which the United States relates. How did they get to be the way they are? What kind of political systems have evolved there? What kind of influence do they have in their own region? What are the dominant political, religious, and cultural forces that move their leaders? These and many other questions are answered in the volumes of this series.

The authors who have contributed to this series have written comprehensive histories of their nations, dating back to prehistoric times in some cases. Each of them, however, has devoted a significant portion of the book to events of the past thirty years, because the modern era has contributed the most to contemporary issues that have an impact on U.S. policy. Authors have made an effort to be as up-to-date as possible so that readers can benefit from the most recent scholarship and a narrative that includes very recent events.

In addition to the historical narrative, each volume in this series contains an introductory overview of the country's geography, political institutions, economic structure, and cultural attributes. This is designed to give readers a picture of the nation as it exists in the contemporary world. Each volume also contains additional chapters that add interesting and useful detail to the historical narrative. One chapter is a thorough chronology of important historical events, making it easy for readers to follow the flow of a particular nation's history. Another chapter features biographical sketches of the nation's most important figures in order to humanize some of the individuals who have contributed to the historical development of their nation. Each volume also contains a comprehensive bibliography, so that those readers whose interest has been sparked may find out more about the nation and its history. Finally, there is a carefully prepared topic and person index.

Readers of these volumes will find them fascinating to read and useful in understanding the contemporary world and the nations that comprise it. As series editors, it is our hope that this series will contribute to a heightened sense of global understanding as we enter a new century.

Frank W. Thackeray and John E. Findling
Indiana University Southeast

Preface

French history, both in the land of wine and pâté and in the United States, has never gone out of fashion. Indeed, the history—containing paintings from the cave paintings at Lascaux to the impressionists to the postmodernists, and with such leaders as Joan of Arc, the sun king Louis XIV, Napoleon, and de Gaulle—remains a growth industry, especially on the Internet. I have presented in these 300 pages a concise, yet comprehensive, history.

As my footnotes indicate, I have examined statistical and journalistic sources, secondary monographs, and previous overviews of French history. These sources provide a running commentary and record of the wealth of sources for students wishing to go beyond the boundaries of this book. I have also produced a continuous narrative so that secondary students, lower-division undergraduates, and the general public may have a clear introduction to this fascinating national history as we enter the twenty-first century. A timeline and an index of notable people in French history facilitate quick access to vital pieces of information.

For this computer age, I have also included a set of important sites for French history, both in English and in French, on the Internet and the World Wide Web. Thus students and the public now have a convenient starting point to explore the new virtual world of French history. The best place to start on the Internet and the Web is with H-France. This electronic resource will always have the most up-to-the-minute material on French history and its electronic resources.

A work of synthesis that ranges from the Gauls to de Gaulle and beyond cannot be done alone. Thus I have incurred, pleasurably, debts among many historians. I wish to thank Bertram M. Gordon who forwarded my name to Greenwood Press to start this project rolling and who provided the essential information on Internet sources and graciously permitted the use of two of the maps from the volume he edited, *Historical Dictionary of World War II France: The Occupation, Vichy, and the Resistance, 1938–1946.* I am grateful to the many scholars who have read all or parts of the manuscript: Carolyn Lougee Chappell, Mary Pickering, Roderick G. Phillips, Michael D. Sibalis, Tyler Stovall, and David Wright. Many thanks, too, to Professor William B. Cohen for his help in finding readers and for his assistance with sources and information. In addition, the following scholars have provided helpful information: F. Bud Burkhard, Bernard-Yves Cochain, Judith de Groat, Ellen Furlough, Leonard Macaluso, Jeremy D. Popkin, Charles Rearick, and A. Whitney Walton. As always, Donna Evleth in Paris has been indispensable in tracking down material and in providing new insights. Helen Solanum, West European Collections librarian at the Hoover Institution, has also been an essential guide through this rich resource.

Across the Internet and close to home I incurred additional debts. I must also thank the participants of H-France and Women in French (WIF) list-servs for their help on matters of fact and judgment. I also thank Polly Tooker who again proved to be a perceptive editor and Tina Hummel for her superb index, and, for the first time, Tom Willcockson, at Mapcraft for a map of contemporary France.

At Greenwood, senior editor Barbara A. Rader, production editor Betty C. Pessagno, and copyeditor Lynn Wheeler have shown, at appropriate moments, patience and critical acumen that made this a better manuscript. Naturally, all remaining mistakes are my own responsibility.

I dedicate this book to my wife, Gano, and our two children, Emily and Bert: They are why I stick around!

Timeline of Historical Events

Ca. 2 million B.C.E.	Earliest human ancestors
Ca. 30,000 B.C.E.	Old Stone Age
Ca. 10,000 B.C.E.	Ice Age ends
Ca. 2,500 B.C.E.	Age of Metal
Ca. 700 B.C.E.	Celtic expansion across France
58–51 B.C.E.	Julius Caesar conquers Gaul for Rome
150–200	France Christianized
400–500	Barbarian invasions and kingdoms
511	Merovingian King Clovis makes Paris his capital
732	Muslim invasion stopped at Poitiers and Tours
751	Carolingian Dynasty established
800	Charlemagne crowned emperor of west by pope
843	Charlemagne's empire divided among three sons
700–900	Rise of feudalism and serfdom

800–910	Viking, Muslim, and Magyar incursions
987	Hugh Capet founds Capetian Dynasty; makes Paris his capital
1095	French Pope Urban initiates First Crusade (eight crusades, usually led by France, take place by 1270)
1130–1400	Gothic architecture flourishes
1209–1229	Albigensian Crusade and incorporation of Languedoc
1226–1270	Reign of Louis IX (Saint Louis), creator of Parlement of Paris (high court of justice)
1285–1314	Reign of Philip IV "the Fair": rise of bureaucratic government and French representative assembly, the Estates General
1309–1378	Papacy moves to Avignon
1328–1589	Valois kings reign
1337–1453	Hundred Years' War versus England
1348	Bubonic plague: over next fifty years population at least halved
1358	Peasant Revolt (Jacquerie) in northern France
1429	Joan of Arc turns the tide of the war
1482	Duchy of Burgundy annexed
1492–1600	Age of European expansion, expeditions of Jacques Cartier in Canada, rise of commerce, and growth of inflation
1515–1547	Reign of Francis I: height of French Renaissance
1539	Edict of Villers-Cotterets: French language declared official language of government
1561–1598	Rise of Calvinism and Wars of Religion
1589–1792	Bourbon kings reign
1598	Henry IV issues Edict of Nantes granting religious tolerance to Protestants

1624–1642	Cardinal Richelieu as head minister consolidates crown's power over nobles and towns and cities
1634–1648	France participates in Thirty Years' War and becomes dominant military power on Continent
1648–1653	*Fronde*, a widespread revolt against growth of royal bureaucracy and its exactions, occurs
1661–1715	Reign of Louis XIV
1672–1713	Wars of Louis XIV; failed bid for European domination
1715–1789	Enlightenment advocates secular, rational society
1715–1792	Reigns of Louis XV and XVI, who were weak kings
1756–1763	Seven Years' War; French Canada lost to England
1778–1783	French become allies of the American colonists in American War of Independence
1789	Bastille falls and French Revolution begins; Peasants abolish last feudal restraints in uprising (Great Fear)
1790	Administrative reorganization of France
1792	War against Austria, Louis XIV deposed, First Republic declared
1793	Government of Committee of Public Safety and the Reign of Terror
1794	Overthrow of Robespierre; end of radical phase of revolution; Thermidorian government established
1795–1799	The Directory government fails to find stability
1799	Napoleon deposes Directory and heads Consulate government
1804	Napoleon crowns himself emperor; establishes legal code
1812	Napoleon's retreat from Moscow
1814–1815	Napoleon's abdication; returns for 100 days; defeated at Waterloo
1814–1830	Restoration of Bourbons

1830	Conquest of Algeria; start of new empire
	July Revolution; ascension of Louis-Philippe, the "citizen king"
1831, 1834	Silk workers of Lyon rise in revolt
1842	Railroad era dawns
1848	Revolution, overthrow of Louis-Philippe, Second Republic declared, Louis Napoleon Bonaparte elected president
1850–1870	Economic growth, transformation of Paris, liberal empire
1851	Louis Napoleon Bonaparte's coup d'état (Second Empire)
1870–1871	Franco Prussian War, Second Empire falls, Paris Commune established, French army cedes dominance to Germany
1870–1876	Third Republic founded
1882	Jules Ferry's educational reforms enacted
1889	International exposition held in Paris, Eiffel Tower built
1895–1914	Belle Époque
1898	Emile Zola's article *J'accuse*, Dreyfus affair
1905	Triple Entente: France, Russia, Great Britain
1914–1918	World War I fought
1916	Battle of Verdun fought
1919	Treaty of Versailles concluded
1920s	"Crazy Years": economic growth, expatriates in Paris
1931	Depression hits France
1934	Stavisky affair and riot of February 6; French right flirts with fascism
	Popular Front (antifascism): Socialists, Radicals, and Communists

1938	Munich agreement with Adolf Hitler signed
1939–1940	World War II: France collapses and Vichy puppet regime established; Charles de Gaulle in London
1944	D-Day and end of German occupation
1945	Fourth Republic formed
1946	Jean Monnet plans industrial modernization
1948	Franco-American agreement reached on Marshall Plan aid
1954	France defeated in Vietnam; Algerian War starts
1957	European Common Market created
1958	Crisis in Algeria sparks fall of Fourth Republic; return of de Gaulle establishes Fifth Republic
1959	France detonates first atomic bomb
1962	Algerian independence granted
1962–1973	Height of "Thirty Glorious Years" of economic expansion
1966	France leaves the North Atlantic Treaty Organization
1968	Student and worker revolt occurs in May–June
1969	De Gaulle resigns; former prime minister Georges Pompidou becomes president
1973–1974	First oil crisis occurs
1974	Valéry Giscard d'Estaing is first non-Gaullist president
1979	Second oil crisis occurs
1981	François Mitterrand is first Socialist president
1983	Socialists make U-turn on economic policy
1986	Right wins parliament; first cohabitation government established
1988	Mitterrand reelected president
1993	Second cohabitation government established

1995   Jacques Chirac elected president

1997   Socialists retake parliament; third cohabitation gov-
                ernment established

1999   France qualifies for European single currency
                (Euro); National Front splits

1

A Fractious and Fascinating Country

For centuries France has fascinated the rest of the world. Its geography and history have embodied a series of creative paradoxes. Spanning both northern and southern Europe—in both climate and culture—the country, with its wide and varied topography of mountains and alluvial plains, offers great cultural and economic diversity. Yet this variegated area is one of the earliest and most continuous nations, dating from the time of the ancient Celts in the third century B.C.E.

GEOGRAPHY, CLIMATE, FLORA, FAUNA, AND PEOPLES

Shakespeare, in *Henry V*, summed up the French landscape as succinctly and successfully as anyone else before or since:

This best garden of the world,
Our fertile France. (*Henry V*, Act 5, Scene 2, ll. 36–37)

Geographically, climatically, and biologically, France has always been a crossroads between the Mediterranean and European worlds. Its agriculture spans the dairy region of Normandy and Brittany on the English Channel, the wheat fields and sugar beet cultivation on the northern

plains, the timber forests of the Massif Central, the sheep-covered hills and mountains in the Pyrenees and Massif Central, and the fruit and olive groves in the Mediterranean region of Provence. Wine, perhaps the agricultural product most associated with France, is produced across most of the nation, but especially in the southern and central regions of France and, in the case of Champagne, Burgundy, and Alsatian wines, near the German border. France follows the United States as the second largest agricultural exporter in the world.

Spanning a region bounded by mountains and rivers between the Mediterranean Sea, the Atlantic Ocean, and the English Channel, France lies at the edge of the European continent. The biggest nation in Western Europe, France encompasses 211,207 square miles (547,026 square kilometers), about the combined size of California and Oregon. Since the 1960s the French have likened the shape of their nation to a hexagon. One of the six sides is bounded by the Pyrenees mountains, which separate France from Spain. To the north, a second side, which includes the Atlantic coast up to the peninsula of Brittany (the Armorican Massif), is a flat plain crisscrossed by rivers, the two most important of which are the Garonne and the Loire. The third side is the English Channel coastline from Brittany to Belgium. This region contains another flat alluvial plain, the principal river of which is the Seine (which flows through Paris). The fourth side, running from Belgium to Germany (to the point where the Rhine River flows through Luxembourg and Germany) has been the least constant of France's borders. On this northern plain, where Belgium, France, Luxembourg, and Germany meet, France has suffered most of its military invasions. The fifth side runs from the Rhine River through the Alps and down to the sea. The sixth side is the Mediterranean, with the Saône and Rhône rivers running through the Alps and emptying in the Mediterranean Sea. West of the Rhône, in the south central region of France, lies the extensive mountainous shelf called the Massif Central. With a current (1997) population of 60,082,000, France is considered underpopulated for its size and resources.[1] The "hexagon" could easily support 75 million.

As its agricultural diversity would suggest, France is home to hundreds of microclimates. Consider, for instance, the range in rainfall. In the Mediterranean regions and parts of Alsace, the average is barely 20 inches per year; in the various mountain regions, on the other hand, rainfall can reach over 80 inches annually. The incidence of rain reveals equally striking differences: in the dairy regions of Brittany and Normandy, rain may fall 200 days of the year, but the scrub regions of the Mediterranean and south may see rain only 50 days of the year.

France's vegetation and animal life also reflect its crossroads position between northern and southern climates. Prior to the age of agriculture, France was covered in forest, up to the treeline of its mountains. In the non-Mediterranean regions, the forests contained predominantly European beech, various types of oak, durmast, and sessile, with hornbeam the primary brushwood on the forest floor. In the mountains of the southern Atlantic section are found forests of pine, spruce, and fir. Vegetation in the Mediterranean area includes Holm and cork oaks and heathland with kermes oak. In lower Provence, Aleppo and maritime pines are found, and in the Pyrenees Scots pine, Mediterranean beech, and mountain pine abound. French animal life also reflects the diverse climates: 90 species of mammals, 400 kinds of birds, 25 different types of frogs, toads, newts, salamanders, and 27 varieties of snakes, lizards, and tortoises.

The people of France also illustrate the varied points of contact with the surrounding environment. Along the southern border with Spain are the Basques, an ancient people with their own language, unrelated to the other peoples of France. On the Amorican Massif, in Brittany, Celts created a culture distinct from that of the Gauls, who were also of Celtic origin. The population of Normandy has been shaped largely by Viking settlements; the word Norman is derived from the term "North men." On both sides of the Belgian border, the population comes from the same Flemish stock. In Alsace, on Germany's boundary line, much of the population is of Teutonic origin. The island of Corsica, brought into France in 1768, boasts linguistic cultural roots of its long Italian heritage. These peripheral populations all have their own languages and distinctive cultures.

Other important cultural and linguistic differences separate the north from the south. During the medieval period, distinctive languages emerged in the two regions defined by the different words for *yes*: the *langue d'oc* in the south and the *langue d'oil* (now spelled *oui*) in the north. Even in the middle of the nineteenth century, as a result of this ethnic and linguistic diversity, a quarter of the population of France did not actually speak French, and another quarter spoke it poorly.

Although France is no longer a formal empire, it still has a variety of small overseas territories, mostly islands, with varying degrees of connection to metropolitan France. Four of these areas have become overseas departments—part of the nation: French Guiana, Guadeloupe, Martinique, and Réunion (in the Indian Ocean). These departments have the same governmental institutions as the rest of France and send representatives to the French National Assembly.

Other possessions include territorial collectivities and overseas territories that vary in their attachment and affinity to France. The two territorial collectivities have a status somewhere between department and territory. Mayotte, in the Indian Ocean north of the island of Madagascar, supports an independence movement and awaited a referendum in 1999 to determine its future destiny, but the islands of Saint Pierre and Miquelon off the coast of Newfoundland in the North Atlantic are content with their present status. Overseas territories include French Polynesia and New Caledonia, both in the South Pacific. Varying degrees of restiveness over French rule are found here as well. In New Caledonia an independence movement has been agitating for independence since the 1970s but has not yet been able to achieve its goal. In the 120 islands that constitute French Polynesia, the resumption of French nuclear testing in 1995 precipitated a drive for greater autonomy.

FRANCE TODAY

France has weathered the storms of the early twentieth century—World War I, the Great Depression, World War II, and decolonization—to emerge over the past few decades as the fourth largest economic power in the industrialized world. Perhaps the greatest revolution France has so far undergone followed World War II, when the nation finally and fully became an urbanized "affluent society," with a standard of living rivaling that of any advanced nation. Peasants have moved to the cities and many small shops have been replaced by supermarkets and malls, without the fanfare or the fighting that accompanied France's earlier political upheavals.

Today the Arianne rocket rivals NASA for putting payloads into space. The European airline manufacturing consortium Airbus, whose final assembly plant is in France, has overtaken the American Boeing in market share for the world's airlines. France's high-speed trains, the TGV (or *train à grande vitesse*), has set standards for the commuter trains of tomorrow. France has also taken a leading role in the creation of a single European currency and monetary union which stands to make the European Union the largest economic unit in the world in the twenty-first century.

France also continues to play an active role around the world, especially in its former colonies. Approximately 140 million people around the world speak French, and French is the official language of 24 percent of the nations in the United Nations. Following large population losses during World War I and the need for rebuilding the nation after World War II, France pioneered in incorporating immigrant labor from other European countries and the rest of the world. This extensive immigration has made France one of the cauldrons in which a new multicultural worldview has been blended with artistic sensibility.

For many people today, France may well be associated with tourism. Indeed, each year France hosts more tourists than any other nation— over 70 million and counting—and Paris is one of the top five most-visited attractions in the world. Tourism accounts for over 8 percent of the French gross national product and, along with agricultural and armaments exports, helps France to achieve its recent record trade surpluses. France has also been a pioneer in the field of leisure activities. Perhaps the greatest innovation for tourists has been the establishment of Club Med. Founded in 1950, this company has become the world leader in rustic holidays. At more than 100 remote hideaways, vacationers live in straw huts or bungalows with no money, newspapers, or televisions; guests are treated to elaborate meals and a constant stream of sports, cabaret entertainment, and other recreations. Club Med has become truly international; over 60 percent of its clientele comes from outside France. Yet the organization, with its clever mix of unspoiled nature and sophisticated sociability, remains distinctively French.

France's standing in the world of contemporary art, literature, and cinema, on the other hand, has declined from its previous lofty heights. Paris is no longer the center of the art world, a title essentially taken over by New York City after World War II. Post-1945 French artists have not achieved the fame, or the greatness, of previous generations. Jean Dubuffet (1901–1985) is generally considered the most important post-1945 painter; Nicolas De Staël (1914–1955) and Yves Klein (1928–1962) are also highly regarded painters of the postwar period. Literature, too, after the generation of Jean-Paul Sartre (1905–1980), Albert Camus (1913–1960), and Simone de Beauvoir (1908–1986), has been productive and innovative but not as influential, especially internationally. Nevertheless, several novelists have gained important honors and a growing reputation after 1970: George Perec, Michel Tournier (1924–), Marguerite Duras, Annie Ernaux (1940–), Jean-Marie Gustave le Clezio (1940–), Patrick Modiano, Philippe Solliers (1936–), and Margaret Yourcenar (1903–1987). French cinema has produced some of the world's great classic films under such pre-1945 directors as Jean Renoir (1894–1979) (*Rules of the Game* and *Grand Illusion*) and Marcel Carné (1906–1996) (*Children of Paradise*) as well as under the New Wave directors of the 1950s and 1960s, such as François Truffaut (1932–1984) (*Jules and Jim* and *400 Blows*), Louis Malle (1932–1995) (*Lacombe Lucien* and *Murmur of the Heart*), and Jean Luc Godard (*Breathless* and *Weekend*). Today, the French cinema, which produces more than 130 films annually, is virtually the only one in Europe to survive the Hollywood juggernaut.

Since 1946 France has had an especially large impact on philosophy and intellectual life. After World War II, Sartre's existentialism captured imaginations around the world with its distinctive blend of commitment to personal choice, economic justice, political liberation, and a bohemian disregard of conventions. Sartre's engagement with Marxism (the primary philosophy of the modern world, he believed) influenced the subsequent generation, too, the one that created the student/worker near-revolution of May 1968. However, in the 1960s, rival philosophies emerged: structuralism, deconstruction, poststructuralism, and postmodernism. In the hands of anthropologist Claude Levi-Strauss (1906–   ), its first great proponent, structuralism examined the "codes" of human culture, based on the assumption that cultural rites and rituals were organized in a fashion similar to human language. A concern with how language shapes, structures, and distorts meaning rather than simply reflects (as Sartre believed) reality has been the common denominator of most recent French thinking. Jacques Derrida (1930–   ), in his philosophy of deconstruction, has argued that all literature and philosophy (indeed all writing) contain gaps and weaknesses that permit critics to take these works apart and reinterpret them in new ways. Michel Foucault (1926–1984), often labeled a poststructuralist, examined the interrelationship between power and knowledge in his studies of discipline, punishment, and confinement (through studies of prisons, hospitals, and mental institutions among other institutions and discourses). Finally, Jean François Lyotard (1924–   ) has helped propagate the notion of postmodernism. This elusive concept, since it eschews precise definitions as part and parcel of the problems of modernity, calls into question modernity's search for truth, utopia, and certainty. Instead, Lyotard argues, today ambiguity, transience, and a pastiche of past cultural styles are all that society can aspire to in a media-driven age. The influence of these philosophers and others across the whole range of intellectual life in the Anglo-American world has been immense.

GOVERNMENT

Many of the key concepts of modern politics—such as left, right, ideology, revolution, even national socialism—developed during the century following the French Revolution of 1789. During France's subsequent nineteenth-century revolutions (1830, 1848, 1871), as well as during the Dreyfus affair (1894–1902) and the Popular Front (1934–1938), France seemed to bubble constantly with ideological passion as the right and the left were sharply divided on almost every issue.

Since the near-revolution of May 1968, commonly known as the "Events of May," the great ideological struggle between the left and the right has lost most of its intensity. The French Communist party has been especially hard hit, going from more than 20 percent in most parliamentary elections in the 1960s to less than 10 percent in the 1980s and 1990s and losing two-thirds of the party's membership as well as control over one-third of the town and city governments it had once run.

Perhaps the best measure of the decline of ideological passion is the generally rising rate of abstention in parliamentary elections over the past twenty years, rising from an average of 20 percent in the late 1960s to 30 percent in the late 1990s. The incessant political corruption scandals of the 1990s have also resulted in increased cynicism. A 1998 poll found that 59 percent of the French believe that their politicians are corrupt.

Although the rooting out of corruption has spawned public disaffection it has also been a necessary cleansing process. A new generation of activist prosecuting attorneys, epitomized by the Norwegian-born Eva Joly, aided by the growing independence of the French media, have rooted out double dealing in both government and industry. Since 1990, 30 government ministers (including former prime minister Alain Juppé), over 100 members of parliament, six heads of political parties, and a quarter of the presidents of France's 40 largest corporations have been brought to court. The cozy connections between government, business, and the courts, in short, are no longer being tolerated. Indeed, current prime minister Lionel Jospin has promised to pass a bill, now pending in the parliament, that will make the French judiciary more independent along Anglo-American lines.

The Fifth Republic has put down deep roots. Formally described as a parliamentary republic under a presidential regime, this republic, founded by Charles de Gaulle in 1958, is commonly characterized as "semi-presidential." The Fifth Republic is a synthesis of the U.S.-style presidential system and the English-style parliamentary system. Despite the potential friction between the offices of the president and the prime minister, the system has operated remarkably smoothly over the last 40 years. What has facilitated the efficient operation of the government is a set of coherent, cohesive, and powerful political parties: first, de Gaulle's UNR (Union for the New Republic, or Union pour la Nouvelle République), during the 1960s and early 1970s, and then the Socialist party under President François Mitterrand and Prime Minister Jospin, during the 1980s and 1990s. The centrality of the presidential election to the French political system and the runoff between the two leading vote getters, if no candidate receives a majority, inhibit party fragmentation and facilitate bipolarity.

Before the 1980s, experts speculated that the Fifth Republic would face instability if the presidency was in the hands of one party and the parliament in the hands of another. Since 1986 France has had three different periods when the presidency and the parliament have been in different hands. This type of mixed government, dubbed cohabitation in France, has proved to be remarkably stable. Twice during the Mitterrand presidency (1981–1995) and once so far under the Jacques Chirac presidency (1995–), presidents and prime ministers have been able to subordinate their differences in the cause of a smoothly functioning government. This has been possible, in large part, because of the narrowing of ideological differences in French politics.

The shift from contestation to deliberation in French politics has also been aided by the emergence of the Constitutional Council. Established at the start of the Fifth Republic to monitor the parliament, the council has increasingly functioned as a "third chamber," which evaluates the legality of government actions on such issues as nationalizing or privatizing companies and abortion and champions human rights on such matters as immigration.

The growth of the civil service over the past two decades has augmented France's already entrenched bureaucratic ethos. Since 1980, during decades when most nations have cut their bureaucracies, the number of government workers has increased by 20 percent and now stands at over 4.5 million. Compared to Germany and the United States (one in six) and Britain (one in seven), every fourth worker in France today works for the government. Although they work shorter hours and have more generous health care, vacation, and pension schemes, French public opinion has a higher opinion of their civil servants than the other countries listed above have of their own.

RELIGION

Religion has both declined and changed. France remains predominantly Catholic, but it has seen the Church's power over daily life recede. The emergence after World War II of an energetic generation of liberal Catholic thinkers and social activists, including worker priests, did not stem the long-term decline of the daily practice of Catholicism. Since the 1950s the percentage of children baptized has plummeted from 90 to 50 percent, and attendance at mass each week has dropped from 32 percent in 1945 to only 10 percent. The Catholic Church also faces a crisis in recruiting new priests and nuns. For example, in 1900, for every 10,000 individuals, the Catholic Church had 14 priests; by 1965, the number of priests had fallen to seven; and in 1999, it was just one. In addition, 85 percent of today's priests oppose celibacy.[2] A sect of "integrationist" Catholics, comprising about 10 percent of the Church in France, has rejected Vatican II and has returned to traditional rites and rituals. Islam, with 4 million adherents, is now the second largest religion in France, ahead of Protestantism and Judaism.[3] After an October 1981 law permitted foreigners to form associations, the number of Islamic places of worship has soared, with the help of oil money from Arab countries, from 11 in 1970 to over 1,000 by 1999.[4] French Protestants currently number over 900,000 in 16 denominations and about 200,000 who are non-demominational.[5] Although a small percentage of the population—at just over 2 percent—Protestants still have, as they always have had since 1789, an important role in French politics. Three of the 14 prime ministers of the current Fifth Republic have been Protestant, including the current (1999) incumbent Alain Jospin. France's 700,000 Jews make up the largest Jewish community in Europe outside of Russia.[6] Although France still experiences incidents of anti-Semitism, the primary targets of religious bigotry today are the Muslims.

The rise of Islam to the status of the second religion of France highlights another important contemporary transformation: the emergence of a multicultural society. Like the United States, France has been a magnet of immigration throughout the twentieth century. Today one in four French people have at least one grandparent who was an immigrant. However, since the 1960s, the places of origin have changed dramatically, with a resulting impact on French society and politics. Between World War I and the 1950s, most immigrants came from other European nations—particularly Italy, Poland, Spain, and Portugal. European by birth and primarily Catholic, these people were easily assimilated. By the mid-1960s, in response to the national labor demand, France has attracted increasing numbers of non-European workers. During the 1973 recession, which ended the postwar expansion, France suspended immigration, except for cases of family reunification.

ECONOMY

In 1997 France's GDP (in U.S. dollars) was $1,396.50 billion compared to Germany's $2,100.1 billion. France is the fourth largest exporter; second on a per capita basis. The diversity of the French economy is indicated by the fact that France is the second largest exporter of agricultural goods as well as of financial, insurance, and other services (in both cases trailing only the United States).

Despite these areas of success, along with those in aerospace and trains, France faces daunting challenges in its automobile, electronic, and farming sectors. Renault and Peugeot, the two largest car manufacturers, export only 15 percent of their products outside of Europe; Volkswagen exports 40 percent and Fiat, 30 percent. In the computer sector, France scored an early triumph when it launched the Minitel system in 1981. This network, which connected the telephone and computer, has become a fixture in more than half of French homes. The great liability of the system is that it is incompatible with the Internet and the World Wide Web. The French have been slow to move into the world of the personal computer; only 15 percent own them in the late 1990s and are not yet able to access the new international communications technologies. Finally, France still lags behind the other major industrialized nations in terms of the size of its agricultural population (about 5 percent as compared to less than 1 percent in the United States) and the paucity of large cities, outside of Paris.

Nevertheless, the 1980s and 1990s have seen French industry streamlined and modernized. Smokestack industries have increasingly given way to the white-collar service sector. The restructuring of industry seems to be paying off as France has recently been growing faster than its neighbors and adding jobs at a rapid pace (see chapter 12). Since 1997 Jospin's socialist government has been able to achieve increased growth and job formation without resorting to cutting government spending on administration or welfare benefits. The coming years will determine whether this traditional French reliance on the state in economic matters proves successful in an age, paradoxically, of both globalization and decentralization.

SOCIETY

French society on the cusp of the twenty-first century is in dynamic flux. Immigration, feminism, youth culture, and economic and social change are reshaping family life and leisure patterns.

For virtually 200 years, France has led the rest of Europe in incorporating immigrants into its society. Indeed, after the United States restricted immigration during the early 1920s, France accepted more immigrants than any other urban industrial country. By 1930 France had a higher percentage of immigrants in its population than did the United States. Today about 14 million out of France's population of 60 million have immigrant parents and grandparents.[7] Immigrants composed roughly the same percentage of the population in 1990 (6.35 percent) as they did in 1931 (6.58 percent).[8] This continuity in the percentage of immigrants highlights an important difference between France and the Anglo-American world in the handling of racial and ethnic questions.

French governments currently emphasize complete integration of immigrants into the nation. When a person receives French citizenship he or she is no longer classified as an immigrant or a foreigner, which makes it difficult to track the economic and social fortunes of immigrants and their children. In addition, the French government does not require that a person's race or original ethnicity be listed on birth certificates or marriage licenses; consequently, it is much harder to study race or ethnic relations in France than in the English-speaking world. This archival practice has assumed more relevance as the origins of French immigration have changed.

Since the 1960s, the source of incoming immigrants has shifted from Europe to the Third World, especially former French colonies in Africa and Asia. Now almost half of the 4.2 million immigrants have come from outside of Europe: a little over 40 percent are Arabs from North Africa, about 12 percent are Asians and about 7 percent come from black Africa.[9] In addition, the number of illegal immigrants has been estimated at 300,000.[10] Since the 1980s a racist political party, the National Front, which typically constituted 15 percent of the electorate during the 1990s, has promoted "France for the French" and has attacked immigrants for taking "French jobs" and "corrupting" French culture. The National Front has failed to win approval for its idea of discriminatory legislation against immigrants (a form of reverse affirmative action), but the Front has prevented the other major parties from promoting multiculturalism.

Instead, the mainstream political parties have continued their emphasis on integration.

Although multiculturalism has not gained much political support, it has become a potent cultural force. In response, second- and soon third-generation Arabs (known in French slang as *Beurs*) and African immigrants have created their own distinctive cultural forms in music, literature, and film and have organized to combat racism. Some of the most innovative cultural fusion today is going on among singers or such musical groups as MC Solaar, Karim Kacel, Carte de Sejour, and Groupe Jungle Gala. The singers combine the traditions of Africa, Europe, and Islam, with the jazz, rock, and rap of the United States.

The growing diversity of French society is also mirrored in the growing variety of family options. After World War II, French families reversed almost 150 years of tradition and chose to have large families. Where prewar mothers and fathers had fewer than two children per family, postwar mothers and fathers had an average of three children. Following the events of May 1968, however, the French opted to return to having fewer children but, at the same time, adopted a more flexible approach to family structures. Couples living together outside of marriage increased from 3.6 percent of all couples in 1970 to 6.3 percent by 1980 and 15.5 percent in 1994. The percentage of children born outside of marriage rose from 6.8 percent in 1970 to 11.4 percent in 1980 and to 37.6 percent in 1995. Divorce jumped from 11.8 percent in 1970 to 22.3 percent in 1980 and to 45.6 percent in 1994; two-thirds of the divorces are initiated by women.[11]

Much of the transformation in the French family has been spearheaded by French feminism. Although failing to win the vote after World War I (as other women's movements did), French feminism has a distinguished history. First to demand political rights (amidst the great 1789 Revolution), French women writers during the nineteenth century developed "perhaps the most radical and thoroughgoing critique of women's subordination in all Europe" and coined the term feminism.[12]

Although French women did not receive the vote until after World War II, French feminists have a distinguished heritage and have inspired women in Central and Eastern Europe. Twentieth-century French feminism has been marked by theoretical sophistication and grassroots organization. The chief theorists are Simone de Beauvoir, the existentialist writer and philosopher, whose *Second Sex* (1949) is universally credited with being a bible of the second-wave feminism of the post-1960s. Subsequently, theorists such as Luce Irigary, Hélène Cixous, Julia Kristeva, and Michelle Le Doeuff have drawn heavily on structuralist and post-structuralist thought to root out male bias in philosophy, psychology, and society. Underpinning these intellectuals is a network of bookstores, publishing houses, newspapers, and local women's groups in universities, neighborhoods, and workplaces. Their steady agitation across the 1950s, 1960s, and 1970s led to the removal of numerous restrictions on women's civil and legal rights and a liberalization of divorce procedures. Women now have the legal right to buy contraceptives, have abortions, and receive equal pay (this last is still unrealized in practice).

Although the main movement devoted to women's liberation (Mouvement de la liberation des femmes, organized after May 1968) had splintered by 1981, women's activism has not diminished. Despite the French populace's having elected fewer women to office than any other European nation except Greece, French women have recently made important political advances. The Socialist party in 1997 entered women in nearly a third of its races, doubling the number of women in parliament. Martine Aubry, daughter of the former finance minister and head of the European Union, Jacques Delors, now runs a powerful "superministry" for employment, social welfare, and health in the Socialist government. Dominique Voynet is head of the Green party and minister of the environment in the government. Lionel Jospin, the current prime minister, wishes to enact into law the principle of parity between the genders in government. Whether he can accomplish this should not detract from his new-found commitment (based in part on political calculation, of course) to achieve equality between men and women.

The status of youth in French society has also altered dramatically since 1945, in both positive and negative fashions. By the 1960s the age for leaving school had been raised from 14 to 16, and the number of students entering college began to skyrocket. At the same time young consumers, as a result of the postwar economy, were purchasing radios, records, televisions, and other leisure-time goods at an unprecedented rate. Soon French youth had created their own form of rock and roll, known as *ye-ye*, with such homegrown singing stars as Johnny Hallyday, Françoise Hardy, and Sylvie Vartan. Radio and television shows such as *Salut les Copains* (roughly translated as "Hello to the friends") became a rite of adolescent passage. An object of fascination for French intellectuals, the youth culture clearly had both conformist and rebellious aspects: as it catapulted the youth into consumerism, it also provided them with a sense of empowerment. The May events of 1968 revealed the revolutionary potential of this sector of the population, but it also gave further impetus to the consumption of clothes, comic strips, and later videos and walkmen. When the Socialist François Mitterrand won the presidency in 1981, his minister of culture, Jack Lang, tried to encourage this new youth culture. For a while Lang subsidized French rock musicians to try to increase their productivity and visibility. Subsequent culture ministers have not been so audacious.

The 1990s have seen increasing numbers of adolescents, defined as those between childhood and full employment. By the late 1990s almost 80 percent of French high school students, double the proportion of the previous decade, were receiving their *baccalaureât*, the ticket to a university education.[13] At the same time, however, unemployment for those under 25 has risen to 25 percent.[14] Much of this youthful free time, in short, is unwanted and leads not to consumption but to delinquency. The rate of juvenile delinquency has risen 81 percent over the past decade; one in five of the defendants now charged in French courts is under 18. The charges range from shoplifting and insulting the police to drug dealing and possessing firearms. Recently, adolescents have rioted in such cities as Strasbourg.[15] Not surprisingly, the major concern pollsters find among the French today, after unemployment, is the problem of juvenile delinquency.

One of the spaces where youth as well as tourists love to "hang out" is the French café, a space that has also been changing radically. In the transformation of French society after World War II, one of the main targets of urban planners was the café. Viewed as a place of drunkenness, debauchery, and poverty, cafés were regarded as eminently expendable. Tough zoning regulations restricted or even eliminated cafés from new housing complexes and from the new towns and cities that were being built. Today, with over 63 percent of the French population living in housing built since 1948, cafés are often hard to find.[16] This may come as a shock to tourists accustomed to visiting the historic areas of French cities where the cafés still flourish. In most new towns, however, a very "American" scene greets the tourist: highways, shopping malls, and fast-food restaurants. The resulting decline of the café is best charted in its total numbers: from over 500,000 before World War II, the number of cafés (as opposed to mere retail outlets selling liquor) has fallen to approximately 50,000.[17] The French government can never let the café die, of course; it is too important for tourism. This was made clear when the famous Fouquet's on the Champs Élysées was recently saved from bankruptcy.

Despite these changes, France is in no danger of becoming an American colony. National traditions of fine wines, exceptional food, and high fashion remain strong and still define the good life. The French drink much less wine today than they did a century ago (75 liters per capita annually compared with 150), but in general the wine is of a higher grade and comes from a specific winery (it thus has an *appelation*). As France has become increasingly middle class, so has its taste for wine, shifting to a choice in between the red of the workers and peasants and the rare wine of the old elites.[18]

Since the 1950s the emergence of refrigeration and better means of transportation and preservation of food have led to what is known as nouvelle cuisine. Pioneered by chef Fernand Point (1897–1955) at his restaurant La Pyramide in Vienne (between Lyon and Grenoble) and by food critics Henri Gault and Christian Millau, nouvelle cuisine emphasizes fresh, natural ingredients (which modern transportation can deliver) rather than heavy, cream-based sauces (which tended to disguise poorly preserved food). In recent decades nouvelle cuisine has been supplemented by a new trend: *cuisine de terroir*, inspired by peasant and regional cooking. This is a hearty, more robust cuisine, introduced by one of Point's students, Paul Bocuse.

French fashion is still a world leader, despite inroads by Italy and the United States. For example, L'Oreal is the largest cosmetics corporation in the world. High fashion is dominated by some 20 houses, virtually all of them owned by large conglomerates. From Christian Dior's "new look" of the late 1940s through the postmodern clothes of Dim in the 1990s, the French have continued to set major trends. Since the 1960s a greater degree of informality and political consciousness has often infused French fashion. The 1980s, for instance, saw the expression of a radical individualism while the 1990s have returned to a more traditional look. Certainly one of the more intriguing recent orders for French designers came from the Chinese army who selected Pierre Cardin to redesign their uniforms.

Over the past decade, the French have become obsessed with the French "distinctive way of life" (*le distinction française*). French distinctiveness is noted especially in their attitudes toward politics and society. Although the French work harder and faster than their grandparents did, they still treasure their leisure time. For example, the government provides five weeks of paid vacation. In a recent poll, two-thirds of the French agreed with the major labor union, the General Confederation of

Labor (CGT), that the retirement age should be lowered to 55. Most French, even among the conservatives, view American-style capitalism as "the law of the jungle." A recent best-seller that attacks globalization and downsizing, Viviane Forrester's *The Economic Horror* has sold 400,000 copies in France. Although the French constantly complain about taxation and regimentation by their government, they also expect the framework to be in place when they need assistance. Two-thirds of the respondents to a 1995 poll, taken before their presidential election, said they wished for more, not less, government intervention.[19] Like many Europeans, the French juxtapose what they call a "social market system," a capitalism with compassion, to what they perceive as heartless American capitalism.

NOTES

1. "Recensement: Sept métropoles contre Paris" *Le Monde*, July 1, 1999, p. 1.

2. John Ardagh with Colin Jones, *Cultural Atlas of France* (New York: Facts on File, 1991), p. 114; and Robert Gildea, *France Since 1945* (Oxford: Oxford University Press, 1997), p. 135.

3. Dominique and Michèle Frémy, *Quid 1998* (Paris: Éditions Robert Laffont, 1998), p. 534.

4. Grace Davie, "Religion and Laïcité" in *Modern France: Society in Transition*, Malcolm Cook and Grace Davie, eds. (London: Routledge, 1999), p. 199.

5. *Quid 1998*, p. 516.

6. Ardagh, *Cultural Atlas of France*, p. 117.

7. Alec G. Hargreaves, *Immigration, "Race," and Ethnicity in Contemporary France* (London: Routledge, 1995), p. 5.

8. Ibid., p. 6.

9. Ibid., pp. 11 and 22.

10. Ibid., p. 21.

11. *L'Etat de la France* 1998 (Paris: Editions la Decouverte, 1998), pp. 67–78.

12. Karen Offen, "Women, Citizenship, and Suffrage in France Since 1789" in *The Transformation of Modern France*, William B. Cohen, ed. (Boston: Houghton Mifflin Co., 1997), pp. 125–126.

13. *L'Étudiant*, June 1999, p. 1.

14. John Ardagh, *France in the New Century, Portrait of a Changing Society* (London: Viking, 1999), p. 196.

15. "The Kid's Revolt," *The Economist*, January 10, 1998, pp. 42–43.

16. "Logement: Époque d'achèvement de l'immeuble," *Quid 1998*, p. 1323.

17. *Cafés, bistrots, et compagnie*. Exposition itinérantes no. 4, 1977 (Paris: Centre de Création Industrielle, 1977), p. 51, and William Safran, *The French Polity*, 5th ed. (New York: Longman, 1998), p. 31.

18. Leo Loubère, *The Wine Revolution in France: The Twentieth Century* (Princeton, NJ: Princeton University Press, 1990), pp. 166–167 and 171.

19. "Monsieur Colbert or Madame Thatcher?" *The Economist*, April 26, 1997, p. 46.

2

Prehistory

"Never say that prehistory is not history. Never say that there was 'no such thing' as Gaul before Gaul, or France before France, or seek to deny that many features of both Gaul and France can be explained by the millennia dating before the Roman conquest."[1] So begins Fernand Braudel, perhaps France's greatest historian of the twentieth century, in his final, most reflective, and extremely controversial work, *The Identity of France*. This statement is not hyperbole when one considers that prehistory in France's case covers 20,000 centuries.

The area's first evidence of *Homo Erectus* is a group of carved quartz fragments discovered at Cilhac in the Massif Central mountains of south-central France and dating from 1,800,000 B.C.E. The fullest record of human prehistory in Europe is to be found in France, for its topography has provided easy routes north from the Mediterranean and its climate was comparatively mild during the late glacial period.

By 100,000 B.C.E. the Neanderthals had replaced *Homo Erectus*. Popularly believed to be a primate brute, this short, stocky species has nevertheless been shown recently to have been the first to bury its dead. Starting from about 40,000 B.C.E., modern humans (*Homo Sapiens Sapiens*) totally supplanted the Neanderthals over a course of 5,000 years. Prehistorians are still uncertain as to the exact cause of the Neanderthals' disappearance.

Successive ages of early humans have been named after their tools. The Old Stone Age lasted from about 30,000 to 6,000 B.C.E. During this era, small bands of hunter-gatherers (numbering no more than 30,000 for all of France) tracked reindeer and horses and collected berries, nuts, and other plants for food and medicine. In this subsistence society, women and men were essentially equal: women took an active role, not only in raising children but also in gathering food. The high status of women is demonstrated by the female fertility goddesses sculpted by these groups. Their homes were usually caves and their tools were not sophisticated, but their artwork may still be seen on cave walls along the Dordogne and Vézère rivers. Often depicting the reindeer so central to their existence, these vivid paintings—the most famous of which are Lascaux—were executed during a 20,000-year time span (30,000 to 10,000 B.C.E.). From this long perspective, as Braudel notes, the historical ages of later painting styles—the Romanesque, the Gothic, the Impressionist— seem like a mere blink of the eye!

The final retreat of the Ice Age—between 10,000 and 9,000 B.C.E.— dramatically transformed human life in the area that would be France. Over the course of thousands of years, humans moved from hunting and gathering to trapping, fishing, and rudimentary farming. Instead of chasing large animals across the tundra, hunters began trapping the stags and boars found in the emerging forests, or catching fish in the warming seas and rivers. Increasingly their diet included vegetables, grains, herbs, nuts, and berries. From around 8,500 B.C.E. evidence emerges of the domestication of dogs and of the use of flint in arrows, hammers, and knives. Knowledge of this Mesolithic Age comes from their garbage heaps, which have indicated, among other things, that the French consumption of snails developed in prehistoric times.

The first indications of an agricultural revolution in this area date from 8,000 B.C.E. By this time, the tundra had fully receded, and forests and fields flourished. In the present-day southern departments of Var and Herault, evidence has been found of the systematic gathering of various grasses, as well as such legumes as lentils and peas. By 6,000 B.C.E. shepherding appeared in southern France having spread there from the Middle East, and in another 1500 years it would be found throughout northern France, too. Soil cultivation, also originating in the Middle East, arrived in France from across the Mediterranean and through the Danube River Valley and into central and northern France. Prehistorians now attribute much of the agricultural revolution to women; planting crops may have been a part of their major gathering tasks.

Southern agriculture, involving the cultivation of corn, barley, and millet, was later combined with transhumant shepherding, or the seasonal migration of sheep between uplands and lowlands. The spread of this Mediterranean style of farming northward into the Massif Central and into the Alps can be traced by the spatial distribution of a specific type of pottery (called "cordial") these people made from seashells.

Northern agriculture developed out of cultural displacement; farmers from Central Europe brought their agricultural techniques with them. By 4,500 B.C.E. they had reached the region of Paris and either had driven out the hunter-gatherers or had forced them to adapt. These middle European farmers built large houses for their large families and lived in villages of up to 200 inhabitants. They burned forest to create farmland and planted wheat and barley. They bred cattle and pigs, but rarely sheep. The northern farmers more closely approximated traditional peasants, with hunting as a mere sideline. By 3,500 B.C.E. only 10 percent of their diet was wild game. They, too, had their distinctive pottery, named "ribbon ware" for its scrolled patterns.

The gradual evolution and expansion of agricultural techniques culminated in the emergence of the "Chasseyan" civilization around 3,800 B.C.E., named after a site at Chassey near Macon. The expansion of this culture is traced to the widespread distribution (all the way north to Brittany) of its distinctive and finely made pottery, knives, sickles, arrowheads and ax heads as well as various types of grinders and millstones. Cultural consolidation seems to have occurred by both peaceful adaptation and interaction, as well as by displacement. Shepherd communities were restricted to mountainous areas of the Alps and the Massif Central. The relative abundance of the agricultural system led to a population expansion, producing what one French historian has called a "national Neolithic culture."[2] Women continued to enjoy high status, as determined by the abundance of statues honoring the fertility goddess.

By 3,500 B.C.E. the cultural homogeneity of the Chasseyan era was disintegrating. The remains of dolmens, great stone megaliths still found in Brittany, indicate a seaborne culture. Over the succeeding 1,700 years other megalithic monuments, possibly burial chambers, were spread across France, believed by historians to represent another peasant culture with its own distinctive pottery, which was smooth and undecorated.

Following periods brought metal working. The Age of Metal in France can generally be delineated as follows: copper was introduced between

2,500 and 1,800 B.C.E.; bronze between 1,800 and 700 B.C.E.; iron after 700
B.C.E. A different set of invading peoples brought each new metal. The
so-called Bell Beaker culture introduced copper. Bronze was brought in
by a people famous for their burial urns. Use of plows and carts and
horses permitted peasants to expand their area of cultivation into hilly
terrain, and typically this increase in agricultural production led to an
increase in the population.

The various tribes described as Celtic (subsequently known in France
as Gauls) brought the Iron Age. Prehistorians designate two major periods of their conquest: the Hallstatt culture, between 800 and 700 B.C.E,
and the Le Tène culture, dating from about 500 B.C.E. The Hallstatt period
brought the arrival of horse warriors with broad swords, whose superior
military technology swept away all before them. Theirs was a more complex society, with merchants, artisans, warriors, and farmers. Their arrival also marked a major shift in religion: a male god of war replaced
the female fertility goddesses. Burial tombs of their warrior nobles contain armor, jewels, and weapons, evidence of growing class stratification.
Individual graves replaced the collective burials of past cultures.

By 400 B.C.E. the various Celtic tribes had imposed their Indo-
European language across all of modern France except the Provence area
close to Italy. Celtic culture and settlement centered in the northeast,
present-day Alsace-Lorraine and Champagne. Ideal for their purposes,
this area contained rich deposits of iron ore and included dense forests,
useful for both agriculture and home building. A class of warrior elite
evolved, with large estates, free and tenant farmers, dependents, and
slaves. In time of war or conflict, the warrior owner could demand that
all able-bodied men on his estate fight for him.

Celtic farming, far more advanced than that of the Romans, included
many efficient and innovative techniques. The Celts introduced heavy
iron plows, pulled by horses, which were used extensively on the warrior
estates. Some farmers enriched their soil with lime to make it more fertile. Iron sickles and reapers made harvesting more efficient, too. More
land came under cultivation and this, in turn, led to expanded production and sparked an increase in population. The population of Gaul rose
from two or three million in 500 B.C.E. to six or eight million by the time
of the Roman conquest.

The warrior society, based on this new set of agricultural techniques,
led to a decline in the position of women. Few, if any, statues of fertility
goddesses are found from this era; the evidence suggests that men increasingly tried to restrict women's activities to bearing and rearing chil-

dren. Although the new and heavier agricultural implements probably required the greater strength of men, women's work continued to be indispensable.

Despite the political instability caused by constant fighting, a cultural unity did develop. One major pillar of this unity was the Druidic religion. Druid priests, who also served as judges and teachers, formed a well-educated elite, exempt from military service. Along with the priestly class, poets and storytellers also flourished. They recounted myths and heroic tales of the society, much as Homer did in ancient Greek society. Road networks also indicated a good degree of economic integration. Although the towns were primitive compared to those of the Mediterranean world, they nevertheless achieved an advanced specialization in labor; highly skilled artisans produced a wide variety of goods in various metals. A type of soap was invented, the first in Europe.

Lack of political organization was a major, but not the only, reason why Rome was able to conquer Gaul. In what is now southern France, Rome had been able to take over the earlier Greek colonies by the time of Julius Caesar. Rome was, indeed, the last in a long line of Mediterranean powers to establish a presence on the southern coast. The Phoenicians, at present-day Monaco and Port Vendres, had been the first to arrive, but their settlements had been trading posts rather than true cities. In contrast, by 600 B.C.E. Greeks from the Asia Minor city of Phocea had established the colony city of Massalia (present-day Marseille). When threatened by Persia, Greece built more colonies on the coast and along the Rhône River. Such modern French cities as Nice, Antibes, and Agde all had Greek origins. Then, when Persia conquered Phocea, much of that city's population moved to Massalia, increasing its importance and prestige. The Greek cities established extensive trade networks across Gaul, as evidenced by the discovery of Greek coins across France. The Romans later used these same trade networks.

When Rome and Carthage battled during the second century B.C.E., Massalia allied with Rome. Rome also provided protection on the occasions when Gallic tribes made incursions. Subsequently, Rome annexed this Greek city and the surrounding area, calling it Provincia (the basis of modern Provence). Provincia would be the springboard Caesar would use to conquer the rest of Gaul.

NOTES

1. Fernand Braudel, *The Identity of France, Vol. 2, People and Production* trans. Sîan Reynolds (New York: HarperCollins, 1990), p. 21.

2. Jean Guilaine's phrase cited by Fernand Braudel in *The Identity of France, Vol. 2*, p. 43.

3

From Caesar to Charlemagne

Colonized by the Romans under Julius Caesar (58–51 B.C.E.), France assimilated and then spread the imperial principle of the Romans. During this period of almost a thousand years, modern France assumed a definite shape, especially in terms of local communal life. This was a dramatic age of Roman imperial conquest, then consolidation and grandeur, followed by disintegration, barbarian invasions, and, finally, the rise of a new religion, Christianity, and various attempts made by French kings to reconsolidate the Roman imperial principle.

Rome's justification for the conquest of Gaul was defense of its boundaries. Within twenty years of consolidating its hold on what would become the province of Gallia Narbonensis (modern-day Provence), Rome had to worry about a whole constellation of marauding Germanic tribes bent on seizing new territory. Two such tribes, the Cimbri and the Teutones, had already been repulsed (109 and 101 B.C.E.). Soon another tribe, the Helvetians, threatened their frontier. Rome, believing it must secure its north border fully from these barbarians, sent the young, ambitious general Julius Caesar to Gaul.

Caesar's conquest of Gaul not only made him famous but also expanded the Roman Empire by more than 30 percent. Roman Gaul now incorporated not only modern France but also Belgium, Luxembourg, and much of Holland, Western Germany, and Switzerland. The area eventually comprised three Gallic provinces: Gallia Belgica (the northern tier), Gallia Iberica (near Spain), and Gallia Celtica (at the center). The already romanized province of Gallia Narbonensis remained separate. Other than minor changes made by Caesar Augustus in 13 B.C.E., these Roman administrative units remained largely unchanged for three centuries. The Romans established the capital of Gaul at Lugdunum (present-day Lyon), an eastern city in the Rhône River valley and the center of the main north-south trade and communications route in the Roman Empire.

After displaying its brutal side in conquest, Rome showed a generous side in administration. Gaul received not only the defending Roman army but also the Roman bureaucracy, language, commerce, and culture. Gaul adopted Latin and developed a written culture. The empire followed Caesar's precedent and used the tribe as the basic unit of their administrative districts. The nobles of Gaul received Roman titles and administrative duties, the warriors were incorporated in the legions, and the peasants paid only light taxes. In 215 C.E. Emperor Caracalla granted Roman citizenship to all the Gauls, who by the fourth century were almost universally called "Romans."

The intimate connection between Roman administration and religion (their emperors were considered gods) resulted in the steady decline of the Druids. The Druids, the priests of the pagan Celtic religion, combined magic, or soothsaying, with religion. Thus on the matter of religion as well as government the elite had a vested interest in dropping its old loyalties. Moreover, the Druids proved unable to maintain a united front, and their religion and oral culture could not compete with Latin literature. In the peasant world, however, religious change was slower, more evolutionary. Although Rome periodically launched anti-Druid campaigns—especially against the practice of human sacrifice—the main strategy was quite literally to cover the old religion with the new. Thus Roman temples were constructed on the sites of Celtic shrines, and Roman thermal spas used springs considered holy by the Druids. Although Christianity did penetrate the cities of Roman Gaul, only after Emperor Constantine's proclamation in 313 of Christianity as the religion of the empire was each *civitas* (city-state) organized also as a diocese and administered by a bishop.

The most decisive reason for the acceptance of Roman rule and the assimilation of Roman culture was the increase in economic prosperity.

Undergoing what we would now term an economic crisis just before the Roman invasion, Gaul soon recovered and enjoyed an extended boom as the empire continued to expand as part of the wider Mediterranean economy. Construction of the famous and still enduring Roman roads in the new provinces put thousands to work and consolidated the already extensive trade network. Romans also transformed the villages and towns of Gaul: marble and stone replaced wood, and enclosed defensive fortifications gave way to free-standing forums, workshops, markets, baths, stadiums, temples, circuses, and theaters. Of the 55 contemporary French cities with a population of 100,000, 37 have Gallo-Roman origins.[1] The cities, although containing only 6 or 7 percent of the population of Roman Gaul, produced a prosperous Gallo-Roman ruling class of merchants and administrators. This wealthy and powerful elite took the lead in transmitting the Roman language and culture.

The Romans increased the scale of the existing agriculture and connected it to a much vaster trading and exchange network. More land came under cultivation, and labor became more intensive, even factory-like, with as many as 400 tenant farmers or slaves working on one villa. Rome's most significant contributions were in the introduction of new Mediterranean crops—especially grape vines, but also olive, cherry, and peach orchards—and in specialization by area. For example, the Beauce region specialized in grain; Languedoc, Roussillon, and Alsace produced wine; the Auvergne grew hemp; Berry concentrated on flax; Artois raised geese and the Ardennes sheep.

The Roman Empire was less successful at reproducing itself. Roman inheritance law and custom did not encourage large families: estates could be left to daughters or an adopted heir, as well as to sons. The decisive factor was the rate of taxation. Until the third century C.E. the Roman tax system, which typically placed its burden primarily on the lower orders, was not too onerous on the Gallic peasantry. But then conquest declined, the steady flow of new slaves and booty dried up, taxes increased, and peasants lost their incentive to have large families. At this point, Rome started sanctioning barbarian settlements, known as *laeti*, to reverse depopulation.

After the third century, taxation became even more oppressive as tax collectors targeted individuals rather than communities. This economic downturn was intensified by epidemics that decimated towns and villages alike. Many small farmers had to sell their property to the great villas; others simply fled. To stop the labor drain, villa owners, with the support of imperial administrators, tightened the regulations tying the peasants to the land. In other cases peasants turned to rebellion and banditry.

In the fourth century C.E. reforming emperors tried to reverse Rome's decline. The Emperor Diocletian (284–305) created two super provinces with capitals in Trier and Vienne and reinforced border defenses. However, his attempt to reduce taxes by allowing peasants to pay in crops and produce rather than in money resulted in a decline in the use of currency which, in turn, reduced the amount of trade and commerce. In short, the international economy of the empire was disintegrating and local autarky, or self-sufficiency, was reemerging. The Roman cult of the emperor and the empire receded, and the Celtic language and culture returned. At the same time, eastern religions, the most important being Christianity, spread throughout Rome and Gaul.

By the early fifth century, barbarian migration had turned into an invasion, caused probably by the movement out of central Asia of a tribe of nomadic horse warriors, the fabled Huns. Their shift into the more fertile steppes of Eastern and Central Europe pushed the various Germanic tribes into the Italian peninsula and thus into Gaul. After 406 a series of cold winters often froze the Rhine facilitating a rapid mass movement into Gaul. The Alamanni moved into Alsace, the Burgundians settled in northern Gaul, and the Vandals and Alans passed through Gaul on their way into Spain and Africa. From the south, in 412, the Visigoths crossed from northern Italy into the Toulouse area. Six years later they proclaimed a Visigothic kingdom and broke Roman administrative continuity.

In most cases, barbarian/Roman accommodation and negotiation provided political and administrative continuity. When the Germanic Franks invaded the regions of Tournai and Cambrai in 430, Roman administrators reached an accommodation with *foederati* (federates), which involved the granting of land and, in return, the performance of military service and protection. In 443 Roman authorities reached a similar agreement with the Burgundians in the Jura-Geneva region and later reached similar agreements with "federation" Visigoths in the southwest.

This symbiosis between Roman administration and Germanic military manpower prevented any dramatic or sudden political transition in Gaul. Only in retrospect have historians dated the "fall" of Rome as having occurred in 476. Probably few shed tears in Gaul that year; probably not even many among the governmental and economic elite because their status and wealth were now protected by barbarian armies. During the 440s the Visigoths crushed a substantial revolt made by peasant rebels (known as Bagaudae) in the southwest, and in 451 a barbarian army fighting under the Roman banner defeated Attila the Hun near Troyes in central France.

Out of the disintegration of the Roman Empire emerged a series of Frankish kingdoms—first the Merovingian Dynasty then the Carolingian Dynasty that ruled until the rise of the Capetians in 980. The Frankish kings saw themselves as continuing the Roman imperium. They may have had their own legal codes, but these were written in Latin and were based on Roman models. In addition, the administrative structures remained essentially unchanged: the old roman *civitates* were simply renamed *pagi* and administered by Frankish counts. The network of bishoprics was left in place.

Aside from bequeathing their name to the nation, the Franks had only a minimal long-term impact on France. Historians estimate the number of invading Franks to have been in the range of from 150,000 to 200,000, perhaps 2 to 3 percent of a population of between 6 and 7 million.[2] The Franks even assimilated the primary beverage of Gaul, wine.

After their initial entrance into the empire, the Franks slowly migrated across the Seine Valley and up the Loire River. By the fifth century they had divided into two groups: the Salian, or "salty," Franks who occupied the area from the British Channel to the Loire Valley, and the Ripuarian, or "river bank," Franks, who seem to have settled between the Rhine and the Meuse rivers. According to legend, but not completely verified by historians, the first king of the Salians was one Merovech, half king, half god. In any case, his name was immortalized in the first Frankish dynasty: the Merovingians.

The true founder of the Merovingian Dynasty was Clovis. His father, Childeric, was one of the top commanders of the joint Roman/barbarian army that had defeated Attila. Already king of the Salians, Clovis had himself elected king of the Ripuarian Franks to create a united Frankish people. In 486 he conquered the Gallo-Romans at Soissons, subsequently the Alamanni, then the Visigoths at Vouille in 507. Ranking with his military victories was his marriage to Clotilda, a Catholic princess and niece of the Burgundian kings. Under her influence he embraced Roman Catholicism and was baptized with 3,000 of his warriors by the bishop Remi at Reims, a city destined to become the coronation site of French kings until the 1820s. Clovis's conversion was a decisive step in the consolidation of his power, for it ensured that the Frankish warriors and the Gallo-Roman officials and principal landowners were all of the same religion. Throughout Gaul the Catholic bishops saw Clovis as their champion. In 511 he made Paris, a city on the northern periphery, his capital. From there he issued a legal code: the Salic Law. The code's prologue reveals sheer physical prowess as the essence of the warrior king and knight: "Illustrious race, founded by God Himself, strong in arms, steadfast in alliance, wise in counsel, of singular beauty and fairness, noble and sound in body, daring, swift, awesome, converted to the Catholic Faith."

Clovis's sons added Burgundy in 536 and Provence in 537 to the kingdom, nearly completing the conquest of Gaul. They also extended their reach into south and central Germany as well as northern Italy. Thus Clovis and his sons unified nearly the whole of Gaul. The only parts of the modern hexagon beyond their reach were the present-day areas of the Breton peninsula, lower Languedoc, and Roussillon in the southwest.

Merovingian royal authority—based upon family ties, physical prowess, and plunder—proved politically unstable and economically primitive. Clovis's rule tended toward political fragmentation, decentralization, and economic devolution. His four sons—Thierry, Clodomir, Childebert, and Clotaire I—divided the Frankish kingdom among themselves, as did their descendants.

Yet the idea of a coherent Gaul remained. For example, Clovis's four sons each chose capitals that were located in the Paris basin: Rheims, Orléans, Paris, and Soissons. The provinces most often divided and fought over tended to be the ones that had been acquired either by Clovis or by his sons: Aquitaine, Burgundy, and Provence. For the first few generations of Merovingian kings, the center of Gaul remained relatively free of strife.

The kings appointed counts to rule the countryside. The steward of the royal domains, called the "mayor of the palace," increasingly became the ruling figure at these ever-smaller courts. Because mayors derived their power from controlling the royal finances, this position, too, in this time of ineffectual royal authority, became hereditary. The position had sufficient significance that one of the mayors was able to found a new dynasty: the Carolingian, so named because of the great number of family members whose first name was Charles. As Austrasin mayor of the palace during the 680s, Pépin II of Herstal waged a decisive battle at Tertry, near Saint Quentin, in 687. Victorious, he then placed one of the feckless Merovingians back on the Frankish throne. Although the Merovingian family may have become ineffectual, the monarchical concept remained sacral.

Pépin II's influence ended with his death in 714; his only fully legitimate heir was a six-year-old grandson. In this power vacuum, Neustrians and Aquitainians revolted, and the Germanic tribes from across the Rhine, the Saxons and the Frisians, quickly invaded. In desperation, Austrasian nobles turned to one of Pépin II's bastard sons, Charles Martel. This was an inspired choice.

Charles Martel was a bold, energetic, and courageous warrior. He achieved a series of swift and decisive military victories across Gaul. First repulsing the Germanic tribes from Neustria, Charles swung into the south to confront a Muslim Arab invasion from Spain. His great victory over the Muslim Arabs at Poitiers in 732 won him the loyalty of the Aquitaine region and heroic status across the Christian world. Through this great victory over the "infidels," Martel amassed large tracts of Church property that he distributed among his followers and warriors.

By 737 Charles Martel, duke and prince of the Franks, had achieved such stature that he was the obvious successor to the Merovingian throne. At the death of Charles Martel, his domains, in the tradition of Frankish kings, were split between his two sons, Carloman and Pépin III (the Short). The brothers first had to suppress local revolts on the periphery—Aquitaine, Bavaria, Alemannia, and Saxony. Such revolts were extremely common after the death of a king or ruler. To secure the loyalty of the most powerful families and potential competitors within the heart of the kingdom, the brothers placed one last Merovingian, Childeric III, on the throne, but retained all the real power for themselves. In 747, Carloman retired to the abbey of Monte Cassino in Italy, and Pépin the Short became the paramount leader.

To gain a transcendent legitimacy—one that would surpass brute physical force and the mere amassing of land and booty—Pépin the Short pursued two strategies. The first, assembling the Frankish nobles to vote him king, was a traditional practice among Germanic tribes in general and the Franks in particular. The second, being anointed not only by a local bishop but also by the pope, was a dramatic innovation. Initially, his friend Bishop Boniface (c. 680–754), Christianizer of German lands and later proclaimed a saint, sprinkled him with sacramental oil in a ceremony inspired by the Old Testament. Three years later, in 751, the new Pope Stephen II (752–757) added his blessing in the basilica of Saint Denis, just outside Paris. This ritual firmly connected the developing Carolingian dynasty to the growing domination of the Roman Catholic Church. Thus the notion that a French king ruled by divine right emerged—a notion that remained dominant but periodically contested until the French Revolution of 1789. At the time, however, the model was not monarchical but imperial. The ultimate goal was the renewal of the Roman Empire.

Pépin the Short, well aware that papal blessing still had to be supplemented by material booty, followed in the footsteps of his father, Charles Martel. He led his armies into Germany, subduing the Saxons, the Alamanni, and the Bavarians. He also consolidated his control over Burgundy and Provence. After his death in 768, his son Charlemagne would complete this synthesis of religion and militarism.

Under Charlemagne, the Roman Empire seemed to revive. Charlemagne possessed not only great bodily size and strength—"just seven times the length of his own feet,"[3] according to his court biographer Einhard—but intelligence, longevity, and great luck. Unlike the Frankish kings before him, he was well educated for his time. Although illiterate, he spoke and understood Latin, comprehended Greek, and had picked up a smattering of mathematics and astronomy. He brought to his court the Saxon monk Alcuin, reputed to be the most learned man in the west. After the death of his brother Carloman in 771, Charlemagne was sole ruler. Like his forefathers, he then turned, to the east. In 782 he smashed the pagan Saxons, a victory that facilitated the work of such Christian missionaries as Bishop Boniface in the conversion of the Germanic tribes. Charlemagne, demanding that the conquered populace show more than mere submission, prescribed death for any Saxon refusing baptism or behaving in a non-Christian manner. As a result of his campaigns in Germany, Charlemagne laid the foundation of Germany just as Caesar had done in Gaul more than 800 years earlier. Charlemagne's role in Italian history was equally decisive. Late in the year 800 he went to Rome to secure the power of Pope Leo III against the machinations of the city's aristocrats. He ceded to the pope the surrounding lands, an area known as the Papal states until Italian unification in the mid-nineteenth century. Not surprisingly, on Christmas Day 800, Pope Leo II legitimated Charlemagne's claims and crowned him Roman emperor, the first western emperor since 476.

By the time of his death in 814 Charlemagne's empire stretched from northern Spain through all of contemporary France, Germany, and part of Italy above Calabria and Sicily. Many of the Slavic tribes to the east were tributary subjects. Only the Romans at the height of their empire had ruled more of Europe; and only Napoleon Bonaparte and Adolf Hitler would later equal this territorial realm. The great problem Charlemagne faced was how to unify his vast holdings. Two of his solutions focused on securing political allegiance. First, he traveled throughout his domains to supervise his officials and to sit as an appeals judge; second, he required that the nobles and clergy meet annually in a general assembly to hear imperial ordinances, report on local life, and advise the emperor.

Charlemagne's answer to the centrifugal forces tending to dissolve any state in this age of migration and economic disintegration was to bind the state and the church in a close alliance. Bishops played a vital role in Carolingian administration and often were more influential than counts. Charlemagne's most original governmental innovation was the creation of a cadre of roving administrators, the *missi dominici*. Teams were sent out in pairs, one layman and one bishop, to oversee the local counts and bishops. They were constantly rotated to ensure that they did not develop local allegiances that outweighed fidelity to the emperor. Another of Charlemagne's strategies to promote unity was an attempt to standardize weights, measures, and money. In another step to combat localism, Charlemagne ceded tremendous amounts of land[4] to the Church: from 751 to 825 Church lands in Christendom appear to have tripled, growing from about 10 to about 30 percent of total arable land.

Charlemagne also facilitated the spread of monasteries and, in an attempt to increase general literacy, attached schools connected to the monasteries and cathedral churches. He also ordered the transcription of ancient manuscripts; the monks assigned to this task are credited with inventing the modern distinction between upper- and lower-case letters (known as Carolingian Miniscule) as well as with developing and standardizing medieval Latin. With the spread of this scholarly language, popular vernaculars developed in each region. One of these was Old French, whose earliest extant book is dated 842.

Despite these Herculean efforts at the restoration of the Roman world, the international economy—the vital glue holding the empire together—disintegrated further. The rise of Islam divided the Mediterranean world in two. As a result, the economic basis of Charlemagne's rule continued to be military conquest and booty. A modest if shortlived economic expansion did occur, facilitated by a population increase from about 7.5 million in 650 to about 9 million in 750.[5] The economic upturn was centered in the monasteries, where monks were now functioning as capitalists through their workshops, farms, and fairs. At the end of Charlemagne's reign, sources of plunder started to run out and the economy once again deteriorated.

After Charlemagne's death, with the economy in decline and the diverse population restive, his son Louis the Pious (814–840) had neither the will nor the desire to maintain the empire. In 817 he decreed that upon his death the empire would be subdivided among his three sons. This proclamation unleashed a dynastic struggle, first pitting sons against father and subsequently the sons against each other. The conflict ended three years later with the Treaty of Verdun (843), dividing the empire among the three brothers. Charles the Bald received West Francia, the nucleus of modern France; the other two, Lothair and Louis, received respectively the kingdoms of Lotharingia and East Francia.

The emergence of West Francia, the name now indicating the official emergence of modern France, would prove more of an ending than a beginning. During the ninth and tenth centuries the population of this nascent France witnessed foreign invasions from all sides: Saracens, Muslim raiders, and warriors from Iberia; Hungarian Magyar horsemen from the east; and Vikings from the north. Vikings, or "Northmen," launched the most sustained, devastating, and consequential raids and pillages. In 844–845, for example, they sacked cities as far south as Toulouse, and in 851 they set up a winter camp in France from which they plundered Paris, Tours, and other cities. Soon they consolidated their hold on the lower Seine estuary. In 911 Charles the Simple, grandson of Charles the Bald, granted Rollo, the Northmen's leader, the territory now known as Normandy. Rollo became a duke, and in exchange the Vikings converted to Christianity and swore allegiance to the Frankish king. These Normans later established kingdoms in England, Sicily, and southern Italy.

The immediate effect of the Viking victory was to hasten the collapse of the Carolingian Dynasty and the emergence of feudalism. Even during the reign of Charles the Bald (ruled 838–877), the Carolingian forces had proved unable to contain the Vikings. By 850 the *missi dominici* system had disintegrated; by 877 counts were no longer reporting to the crown, the royal decrees known as "capitularies" ceased after 884, and no national assemblies convened after 889. Local nobles and large landowners filled this power vacuum as they had during the time of Rome's decline. Counts, placed or removed at the discretion of a strong ruler like Charlemagne, now achieved lifetime or hereditary tenure and in some cases declared themselves princes or kings and supported their own armies. Peasants and townspeople turned to these local magnates because their fortified keeps and castles provided the only source of protection. Hincmar, Bishop of Reims, told Charles the Bald at the end of his reign: "You have so many partners and rivals in that part of the kingdom that you rule more in name than in fact."[6] Out of this maelstrom came the figure

Robert the Strong, one of the generals Charles appointed to stem the Viking onslaught. Famous for his bravery and valor in battle, Robert the Strong would lay the foundations for a new dynasty.

This period of political disintegration and foreign invasion also gave birth to cultural and linguistic differentiation, not only in the kingdoms of West and East Francia but also in the northern and southern parts of France. In the north the Franks maintained their power base and produced a French dialect that became known as the *langue d'oil*. In the south, where laws, customs, and language remained closer to their Roman origin, a different language emerged known as the *langue d'oc*.

In 888, like the Merovingian Dynasty before them, the Carolingian Dynasty was terminated when a noble assembly voted for Eudes, son of Robert the Strong, as their new king. During the following century, currents of royal authority flowed back and forth between this line of Robertians (after Robert the Strong) and the last of the Carolingians. By the time Hugh Capet of the Robertian line was crowned king in 987, "France" comprised no more than a few hundred kilometers around Paris. Ironically, this small principality under the Capetian Dynasty would prove to be the nucleus of modern France.

NOTES

1. Colin Jones, *The Cambridge Illustrated History of France* (Cambridge: Cambridge University Press, 1994), p. 37.

2. Patrick J. Geary, *Before France & Germany: The Creation & Transformation of the Merovingian World* (Oxford: Oxford University Press, 1988), p. 115.

3. Einhard and Notker The Stammerer, *Two Lives of Charlemagne*, trans. and intro. Lewis Thorpe (Harmondsworth, Middlesex, England: Penguin Books, 1969), p. 76.

4. Jones, *The Cambridge Illustrated History of France*, p. 64.

5. Ibid.

6. Jean Dunbabin, *France in the Making, 843–1180* (Oxford: Oxford University Press, 1985), p. 13.

4

Building the Nation: From Hugh Capet to Richelieu (987–1642)

The foundations of the modern French nation were put in place between the reign of Hugh Capet who ascended to the throne of the Carolingian territories around Paris in 987 and the death of Cardinal Richelieu in 1642. The process took almost 700 years and was achieved despite periodic intervals when the monarchy seemed on the verge of collapse. Each time, however, a king, a powerful minister, or a great military leader was able to reestablish and even strengthen royal power. By the birth of Louis XIV in 1638, the French state was the most centralized and developed in Europe.

Why did France emerge as a nation-state sooner than the neighboring Italy, Germany, Belgium, or Holland? Noted historian Fernand Braudel believes that the precocious development of trade and manufacture in the cities of these areas worked to their economic advantage, but the political freedom that prosperity brought meant that these cities resisted the centralizing efforts of the monarchs and thereby retarded national development.[1]

Why would the Paris region provide the nucleus of modern France? Again Braudel, following the American historian Edward Whiting Fox, provides insight. He argues that the Capetians, like the Carolingians before them, found this area to be the center of a particularly rich agricultural region. In an age when the mounted warrior was the decisive element in military strategy, an abundant supply of oats for their steeds gave the Capetians a decisive military advantage.[2] The capital city of Paris, located at the center of trade routes, became the biggest city in the region, and, indeed, the kingdom. No other region or city could challenge the predominance of Paris or its agricultural region.

Complementing these geographic and economic opportunities was the combined wisdom and luck of the Capetian dynasty. In this tumultuous and violent age, with high infant mortality and low life expectancy, dynastic discontinuity was the norm for most monarchies. But for 11 consecutive generations, the Capetians produced male heirs. They also proved to be masters at statecraft, not only in the matter of political and military power but also in the realm of political imagination. Indeed, they were past masters at what would become distinctive in French life: the uncanny ability to infuse politics with culture.

The Capetian line had to start from scratch. When Hugh Capet came to the throne in 987, he did not even control Paris. He wielded more significant power as a landowner than as a king and had barely an entourage, much less a bureaucracy. So insecure did he feel that he crowned his successor during his own life, an action with a far-reaching result: annulment of the disputatious Carolingian customs of elective kingship and divisible inheritance. Under Hugh Capet's successors— Robert II (the Pious, 996–1031), Henry I (1031–1060), and Philip I (1060–1108)—the monarchy did little more than survive. Philip I was the first king to extend the rights of self-government to a city (Le Mans in 1070), and he was little more than a spectator when one of his vassals, William of Normandy, conquered England, and when another Frenchman, Pope Urban II, initiated the First Crusade against the Muslims in 1096 to retake the Christian Holy Land (where Jesus was born).

The rise of the Capetians coincides with what historian Marc Bloch titled "the first feudal age."[3] Political authority had devolved into bonds of personal loyalty and dependence between the powerful (the lords) and the weak (the vassals). Power in this age was exercised especially through land ownership. The surest way for the nobility to build a powerful army was to promise land to the mounted warriors. By doing an act of "homage," a warrior could be "invested" with land. Once the land was given, the new owner in essence became "lord" (*seigneur*) over the peasants and townspeople within his territory. In effect, almost all the functions we now associate with government—especially police and judicial functions—were in the hands of the new lord rather than in the hands of the king or his agents. The only other official at the local level was the parish priest. Although between one-fifth and one-third of landed property was in Church hands, this property was administered under feudal forms of land management. Even medieval liturgy had a feudal cast: saints functioned as spiritual lords to their earthly vassals.

The castle and the church thus symbolized a world that was profoundly local and insular. The peasant submitted to the superior weaponry of the mounted knight in return for his protection. By 900 few allodial peasants (i.e., those who farmed their own land, free of seigneurial dues) remained, especially in the north. Most had become "serfs" and had to work on the lord's fields and properties a set number of days each year. In addition, the lords extracted profit from such other enterprises as the local winepress, the flour mill, and the bakery. Peasants only slowly come out from under this yoke: following the Hundred Years' War (1337–1453—between France and England), they began to pay off their obligations with cash rather than personal services. Some bought their own land. But the feudal system would not be fully abolished until the French Revolution in 1789.

The other great institution of the feudal age, the Catholic Church, also played a significant role in state building. The Church helped maintain order, developed economic infrastructure, and promoted the stability and expansion of the family. The rise of monasteries, especially the extensive Cluniac network (started in Burgundy in 909) and the Cistercian (founded in 1098) encouraged economic and social development through their land clearing, farming, schools, and ongoing pastoral care. In 989 church councils started the Peace of God movement in an attempt to stem the endemic violence and pillage of feudal knights. This movement was superseded in 1027 by the Truce of God movement, dedicated to prohibiting violence on Lent, Advent, Sundays, and other holy days.

The eight European Crusades, whose purpose it was to retake the Holy Land from the Muslims (1095–1270), also brought prestige to the Capetian monarchy and peace to France. A French pope, Urban, launched the First Crusade and a French king, Saint Louis, led the last one. For almost two centuries French knights composed the largest of the Christian forces fighting first to win and then to retain sacred sites including Jerusalem, the birthplace of Jesus. As a result, the Church and the crown exported noble violence overseas. In addition, the crusading experience built a sense of fraternity and loyalty to the king among the warrior nobility.

Perhaps the most direct way in which the Church facilitated state building was by providing capable and astute royal advisers. In the medieval period, these advisers infused the Capetian[4] dynasty with a sacred charisma and ideology. Advisers to Hugh Capet's son, Robert II (the Pious), promulgated the belief that the king could cure scrofula, a lymphatic skin disease, by his mere touch. Soon the royal touch became one of the most dramatic ways in which the king mixed with the population. Most important among these early advisers was Suger, the abbot of Saint Denis. Counselor and strategist for the first two significant Capetian kings—Louis VI (the Fat) (r. 1108–1187) and his son Louis VII (r. 1137–1180)—Suger depicted the king as God's Anointed, and in a linguistic move fraught with future implications referred to him as the "King of France" rather than the "King of the Franks." Suger also helped give tangible form to the Capetian Dynasty's claims of power and sanctity when he invented and promulgated the Gothic architectural style, of which Reims Cathedral, site of the kings' coronation, provided a particularly fine example. The style's diffusion across Europe added to the monarchy's reputation. Moreover, Church and state in the eleventh and twelfth centuries also constructed a new matrimonial order; marriage, as a sacrament, fused well with the rules of feudal property.

Under Louis VI and Louis VII, not only were Paris and its environs (the Île de France) consolidated as the locus of royal power, but Paris was expanding to become a major city. From a population of 15,000 to 20,000 under the Carolingians, it grew under the Capetian rule to 200,000 by 1300 and, as well, boasted one of the most important universities in Europe, the University of Paris. Louis VI took an important first step in the creation of a royal bureaucracy with the office of provost, charged with administration of small districts, collection of royal revenue, recruitment of troops, and preservation of order. Louis VI was also known as "father of the communes," in recognition of the large number of such municipal franchises he granted, including Laon, Beauvais, Noyon, Soissons, and Reims.

The following king, Philip II (Augustus, r. 1180–1223), dramatically augmented royal territory and power. During the decades-long struggle with the Norman kings of England known as the First Hundred Years' War (1159–1299), Philip increased Capetian territories fourfold, incorporating the provinces of Anjou, Maine, Touraine, Brittany, Poitou, Auvergne, Artois, and Picardy. The foundations of royal expansion to the Pyrenees were laid during his reign. In the southwestern region known as Languedoc, including the cities of Toulouse, Albi, and Carcassone, a religious heresy known as Catharism had taken hold. The Catholic Church viewed the heresy as a mortal threat to its power especially because the Cathars denied the legitimacy of the Church's hierarchy of bishops and priests. Instead of the Catholic clergy, Cathar doctrine held that God had selected a special sanctified elite known as the perfects who did not need to follow Catholic teaching concerning marriage. In 1208 Pope Innocent III launched a crusade against the heresy. Within a year, French knights from the north had essentially crushed the Albigensians, and, by the end of the 1220s, the French crown had incorporated the region.

Central to Philip's consolidation of royal power and authority was the renewed study and application of Roman Law, with much of this scholarship centered at the University of Paris. Indeed, by adding "Augustus" to his name, Philip acknowledged a desire to ground his sovereignty upon Roman law. The territorial expansion of his kingdom was paralleled by an increase in tax receipts—an 80 percent jump between 1180 and 1203. To administer these new lands and revenues, Philip created a new administrative level: *baillis* (bailiffs) to oversee matters of finance and justice. He used the growing corps of lawyers to wring every possible advantage from the feudal ties binding him and his noble vassals. He also increased his power by granting royal patronage charters to monasteries and towns, making these entities loyal to him rather than to the local lords.

His successors Louis VIII (r. 1223–1226) and "Saint" Louis IX (r. 1226–1270) built upon Philip's achievements. For example, both the short-lived Louis VIII, who died of dysentery on his return from a trip south, and the long-lived Louis IX consolidated royal control over Languedoc. Saint Louis, in particular, furthered the specialization of the royal bureaucracy. A branch of the administration devoted to royal justice laid the groundwork for the later emergence of the high courts of justice known as Parlements, and a branch of the administration which regulated finance produced the Court of Accounts (*Cour des Comptes*). Saint Louis also brought clearer definition to the duties of the bailiffs. In 1190 he assigned them to specific locations rather than allowing them to roam through the kingdom, and he issued more detailed instructions concerning their supervisory duties and reports. Louis also introduced a large silver coin, the *livre tournois*, which was the basis of French currency until 1789.

As his name implies, however, this king was most renowned, during his lifetime and later, for his sanctity. He crushed the Cathar heresy in the south and launched the last crusade against the Muslims. In a series of major ordinances he forbade his vassals to use arms or to harm their vassals, and on his own agents he imposed a strict and detailed moral code. His sanctity was offset by his growing intolerance and his systematic surveillance, incarceration, or banishment of all that seemed to him unchristian or deviant: Jews, lepers, prostitutes, tavern keepers. Women's normative roles became increasingly restricted to the idealized woman of courtly love literature or limited within the growing cult of the Virgin Mary, which emphasized sexual purity and a narrow range of female behavior. Male clerics increased surveillance not only of lay women but also those in convents. The changing structure of government administration also reduced the influence of queens and princesses. Medieval Christian marriage seemed to make aristocratic women pawns and tempted them down the path of heresy. Catharism, which allowed women greater freedom than Roman Catholicism, was especially attractive.

The reign of Saint Louis would gather even more luster when his successors proved short lived, overreaching, and sterile. The uneventful fifteen-year reign of Philip III makes one wonder how he has gone down in history as "the bold." Philip IV (the Fair) embarked in 1285 on an ambitious but abortive scheme to implement a principle his lawyers found in ancient Roman law: "The King's wish is the law's wish."

Philip's ambition, abetted by a cluster of legal advisors, quickly crashed upon the reef of papal pretension. Pope Boniface VIII, also a legalist, asserted the authority of the Church over all temporal rulers. In 1301 the pope created a new French bishopric at Pamiers without the advice or consent of Philip. A complicated, eight-year conflict ensued, ending when Philip arranged for Boniface's death by poison and for the subsequent election of a friendly French pope. By this time (1309), the papacy had moved to Avignon, although having the papacy on his territory added little, or nothing, to Philip's power. Indeed, ensuing schisms in the Church may ultimately have helped to precipitate the Protestant Reformation.

At the same time, Philip tried to gain territory at the expense of the English crown to the south and the Count of Flanders to the north. Both campaigns were expensive failures. Philip and his advisors claimed that the feudal obligation of military service could be achieved through a tax called "army aid," on the principle (not fully achieved until the nineteenth century) that the upper classes of society as well as the lower should be subject to taxation. To legitimize this taxation, in 1302 Philip formally convened the three estates of the realm—the first (the clergy), the second (the nobility), and the Third Estate (everyone who was a member neither of the clergy nor of the nobility). This representative body, which became known as the Estates General, was France's national representative body until 1789. The following year, the body approved the first permanent taxes of the Capetian monarchy. Even so, Philip, always desperate for money, manipulated exchange rates and forced Italian and Jewish bankers to provide loans.

Perhaps Philip's most infamous act was to confiscate the property and wealth of the Knights Templars. This religious and military order, which had been created two centuries earlier in the Holy Land to defend Christian shrines, had become bankers and merchants for European royalty and had amassed extensive wealth. The trumped-up charges of immorality and heresy were obediently ratified by Philip's hand-picked pope Clement V (1305–1314) and confirmed by confessions extracted through torture.

The power and pretensions of these later Capetians had been underwritten by a dynamic and expanding economy. Indeed, the period between 1000 and 1300 has often been called a medieval renaissance. Western Europe experienced an unparalleled rate of expansion, facilitated by such diverse factors as climatic improvements, an increase in the supply of gold and silver, cessation of barbarian invasions, and the widespread diffusion of more efficient agricultural methods and tools (heavy plow, three-field system, and more efficient collars and harnesses). In the absence of specific economic data, our best indication is the dramatic jump in population: from 5 or 6 million in the time of Hugh Capet to around 15 million subjects under the later Capetians. Whereas half of France's total landmass had been wooded in 987, by 1300 forests had been cut dramatically to provide arable land to feed all the new mouths in some 30,000 villages. Political stability and agricultural productivity produced dramatic urban growth. Early medieval cities, essentially religious and military centers, now developed strong economies. Urban merchants and craftsmen created a set of interests and values quite separate from those of the agrarian nobility.

The booty system gradually disappeared, resurfacing during times of severe turmoil, and a stable monetary economy emerged. Rude and illiterate warrior nobles became literate and cultured aristocrats who engaged in a stylized existence of hunts, tournaments, feasts, and courtly festivities. The growing expense of this lifestyle made the seigneurs often as profit-conscious as any merchant or artisan. Aristocrats often wrung every ounce of profit out of their extensive legal rights and judicial powers. This increased seigneurial greed drove the peasant, in turn, to be more innovative and productive. The conception of a three-way division

of society—those who pray (clergy), those who fight (nobles), and th
who work (peasants)—was coming to look archaic even as it becai.
fully established in the Estates General.

By 1314 the Capetian Dynasty had helped to make France one of the
foremost states in medieval Europe, but the dynastic luck had finally run
out. The French economy suffered as the main European trade routes
shifted east to Germany. Then famines, caused by the population
growth's outstripping agricultural resources, hit in 1315 and 1317. The
gabelle, a tax on salt, was introduced in 1341 to bolster royal revenues.
In 1348 a devastating strain of bubonic plague, known as the black death,
descended on Europe. By 1400 an estimated one-third of France's population had died from the plague. The depopulation ravaged the economy: agricultural and artisanal production sank, tax revenues dropped,
and labor costs rose. In the face of such catastrophic losses, the crown
and the wealthy tried to maintain revenues by raising taxes, devaluing
money, or placing a limit on wages. A series of dramatic and furious
peasant and urban revolts resulted. The most impressive of these was
the *Jacquerie* of 1358, when peasants in northern France attacked seigneurs and burned down castles. Panic reached the upper classes as
well; nobles and warriors faced with poverty pillaged peasants and
townspeople thus reverting to a booty economy. Desperation among
some reached such levels as to lead to cannibalism.

Within this context of economic and social devastation, the Hundred
Years' War (1337–1453) erupted. In 1328 the line of 11 uncontestable
Capetian heirs ended with the death of Philip the Fair. His three children
ruled consecutively, but not fruitfully: none could produce a durable
male heir. The succession debate was eventually decided in favor of
Philip de Valois, a nephew of Philip the Fair, who took the title of Philip
VI (1328–1350) but not before the ruling English dynasty (the Plantagenet
line running from Henry II to Richard II) had determined to make good
on their claim to the throne of France. The war started in 1337 over
interlocking territorial claims, dating from the Norman Conquest of England (1066) through to Henry Plantagenet's marriage to Eleanor of Aquitaine (1154). In 1340, when Philip VI attempted to confiscate Edward
III's lands in the Guyenne, Edward declared Philip a usurper and added
the kingship of France to his own titles.

During the course of the Hundred Years' War, the French crown suffered dramatic military defeats—from the destruction of the French fleet
outside Bruges (1340) to the annihilation of the French cavalry at Agin-
court (1415). Mutiny, rebellion, and plunder were common in both the

French and British armies. The resulting devastation of some areas—Normandy, for instance—has been compared by some historians to the ruin of Hiroshima. In the darkest days of this war, France's very existence seemed in question.

Then, in the spring of 1429, in a moment that makes even Hollywood kneel at the feet of history, the English, poised to take the city of Orléans and the entire Loire valley, were confronted by a young peasant woman from the region of Lorraine, Joan of Arc. Charles VII, the French king whom she inspired and empowered, was able to create in 1439 the first standing, professional army in a European country since the fall of the Roman Empire.

The cost of warfare had risen dramatically during the Hundred Years' War. The relatively inexpensive and small-scale nature of knightly warfare—with each warrior supplying his own equipment—was displaced by the rise of costly civilian infantries equipped with longbows, crossbows, or pikes, and gunpowder and cannons. As feudal obligations declined, soldiers demanded to be paid and insisted on cash when booty was unavailable.

Facing destruction, a desperate French crown levied a new tax directly on peasant families. Originally called *fouage*, from the word "hearth," it was later known as the *taille*, from the verb to cut up or divide. Imposed without consultation with the Estates General, this tax was a major step in the growth of royal sovereignty. Nobles and clerics—the first two estates—had little objection to this direct tax because they were to be exempt from it, and therefore had little incentive to convene the Estates General. In 1438 Charles VII gained additional powers of taxation and patronage with the Pragmatic Sanction of Bourges. The pope granted French kings much discretion in appointing bishops and power to tax some Church revenues.

The royal standing army, which became one of the key agents of royal absolutism, was financed by the *taille*. Permanent companies of regularly paid and strictly disciplined cavalry replaced the old feudal ties. Artillery forces were organized into fifteen companies of 660 men each. Finally, every 60 "hearths" had to train and maintain one archer and one crossbowman for service in the army. Charles VII used his newly created army to push the British out of France in the 1440s and bring the war to a conclusion in 1453.

In the following decades, under Charles VII (1422–1461) and his ugly but crafty successor Louis XI (r. 1461–1483), the crown continued to become more bureaucratic and less feudal. Professional lawyers increased in both numbers and influence. Financial and judicial duties became more clearly defined, subdivided, and monitored. A hierarchy of royal tribunals emerged, with the Paris Parlement at the top. A series of "generals of finance" administered finances through an accounting office (*chambre des comptes*) and monitored taxes with a tax court (*cour des aides*). The courts of bailiffs (*baillis* in northern France and *senechaux* in the south) were also increased in number, and their business expanded. In this spirit of rationalization, Louis XI created the first royal postal service and conceived, but could not carry out, a standardization of weights and measures. Some feudal elements remained: the feudal levy was periodically invoked until 1695, and patronage remained intimately connected to aristocratic status.

The recharged and reconstituted Valois Dynasty utterly transformed the shape and size of France. The wealthy and sophisticated duchy of Burgundy, containing a court and administration that rivaled those of France, fell into the grasp of Louis XI following the defeat and death of Charles the Bold outside the walls of Nancy in 1477. The treaty of Arras five years later (1482) specified the incorporation of the duchy and a number of cities along the Somme River. The intrigues of Louis XI also brought the Dauphiné, Provence, and a duchy in Lorraine under the French crown. These last acquisitions were particularly significant, as they constituted the first extensions of France beyond the boundaries of West Francia laid out at the Treaty of Verdun in 843. After the 1472 annexation, French kings moved cautiously to ensure the loyalty of their new subjects; traditional laws were respected, and the people retained their own high courts of justice.

The dynamism and expansionism of these Valois kings resulted not only from increased powers of taxation but also from a renewed economy. Both the population and farm production bounced back from the disasters of the black death. After reaching its low point around 1450, the population grew steadily, especially in the south (the midi), and had recovered its medieval high point by the latter half of the sixteenth century. The explanations for this population rebound are numerous. For reasons that are not entirely clear, the incidence of plagues and famines dropped in the first half of the sixteenth century. Moreover, war after the 1490s was conducted outside of France, and the populace thus avoided horrors like the Hundred Years' War. In addition, after 1600, farmers adopted two new high-yield crops: buckwheat, raised by peasants in the west, and maize, introduced from the Americas. Agrarian expansion again triggered urban growth: the population of Paris soared to over a quarter of a million by 1550, and in the next fifty years Rouen expanded from 40,000 to 75,000, Lyon from 40,000 to 58,000, and Bordeaux from 25,000 to 35,000.[5] Urban life became more lively and sophisticated as nobles built town houses, the new Italian Renaissance culture moved northward, and the printing press quickened the pace of intellectual and religious life.

Art and culture were not the only Italian matters that interested the French in this era, however. The restless and ambitious Valois king Charles VIII (1494–1555) was raised during a period when the horrors of war had been forgotten and only its heroism remembered. Upon the death of King Ferdinand I in 1494, Charles acted on the Valois claim to the throne through the house of Anjou. On the invitation of the Borgia pope Alexander VI, Charles marched the royal army into the fractious and divided peninsula. But after a series of triumphal victories, including an entry into Naples on a chariot drawn by four white horses, he faced a wave of anti-French feeling that led to the formation of a military alliance against him by the city-state of Venice. In short, triumphal advance quickly turned into a quagmire that would embroil him and his Valois successors—Louis XII, Francis I, and Henry II—until 1559.

About the only benefit the French crown derived from the Italian wars was a measure of internal peace, largely because the great nobles directed their energies at foreign conquest rather than local intrigue and aggression. In addition, through the Concordat of Bologna in 1516, Pope Leo X granted Francis I royal control over the French Church, as a reward for the decisive victory over the hitherto invincible Swiss infantry at Marignano the previous year. At the war's end, France had not only failed to gain territory but had also entered into what would be a long-term struggle with the Habsburgs who sat on the thrones of Spain and the Holy Roman Empire. Finding himself surrounded, the "Most Christian King" strategically accepted alliances with German Lutheran princes and in 1543, for the first time in the annals of European diplomacy, the Ottoman Turks. Reason of state was starting to replace reason of religion.

The Valois monarchs, particularly Francis I who ascended to the throne in 1515, continued to be innovative state builders. Within an economy increasingly based on money rather than simply on ownership of land, the power of the crown increased relative to their nobility. Because the king had the ability to increase his revenue steadily through taxation (especially in such an age of inflation as the sixteenth century) kings could keep ahead of the ravages of inflation much better than even the biggest of the noble landowners. At the same time, tax collection was becoming more organized, coherent, and aggressive.

In 1522 Francis I established a single collection agency, the Treasury, supervised by a controller general who was a finance minister in embryo. In the same year, he required all his subjects to lend him money at 8 percent interest, to be paid out of the receipts of indirect taxes. And still the unquenchable royal thirst for money was not satiated. Kings tapped the growing wealth of urban merchants and manufacturers by selling such government offices as positions on the provincial high courts of justice, or parlements. The sale of offices led to the creation of a new type of nobility based on bureaucratic service to the state, called the "nobility of the robe" as opposed to the "nobility of the sword"—those who had won their status through the bearing of arms. Increasingly kings drew their inner circle from these bureaucratic nobles rather than from princes of the blood and others of high birth. The most trusted nobles of the robe were gathered into a "council of affairs," the most energetic member of whom assumed the functions of prime minister. To stem the discontent of the nobles of the sword, Francis I, after the Concordat with the pope, gave them high church appointments or provided them with subsidies that allowed them to grace his court in ceremonial but not practical ways. Francis I (and later his son Henry II) did not allow the discontented ones to assemble in the Estates General, which consequently did not convene between 1506 and 1560.

To increase his revenue, Francis I also engaged, as did his Portuguese, Spanish, and English royal counterparts, in exploiting European discoveries in the New World. The foundations of the French colony of Canada were laid by the most important of the French explorers, Jacques Cartier, in his voyage of 1534. At the same time, French explorers, merchants, and raiders searched the west African coast for ivory, gum, and gold, and started the French trade in enslaved Africans. Francis I's attention, however, remained focused primarily upon Europe and neither he nor his successors devoted the same efforts to overseas expansion as did the Iberian countries, England, or the Dutch.

Francis I, a great patron of learning and the arts and a champion of the French language, was thoroughly imbued with the spirit of the Renaissance. In 1530 he created a college, free of the restraints of the Sorbonne. At this new institution, later known as the Collège de France, such innovative subjects as Hebrew and Latin philology were taught. An ordinance of Villers-Cotterets in 1539 stipulated that royal business be "pronounced recorded and delivered . . . in the native France language, and not otherwise." The same ordinance also required the systematic recording of births, marriages, and deaths. Finally, Francis I brought Italian architects to France to rebuild rustic hunting lodges at Fontainebleau and Chambord into sumptuous châteaus and thus introduced the Italian Renaissance style to France.

The end of the Italian wars brought another period of crisis for both the country and the monarchy. Although not as severe as those during the Hundred Years' War, a series of calamities again befell the economy. The climate turned colder—a "little ice age" that lasted until 1830—which led to a series of major harvest failures and consequent inflation. Then, in the 1580s and 1590s, famine and plague returned. These calamities made the tax burden unbearable, and the peasants revolted, especially in the southwest, in Normandy, and the northwest, in Brittany, with resentments continuing into the 1650s. In addition, the warrior nobility, returning from the Italian wars, recommenced their feuds and intrigues. Out of this cauldron of catastrophes emerged the Protestant Reformation, especially Calvinism, a French version, propagated from nearby Geneva.

Just when the steady hand of the king was most needed, Henry II (r. 1547–1559) died in a jousting accident in 1559, leaving his oldest child to be king under the regency of his wife Catherine de Medici. Henry II's three sons—Francis II, Charles IX, and Henry III—would each wear the crown, but none would wear the crown with distinction or for long. When the last of them, Henry III, died in 1589 without an heir, the male line was extinct. Their weak rule had exacerbated aristocratic intrigue, which found expression in religious differences. Initially, much of the nobility converted to Protestantism. Members of the Condé, Montmorency, and Bourbon families, for example, converted. Nobles thus argued and fought not only over Protestantism, but also over the monarchy.

For 36 years (1561–1598), France rocked under an intense if intermittent Catholic-Protestant conflict. The most dramatic moment was the famous Saint Bartholomew's Day Massacre in Paris in 1572. French Protestants (known as Huguenots) had gathered in large numbers (more than 3,000) to attend the marriage of the Protestant prince Henry of Navarre to the king's sister Marguerite. Henry of Navarre was a member of the Bourbon family who traced their royal lineage to Louis IX (1214–1270). Henry's father, Anthony, duke of Bourbon, in 1572 had married Queen Jeanne of Navarre. During the slaughter of the Protestants during the Saint Bartholomew's Day Massacre, Henry of Navarre was brought at sword's point to the king and was forced, upon pain of death, to convert to Catholicism. Once out of Paris, however, Henry reverted to his Protestantism. His retraction brought a papal disqualification: Henry was barred from the throne. Succeeding years brought the formation of a Calvinist Union under Henry as well as a Catholic Holy League headed by members of the power-seeking Guise family, fanatical Catholics whose Carolingian ancestry provided a claim to the throne. The Guise family seemed to be fighting as much to gain the throne as to crush Protestantism. In 1589 the childless Henry III recognized Henry of Navarre as the legitimate heir. Soon after, the king was assassinated by a zealous Dominican monk, and Protestantism remained the sole hurdle between Henry of Navarre and the crown. In an act caricatured in one of the most famous phrases in French history—"Paris is worth a mass"— Henry renounced Protestantism in 1593 and entered the capital the following year, 1594. (In reality Henry did not say this.)

The great problem still remained: how to handle French Protestantism. With some 2,150 churches, a total membership of between one and two million, and its special appeal to women, French Calvinism was simply too big for a government to adopt the liquidation policy of Spain and the Italian states, but not big enough to dominate the state.[6] Henry's answer was the Edict of Nantes, issued on April 13, 1598, which granted the freedom of conscience to all French people, the right of Protestants to religious worship in certain specified locations and to hold provincial and national synods, equal opportunity for Protestants in royal appointments and awards, a special bureau in each high court of justice (parlement) to protect Protestant rights, and permission for the Protestants to retain 100 fortified cities and towns for Protestants for eight years. Although disdained by the pope and much of Catholic France, this edict brought peace to the ravaged country. Unfortunately, the tolerant Henry died of stab wounds received at the hand of a Catholic fanatic in 1610.

During his reign, Henry IV restored the power and luster of the monarchy. He rebuilt Paris and made it a permanent capital. Sully, a frugal Huguenot, was made superintendent of finance in 1598. He doubled the state's net revenues, mainly by cutting expenses, shifting to indirect taxes, and rationalizing tax farms (establishing permanently the five great tax farms around Paris). The most important institutional development of the reign was the introduction in 1604 of the *paulette*, named for the person who first collected the tax. The sale of government offices, a century-long practice, was stabilized by this tax, and an officeholder was permitted to bequeath the position to his son. This measure not only increased the crown's income, but also decreased the meddling of the nobles in governmental appointments. Sully also reinstated 40,000 taxpayers dropped from the rolls of the *taille* during turbulent times. Beyond balancing the budget, these measures created a surplus of 30 million livres. French colonization in Canada also continued. Samuel de Champlain founded Québec in 1608, and French peasants started to emigrate to this territory that became known as New France.

After Henry IV's assassination in 1610, the queen mother, Marie de Medici, headed the regency for her nine-year-old son Louis XIII. Typically, the nobles schemed to gain power at her expense. To defuse the situation, she convened the Estates General in October 1614. As she hoped, the nobility and the Third Estate fell into heated argument almost from the start. She dismissed the Estates in February 1615 after six futile months; the body did not meet again until 1789. The most decisive moment of her regency—or, for that matter, of her son's reign—occurred in April 1624 when one of her confidants, Cardinal Richelieu, was admitted to the king's council. Three months later, he became prime minister and held this position until his death in 1642. From the start he promised the young king to "ruin the Huguenot party, humble the pride of the nobles, compel all subjects to do their duty, and raise the name of the king among foreign nations to the point where it should be."[7]

Richelieu presided over yet another defining moment in the development of royal power. The Thirty Years' War (1618–1648), a European war arising from religious and dynastic conflict—particularly pitting the Habsburgs against France—ranks as a great moment in governmental innovation. Although a cardinal himself, Richelieu subordinated religion to national interest. To counter the Habsburg power that threatened to envelop France, he subsidized the entry of Protestant Sweden into the German maelstrom in 1630 and five years later brought the French army into battle. After initial reversals, the French won a series of brilliant victories. The victory of Prince Condé over the Spanish at Rocroi (1643) consolidated France as the dominant military power in Europe for more than 200 years. The peace treaties of Westphalia (1648) and Pyrenees (1659) granted land to France from Spain on the southern border and from the German territories of the Holy Roman Empire on the northern border.

To achieve this triumph, Richelieu had to modernize the French army. A military revolution between 1500 and 1650 not only increased the use of gunpowder but also developed new strategies using cavalry, infantry, and artillery, resulting in larger and larger armies. In the early 1630s, the

French army stood at around 20,000 men; by the late 1640s, the total was nearly 100,000 and reached a quarter of a million after the 1650s.[8] This staggering expansion required a massive increase in centralized and bureaucratic government. Richelieu, and later his successor Cardinal Mazarin, further distanced feudal dignitaries from important decisions. Secretaries of state and subordinate masters of requests (*maîtres des requêtes*) gained increased autonomy. From the latter group, Richelieu in the 1620s drew his *intendents*, agents sent into the provinces to supervise the state machine. Earlier monarchs also had sent officials into the provinces, but Richelieu equipped his men with ever wider powers. They collected taxes, raised conscripts and administered the army, oversaw the demolition of Protestant fortified cities and noble castles, and could curtail or eliminate local privileges and liberties. In essence the *intendent* became Richelieu's eyes and ears.

Military growth and the resulting administrative innovations dramatically expanded the size of government. Tax levels increased threefold between 1630 and 1648 and another 50 percent in the remaining years of the seventeenth century. Richelieu complemented the tax increase with a gamut of other financial stratagems: lowered value of government bonds, special tax demands, loans, and monetary devaluation. The sale of offices jumped from some 12,000 officeholders in the sixteenth century to approximately 50,000 by 1650. In one 30-year period, state income from this source quadrupled.[9]

Richelieu's penchant for reorganization and systematization also affected French colonial policy. He created trading companies, on the models of the Dutch and English, to develop Canada's economic potential and to develop colonies and plantations in the Caribbean (Company of the Islands). To encourage colonial entrepreneurship, nobles were permitted to engage in colonial trade and commerce without losing their noble status.

At Richelieu's death in 1642, France was on the verge of its greatest hegemony over the rest of Europe, although the country would first have to face an era of turmoil and rebellions. Louis XIII survived his extraordinary prime minister by only seven months. The death of the king left a five-year-old child on the throne facing immediate and dramatic challenges. We now turn to Louis XIV.

NOTES

1. Fernand Braudel, *The Identity of France, Vol. 2, People and Production*, trans. Sîan Reynolds (New York: HarperCollins, 1990), pp. 422–423.

2. Ibid., p. 304.

3. Marc Bloch, *Feudal Society, Vol. I, The Growth of Ties of Dependence*, trans. L. A. Manyon (Chicago: University of Chicago Press, 1964), pp. 59–72.

4. Colin Jones, *The Cambridge Illustrated History of France* (Cambridge: Cambridge University Press, 1994), p. 100.

5. Ibid., p. 132.

6. Ibid., p. 140.

7. G. de Bertier de Sauvigny and David H. Pinkney, *History of France* Revised and Enlarged Edition, French text trans. Jams Friguglietti (Arlington Heights, IL: Forum Press, 1983), p. 132.

8. Jones, *The Cambridge Illustrated History of France*, p. 153.

9. Ibid., p. 154.

5

Absolute Monarchy: From Apogee (Louis XIV, Ruled 1643–1715) to Catastrophe (Louis XVI, Ruled 1774–1792)

The decades of the 1640s and the 1780s, encompassing the beginning and end of this chapter, saw general crises in both the French monarchy and society in general. Resolution of these two convulsions could not have been more different for the monarchy. The rebellion of the 1640s, the *Fronde*, occurred during the minority of Louis XIV and resulted in the consolidation of an ever stronger monarchy under the mature Louis, called the "Sun King." (Just as the planets circled the sun, so the royal court and French kingdom circled Louis.) Louis XIV would define and embody the European ideal of the absolute monarch. Once again in times of travail, the monarchy proved to be the only source of authority and stability. The turmoil of the 1780s, however, would see the monarchy shatter.

Why did the monarchy not rise to the crisis as it always had in the past? Why had it ceased to be the source of stability in French society? After 1750 the symbiotic relationship between the Catholic Church and the absolute monarchy lost the allegiance of much of the elite, who turned to the secular, rationalistic, and emerging republican philosophy of the Enlightenment. The result would be the birth of modern political thought as well as the modern nation-state.

Certainly all the ingredients for a modern revolution seemed to be in play in 1648 when the *Fronde* rebellion erupted. *Fronde*, literally "sling-shot," refers to the children's game of hurling mud at passing coaches. The ten-year-old king was still under the tutelage of his mother, Anne of Austria, and the prime minister, the Italian-born Cardinal Jules Mazarin, a protégé of Richelieu's and Anne's confidant (and perhaps lover). Mazarin had no legitimacy in the eyes of the French population because of his Italian origins, his papal connections, his corruptly amassed fortune, and his romantic involvement with the queen mother. Innumerable poison pamphlets, called the *Mazarinades*, mocked and denounced his tyranny. Satire turned to struggle and denunciation to disorder when, in early 1648, Mazarin announced that the royal coffers were empty—as a result of the Thirty Years' War according to Mazarin—and that the salaries of many royal officials would not be paid for the next four years. The highest court of justice in the realm, the Parlement of Paris, took the lead in denouncing this high-handed act.

As had the English Parliament during that same decade, the Parlement demanded an end to royal tyranny: abolition of the office of *intendent*, among other posts; veto power over new taxes; and implementation of a habeas corpus law. When Mazarin had the parlementarians arrested, Paris rose in revolt, forcing Mazarin and the royal family to flee. Although Mazarin returned the following year and compromised with the Parlement, the old "sword nobility" engaged in their own *fronde* and the revolt spread throughout the country. A major urban revolt occurred in Bordeaux, with a resurgence of peasant revolts in the north, northwest, and south. Despite the widespread repugnance toward absolute monarchy, however, no political entity provided a coherent alternative. Justices of the parlements, the "robe nobility," famous generals Henri de Turenne and the Prince of Condé, "nobles of the sword," each group thought only in terms of its own advantages and produced only disorder. At least, that was the experience of the child-king when the Parisian crowd invaded his bedchamber one night in 1651 to see if he had fled the city with Mazarin. Although the crown was forced to cope with the belligerence of the nobles and the tax revolts of the peasants through 1661, Mazarin and Anne of Austria were back in power by 1652. Once again, the crown had provided the only stability in the kingdom. Indeed, by 1650, the cardinal ministers Richelieu and Mazarin had developed the most efficient and centralized state on the Continent.

On the death of Mazarin in 1661, therefore, when Louis XIV assumed full power, he could consolidate an already considerable governmental achievement. The young king took the audacious step of declaring that he would be his own prime minister. His reign would represent the apogee of centralized monarchical government: all his ministers paled in comparison with the regal figure of the king. Louis summed it up in his most famous statement, "I am the state" (*L'état c'est moi*). State power under Louis would achieve a hitherto unknown amount of control over three critical administrative functions: use of armed force, formulation and execution of laws, and collection and expenditure of revenue.

Concerning the first, coercion, Louis created a finer network of surveillance and repression than his predecessors or any other contemporary ruler, when, in 1667, he created a lieutenant-general of police in Paris. This lieutenant-general was appointed by and responsible to the king, whereas the earlier provost of Paris, responsible for order in the city, had been under the supervision of the Parlement. By 1699 Louis had established the same system in all major cities. In rural France he mounted a national police constabulary, the *maréchaussée*. At the least sign of revolt in either city or country, Louis sent his police or his army. For example, the 1670 peasant uprisings in the Boulonnais and Languedoc were swiftly crushed. Thereafter no serious revolts threatened, even though the country periodically suffered devastating famines in the final two decades of his reign.

As for the formulation and execution of laws, Louis made his mark less in the realm of juridical innovation than in the forceful imposition of his will. He did create another layer of administration: the commissioner, appointed by the king. The position could not be inherited or purchased, which guaranteed subjugation to royal authority. In addition, each province now had a permanent *intendent* (an official who could be appointed and dismissed at the whim of the king) with assigned subdelegates to enforce royal orders. The last province to receive a permanent *intendent* was Brittany in 1689.

The traditional consultative bodies and the parlements became moribund under Louis. The Estates General, which had last met in 1614, and the Assembly of Notables, which had last been consulted in 1626, never convened under Louis's long reign. Moreover, the Assembly of the Clergy was tightly supervised, and provincial estates (Dauphiné after 1628, for example, and Normandy after 1655) were dissolved at the slightest sign of protest. With the memory of the *Fronde* fresh in his mind, Louis virtually eliminated the rights of the parlement to question or obstruct the implementation of royal edicts. In this way, he ensured that these high courts of justice could not become rallying points for his opposition.

In place of consultation Louis erected an elaborate patronage system. In short, he pacified the nobility, intellectuals, and artists through subsidization rather than representation in a deliberative body such as the English Parliament. Indeed, it was as much through representation as repression that Louis achieved a virtual domination over society. In his *Memoirs for the Instruction of the Dauphin* (that is, his young heir), he noted, "What makes for the greatness and the majesty of kings is not so much the scepter that they bear as the manner in which they bear it."[1] Some historians have characterized his reign as that of a "theatre state," in which the king constantly performed his role. All kings had naturally been concerned about portraying an image of majesty and power—remember the king's touch—but no previous or future king would so systematically construct his reign around performance or so control the image he projected. Louis made sure that his image circulated widely in society in paintings, engravings, medals, coins, sculptures, plays, ballets (in which he often participated), and operas. These representations were created not only in his palaces but also even on the battlefield.[2]

More than any other king he inspired a style that spread across Europe and through all realms of artistic expression. In Paris he made the Louvre even more palatial, constructed the Place Louis-le-Grand (currently Place Vendôme and Place des Victoires), tore down old walls and laid out new boulevards in their place, and founded Les Invalides, a home for retired soldiers. Under his patronage, Paris became a center of the luxury trades and topped half a million in population.[3]

The ultimate expression of Louis's synthesis of stagecraft and statecraft was the palace he built in the village of Versailles, 12 miles west of Paris on the site of his father's hunting lodge. Here the monarchy was removed from any interference from the Parisian crowd that had traumatized his childhood. Louis created a space calculated to give architectural form to his majesty. From 1682 when he moved in until his death in 1715, architects such as Louis Le Vau and Jules Hardouin-Mansart constructed the largest building in Europe, with a front facade one third of a mile long. Landscaper André Le Nôtre diverted a river, dug a canal, and created a garden with 1,400 fountains and an orangery with 1,200 orange trees. The interior decoration and painting were under the supervision of the famous Charles Le Brun. Construction and decoration of the palace employed the best architects, painters, sculptors, weavers, and furniture makers of the age and cost over 5 percent of the royal budget during the 1670s and 1680s.

At this grand palace Louis not only conducted government but also domesticated the fractious French nobility. By 1700, 10,000 noblemen, officials, and attendants lived at the palace. One disgruntled nobleman, Saint Simon, wrote in his memoirs,

> Upon rising, at bedtime, during meals, in his apartments, in the gardens of Versailles, everywhere the courtiers had a right to follow, he would glance right and left to see who was there; he saw and noted everyone; he missed no one, even those who were hoping they would not be seen.[4]

Louis devoted more than half of each day to ceremonial duties at which his nobles competed to gain royal favors. According to Colin Jones, "The rectilinear angles of classicism converged on the eye of the ruler. . . . Louis XIV had built a gilded cage in which the turbulent warriors of the Wars of Religion became foppish courtiers of the Sun King."[5]

Louis brought the long-standing art of royal patronage to peak perfection. During the early years of his reign he subsidized such writers as Pierre Corneille, Jean Racine, Molière, La Rochefoucauld, Jean de La Bruyère and Jean de La Fontaine—authors who defined the "classic" period of French literature. To house their plays he established the Comédie-française, the French national theater, in 1680. He expanded Richelieu's idea of the academy by creating academies of dance (1661), inscriptions (1662), science (1666), architecture (1671), and music (1672). These expert bodies codified standards for the arts—such as the "three unities" of time, place, and action for drama—and helped popularize science among the nobility and upper classes of the cities. Louis clearly understood the intimate relation between knowledge and power. Under the Sun King, the scientific revolution reinforced royal authority. Science, like social criticism in the following generation of the Enlightenment, however, would undermine the crown.

Louis XIV's diverse and ambitious projects were made possible by the greater efficiency that his ministers brought to the third vital function of government: the collection and expenditure of revenue. One striking example demonstrates this point. Louis's finance minister, Jean-Baptiste Colbert, discovered on taking office that only 25 percent of the tax money actually reached the royal treasury; the other 75 percent disappeared into the pockets of tax farmers and corrupt officials or were swallowed up in interest payments on the royal debt. Colbert clamped down on the tax farmers and repudiated part of the debt. At the time of his death in 1683, the crown was collecting 80 percent of the tax revenue raised.

Louis's power was further enhanced by the fact that he lived during a time when the Catholic Church had reinvigorated itself through the Catholic Counter-Reformation, the reform movement in the Roman Catholic Church following the Protestant Reformation. The Counter-Reformation received its impetus at the Council of Trent (1545–1563), which tried to reform the Church and reconvert the Protestants. This reenergized Catholicism not only provided a more systematic justification for his own rule but also ensured that his population was more docile, dutiful, and productive. The alliance between throne and altar, intimately interconnected since the time of Clovis, reached the height of its development.

The line between succor and social control was often very fine. Les Invalides not only sheltered infirm soldiers and the aged, but also incarcerated those who could be belligerent and rowdy. Civilian hospitals, which the crown had also helped to establish, did indeed assist the destitute, but also often punished the lazy and those deemed to be heretical. By 1700 some 200 hospitals participated in what historian Michel Foucault has called "the great confinement"; within their walls resided 100,000 people considered outcasts: Gypsies, Protestants, beggars, the unemployed, the transient, the insane, and those deemed to be witches, prostitutes, and juvenile delinquents.[6] Under Louis, obviously, public order and religious conformity were two sides of a single coin.

Social historians have found that Louis XIV and the Catholic Church did create, for the most part, a more dutiful and docile population. Their study of parish registers reveals a remarkably low rate of out-of-wedlock births, for example. Moreover, the decline in rioting and social revolt after 1670 may be due in part to the growing moral authority of the clergy.

The one great failure of Louis XIV's religious policies concerned the Protestants. Despite decades of effort he achieved neither their submission nor their eradication. In 1659 he banned national synods and embarked on a campaign of tearing down Protestant houses of worship, eventually destroying almost 700 of them. In the Edict of Fontainebleau (1685) he nullified the Edict of Nantes. Although acclaimed throughout the Catholic world, the new measure did not lead to wholesale conversion of the Huguenots, as Louis XIV had hoped, but led instead to a Huguenot emigration numbering in the hundreds of thousands. Revolts arose, particularly in the south, among diehard Protestant peasants, known as Camisards. Louis XIV's actions ultimately drained France of some of its most entrepreneurial and skilled workers and delivered them into the hands of his enemies: England, the Netherlands, and Prussia. In 1788, when religious toleration was again granted to them, the Huguenot population totaled 600,000.

Although unquestionably devout, Louis never lost sight of politics. He had learned this lesson well, of course, from the cardinal ministers who preceded him. He often played a double game in his dealings with the Hapsburg emperors in Vienna and with the Ottoman emperors, hoping the "infidels" would smash Hapsburg power and then he, "the Most Christian King," could defeat the Turks and gain mastery over Europe. In addition he fought a long, drawn-out battle, from the 1670s to the 1690s, with the pope over his right to appoint bishops in dioceses in southern France traditionally under papal control. When the pious, but potentially seditious, movement known as Jansenism developed among the nuns at the Port-Royal-des-Champs monastery outside of Paris, he had the buildings demolished in 1710 and its members dispersed.

The Sun King's long personal reign can be divided into three periods. The first (1661–1672) was a time of peace, prosperity, and cultural creativity. During the next two periods, Louis tried to satisfy his virtually inexhaustible thirst for glory and power by waging war. The period between 1673 and 1688 saw a measure of success as French power and territory expanded. But then, from 1688 until his death in 1715, his ambition far exceeded his power, and his reign ended on a note of frustration.

His two most important ministers reflect his goals: cultural magnificence and economic expansion, on the one hand, and military prowess and territorial expansion, on the other hand. Finance Minister Jean-Baptiste Colbert (1661–1683) gained Louis XIV's favor early on. An assiduous and systematic practitioner of the theory of mercantilism, he pursued every possible strategy to achieve the economic goal of amassing gold, the only true source of wealth, through extensive exports and minimal imports. To overtake Holland, a major rival, Colbert aggressively raised tariffs on Dutch and other foreign products entering France. He established luxury industries: silk weaving in Lyons and glass and tapestry factories around Paris. To stimulate commerce within France,

Colbert abolished or diminished internal trade barriers and tolls and dug the impressive Canal du Midi (1665–1681) to connect the Atlantic Ocean with the Mediterranean Sea.

Colbert, even more than Richelieu, believed that the French economy could be substantially increased through the expansion of its colonies. He created new or reorganized old trading companies. France now had a company for each of the following areas: East India, West India, northern Europe, and the Levant. Colbert also expanded the merchant marine and the navy. Under his direction, France became a major exporter of enslaved Africans in the European slave trade. Most of those enslaved were shipped to France's Caribbean plantations whose sugar production expanded dramatically. The booming plantation economy, as well as the vigorous increase in the slave trade, led to a boom in the French Atlantic ports of Nantes, Bordeaux, Brest, and Saint-Malo. In Canada, French explorers, businessmen, and priests (often one man combining all three functions) expanded France's domains. Louis Jolliet and Jesuit Father Jacques Marquette explored south from Québec into present-day Illinois and Iowa. Robert La Salle went down the Mississippi all the way to the Gulf of Mexico and founded the colony of Louisiana, named in honor of Louis XIV. In East India, French merchants established trading posts along the coast, the most important of which were Pondichéry and Chandernagore. Nevertheless, despite France's impressive economic growth, Holland retained economic dominance.

In 1672 a frustrated Colbert, chafing under the continued dominance of Dutch shipping even in French waters, advised Louis to invade and conquer the neighboring economic powerhouse. After a decisive initial victory, the road to Amsterdam seemed open, and Louis decided to celebrate. Meanwhile, William III, the youngest member of the House of Orange, whose army had won Holland its freedom from the Spanish Hapsburgs, seized power and opened the dikes. The ensuing flood turned Amsterdam and other Dutch cities into islands and rendered the French army powerless in the face of the formidable Dutch navy. Although Louis XIV fought on and made some compensating territorial gains—Franche Comte in the northeast and in Flanders at the expense of Spain—he lost his bid to crush and annex his major trading rival. He gained as well a relentless foe who would organize coalitions against him for the rest of his life.

After Colbert's death in 1683, the Marquis of Louvois became the most trusted advisor to Louis XIV. The Sun King embraced Louvois's doctrine of military strength as the foundation of French power and proceeded to develop the largest, best-trained, and most professional army in Europe. This superb military machine allowed Louis to engage in a succession of wars over a 30-year period, from 1682 to 1712. During the first war, the war of the League of Augsburg, and even more during the second, the war of the Spanish succession, Louis XIV displayed overwhelming ambition but achieved minimal territorial annexation. Eventually almost all of Europe was allied against him, France's public debt skyrocketed tenfold, and famine swept across the land in 1693–1694 and again in 1709–1710 in the wake of harvest failure. Bankruptcy was averted only by an augmentation in venal governmental offices and the imposition of new taxes—a poll tax (*capitation*) in 1701 and a "tenth tax" (*dixième*) in 1710. "All France is now no more than one great hospital, desolate and unprovided," lamented the Bishop, writer, and royal tutor François Fénelon.[7] The increased efficiency and order of Louis's government prevented any serious revolt. But all of Louis's power could not prevent a smallpox epidemic in 1711–1712 that killed three princes, or dauphins, in rapid succession, leaving only one frail five-year-old to inherit the throne.

During his lifetime, Louis XIV had succeeded in suppressing all significant dissent, but cheers and celebration greeted the news of his death in September 1715. The Sun King's dream of neutralizing the great nobility's political power was dashed when his nephew Philip Duke of Orléans became regent.

In 1723 Louis XV celebrated his thirteenth birthday, and the regency formally ended. Philip remained briefly as first minister. When he died later that same year, he was replaced by another royal prince, the duke of Bourbon, who lasted less than two years, thanks to his intrigues against Louis's tutor. In 1726 the young king turned over effective power to his wily seventy-three-year-old tutor bishop André Hercule de Fleury.

Under Fleury France participated in the dramatic economic expansion underway in Western Europe, a growth unparalleled since the thirteenth century.[8] Under Fleury's wise and pacific counsel, France enjoyed a sustained period of peace, from 1726 to 1741, with economic expansion continuing into the 1770s. European commerce jumped 400 percent and colonial trade by the even more amazing figure of 1000 percent. Indeed, France's growth rates in many sectors of the economy were higher than those of England, which was already starting into the Industrial Revolution. Colonial exportation of slaves, sugar, coffee, and tea were vital to this expansion and ignited especially rapid growth along France's Atlantic coast. Agricultural production also increased, rising 40 percent over the century. Maize cultivation continued to spread in the south, and the potato found increased value in the poor regions of the center and east. Scientific farming on the large farms of the Paris basin and other areas of northern France after 1750 brought ever more produce to city markets.

Economic expansion led to a dramatic jump in the urban middle classes, the *bourgeoisie*, and to increased entrepreneurial activity. From around 700,000 in 1700, this diverse class—ranging from large merchants, manufacturers, and bankers to small shopkeepers, crafts-people, and wealthy peasants—grew to approximately 2.3 million by 1789.[9] Nobles also profited from the expansion of colonial and whole-sale commerce as well as from mining and metallurgical enterprises. Nobles introduced to their estates the new methods of animal husbandry, fertilization, and crop rotation that were hallmarks of scientific agriculture.

The French population expanded from a high of 21.5 million around 1720 to 28.6 million on the eve of the French Revolution.[10] The primary causes of the increase were the cessation of wars and the elimination of famine and plague as serious scourges. With minor exceptions, wars even in the last years of Louis XIV's reign were fought outside of France. Famines seldom occurred after 1710, and the bubonic and pneumonic plagues had receded from most areas of France by the 1720s.

The royal bureaucracy—especially the reforming and innovative *inten-dents*—also helped spur this economic expansion. Continued construction of canals, dramatic improvements in road construction, and the creation of a national network of turnpikes had cut travel time in half by the 1780s. A trip from Paris to Marseille, instead of taking two weeks, now took less than one. The crown also learned the efficacy of cordoning off areas affected by the plague or other epidemics so as to supply grain more quickly in times when famine threatened.

Based upon this rapid and sustained recovery, Louis XIV's wars turned out not to be as devastating to the kingdom as they seemed initially. After Fleury's death, however, Louis XV was unable to find a singular focus or purpose as king. Reluctantly—for he much preferred hunting and court life, especially entertainments and beautiful women—he returned to the crown's field of battle. Although he failed to exercise the imagination or resolve of his royal ancestors, his armies in the war of the Austrian succession (1741–1748) conquered Belgium, Nice, and Savoy. But Louis gave them up again in the Treaty of Aix-la-Chapelle (October 1748) in a futile attempt to end a war he had grown tired of fighting. During the Seven Years' War that immediately followed (1756–1763), Louis XV suffered an unmitigated defeat: the crown won, no new territory on the Continent and lost most of its colonial empire, including Canada. In sum, the only territory gained during his reign—the province of Lorraine in 1766 and Corsica in 1768—were won through diplomacy and purchase, respectively. The crown was virtually helpless when Poland, its traditional ally in the east, was annexed by Prussia, Russia, and Austria. Only at the end of the century did his grandson Louis XVI regain some honor by allying with the fledgling American nation in its struggle against England, during the War of American Independence (1776–1783). Although the crown also retrieved Senegal and a number of West Indian islands, the debt contracted to finance these operations helped drive the country further toward a bankruptcy that led to momentous consequences.

A primary reason for the Bourbon monarchy's reverses was an inadequate system of finance and taxation. Lacking a national bank, due to the fiasco of the shady Scots financier John Law, the crown instead took short-term loans, ordering their financial agents to make payments in advance or in excess of the tax revenues they collected. Although the French nobility failed in its attempt to reverse royal absolutism, for decades they were able to block—with the help of the parlements—any significant new taxes, especially any that would apply to them. For example, in 1749, Louis XV's finance minister, Machault d'Arouville, hoping to stem the growing budget deficit generated by war, levied the *vingtième* ("twentieth"), or 5 percent tax, on all incomes—noble, clerical, and commoner. Lacking the resolute support of the king, however, Machault had to settle for collecting the tax only from the commoners—from the peasants rather than the wealthy townspeople (who could usually find ways to avoid paying taxes). Subsequent additional *vingtièmes* were imposed in 1756 and 1760 in a vain attempt to keep up with wartime expenses. Once again, the privileged classes were exempt: at every turn, the parlements, especially in Paris, defended the nobility and clergy against the king.

In the last years of his reign, Louis XV, determined to break the power of parlement and revamp the tax structure, chose new ministers: René de Maupeou, chancellor; Abbé Joseph Terray, controller-general of finances; and the duke of Aiguillon, secretary of state. They abolished the parlements in 1771, held firm during the ensuing crisis, and appeared to gain the upper hand just as the king died of smallpox in May 1774. Louis XVI, as a step toward national unity, decided to dismiss Maupeou and recall the parlements. He would live to regret this act, for the parlements would lead the opposition to the crown's attempts to solve its financial problems in the late 1780s.

The new king faced a much more formidable opponent than any of his predecessors had faced. In previous centuries nobles, parlements, townspeople, and peasants had defended narrow, corporate, or local interests. The king, on the contrary, could pose—usually with reason—as the only unifying force in the realm.

After 1750 this situation changed, largely because of the increase in literacy, the emergence of a new critical philosophical movement called the Enlightenment, and the advent of what is known today as the "public sphere." The Enlightenment was a literary and philosophical movement that aimed to diffuse the empirical and critical method of the natural sciences (the physicist Sir Isaac Newton was the great hero) to the study and transformation of political, economic, and social institutions. The concept of the public sphere encompasses various public institutions and places where individuals gather to discuss the current issues and where their arguments are judged on the soundness of their ideas rather than on their status in the social and economic hierarchy. The growing rate of literacy among the French population allowed for an expansion of the public sphere. By the 1780s, over 65 percent of the male population in the more advanced north could read, and even in the less developed south, the rate was above 50 percent. Although below these male rates, women's literacy had also increased substantially across the eighteenth century.[11] Equally important, the amount and type of material being published also increased dramatically. Consequently, readers shifted their habits: instead of reading and rereading a few sacred and devotional works, they now branched out into novels, travel literature, philosophy, politics, and science. In the writings of the major and most popular writers, such as Voltaire and Jean-Jacques Rousseau, these genres intermingled. This shift in reading material signaled the decline of the Catholic Counter-Reformation and the rise of the Enlightenment. Increasingly after 1700 philosophers and writers applied the critical empirical methods of science to society rather than to the stars. As a result, the pretensions of the absolute monarchy and the divinely inspired Catholic Church were questioned and found wanting. Science had been viewed by Louis XV and Louis XVI as simply a means of increasing royal technology and military prowess. Now the crown realized that these doctrines could contain philosophical dynamite that might blow the monarchy to bits. During the eighteenth century, critics of the regime from Voltaire to the Marquis de Sade were sent to the royal fortress and imprisoned in the Bastille in eastern Paris.

The Enlightenment not only produced the notion of strong public opinion but also articulated an alternative theory of the good and orderly society based not on divine right monarchy but on critical reason and popular sovereignty. This new embryonic republicanism was most dramatically illustrated by the great writers of the age, but scores of pamphleters, journalists, and hack writers also disseminated this new critical view of the social hierarchy. In the first half of the eighteenth century, Charles de Secondat, baron de Charles-Louis de Montesquieu, a member of the parlement of Bordeaux, satirized French society in *Persian Letters* (1721); then, in his *Spirit of the Laws* (1748), he defended the role of "intermediate bodies" as a check on royal absolutism and a "separation of powers" as the best way to ensure public liberty. The multitalented Voltaire—poet, dramatist, essayist, novelist, and popularizer of Newtonian science—set the standard in his productive, 50-year career. He ceaselessly attacked the Catholic Church as a force of obscurantism and oppression in society, fought for a more humane and rational government, and championed the rights of the persecuted. Denis Diderot, editor of the 35-volume *Encyclopedie* (1751–1772), systematized and disseminated Enlightenment views on everything from Adam to zoos. Finally, the self-taught iconoclastic outsider Jean-Jacques Rousseau, a Genevan of humble Protestant origins, provided the strongest arguments for popular sovereignty and the power of public opinion in *The Social Contract* (1762). The "General Will" of the people, he argued, rather than the divine right of a monarch, should be the governing principle of society.

These secular, rational, and republican ideas became powerful as they were diffused in society. After 1700 a wide variety of institutions, organizations, and public places—academies, salons, cafés, masonic lodges, and clubs—not only proliferated the ideas but also, especially after 1750, became bastions of Enlightenment thought. Even theaters became a forum for Enlightenment ideas, staging such plays as Pierre-Augustin Beaumarchais's *Marriage of Figaro* (1784), in which a resourceful domestic servant outwits an aristocratic master.

During the first half of the eighteenth century, aristocratic and upper-class women achieved a visibility and power that they had rarely obtained previously. For twenty years, at Versailles, between 1745 and 1764, Madame de Pompadour was not only Louis XV's mistress but also his principal political advisor, organizer of court life, and a great patron of literature and art. In Paris such women as Madame Geoffrin, Madame Necker, the Marquise Du Deffant, and Madame Helvetius held salons where much of the Enlightenment thought was formulated and disseminated.

In the late 1770s Jacques Necker, one of Louis XVI's many finance ministers, called public opinion "an invisible power that, without treasury, guard or army gives its laws to the city, the court and even the palaces of kings."[12]

Until 1788 the Parlement of Paris proved the most adept government institution at winning public opinion. It drove a series of reforming ministers from office—Maupeau and Terray under Louis XV and then Turgot and Calonne under Louis XVI—by portraying itself, like Montesquieu, as the champion of liberty against royal despotism. Were the parlements merely defending their particular privileges? Or were they promoting the general will? The language of politics had already changed; what would happen to its institutions?

NOTES

1. Louis XIV, *Mémoires for the Instruction of the Dauphin*, intro., trans., & notes Paul Sonnino (New York: The Free Press, 1970), p. 130.

2. Peter Burke, *The Fabrication of Louis XIV* (New Haven: Yale University Press, 1992), p. 7, and passim.

3. Orest Ranum, *Paris in the Age of Absolutism, An Essay* (New York: John Wiley & Sons, 1968), pp. 293, 66–67, 76, and 294.

4. Norbert Elias, *The Court Society*, trans. Edmund Jephcott (New York: Pantheon, 1983), p. 197.

5. Colin Jones, *The Cambridge Illustrated History of France* (Cambridge: Cambridge University Press, 1994), p. 160.

6. Michel Foucault, *Madness and Civilization: A History of Insanity in the Age of Reason*, trans. and abridged Richard Howard (New York: Vintage: 1973), pp. 38–64.

7. Pierre Goubert, *Louis XIV and Twenty Million Frenchmen*, trans. Anne Carter (New York: Vintage: 1970), p. 220.

8. Jones, *The Cambridge Illustrated History of France*, p. 170.

9. Ibid., p. 171.

10. Ibid., p. 170.

11. Jeremy D. Popkin, *Revolutionary News: The Press in France, 1789–1799* (Durham, NC: Duke University Press, 1990), p. 80.

12. Jones, *The Cambridge Illustrated History of France*, p. 175.

6

The French Revolution and Napoleon

In 1789 France produced the first modern revolution. It set the model for all subsequent revolutions not only in nineteenth-century France but also across the world in the twentieth century. Not only did the French Revolution produce modern politics, it also led to the rise of modern nationalism, an idea that has far from run its course.

The French Revolution, in essence, was driven by a broad cross section of the French middle class, the bourgeoisie. Ever since the outbreak of the revolution, controversy has raged over what exactly constituted the bourgeoisie and whether this class created and benefited from the upheaval. This debate shows no signs of letting up, even 200 years after the revolution. The French bourgeoisie had grown dramatically as an economic class since 1700, but became a distinct and coherent political class only during the crisis of the monarchy in the 1780s. In this sense, the revolution made the bourgeoisie as much as the bourgeoisie made the revolution.

The most fundamental cause of the revolution was an economic depression that hit France after 1770. After a half century of unprecedented growth, the French economy suffered a series of severe setbacks. Just when a dramatic population expansion from 1730 to 1770 had produced millions of new mouths, French agriculture failed to feed them. Lacking, for the most part, the innovative farming of England, the French were hard hit when climatic conditions worsened after 1770 and a series of poor harvests resulted. There followed impoverishment and unemployment—in some cities and in some years reaching 50 percent of the laboring population–and inflation caused by more people competing for limited farmland and jobs.[1] Peasants who had become prosperous during the good times now feared that all their gains might be wiped out. At the same time, the economic downturn resulted in a drop in tax revenues for the royal treasury, which was already running a deficit from the War of the Austrian Succession and the Seven Years' War.

In 1777 Louis XVI appointed an eminent Swiss banker, Jacques Necker, controller general. Necker tinkered with French finances rather than attempting wholesale reform. All the while the royal debit climbed, exacerbated by France's entry (1778) on the side of the fledgling United States in their revolutionary war. By the 1780s the mounting royal debt was consuming more than half the state's tax income. Expenditure jumped over 250 percent between 1770 and 1788. The crown could no longer repudiate this debit as they had done before the 1720s because the financiers, accountants, and tax collectors who held this debit—Farmers General, Receivers General, Treasurers General, Payers of the Renters, and other high accountants—had become noble and had merged with the ruling class. Their noble status prevented the crown from using the traditional expedient, a Chamber of Justice, to cancel their claims. The royal aura simply could no longer overmaster financial logic.

In 1787, came Louis's new finance minister, Charles Alexandre de Calonne, proposed a single land tax payable by all landowners. Knowing that the Parlement of Paris would veto the idea, Calonne persuaded Louis XVI to call an assembly of notables, the first since before the reign of Louis XVI. Even though the crown chose this assembly with great care, when the group met in February 1787 they voiced the now common refrain: no taxation without representation. Shortly thereafter Calonne fell, and Louis XVI appointed the archbishop of Toulouse, Lomenie de Brienne, who tried the parlement once more. When this parlement, too, rejected the proposal, he took the fateful move of convening the Estates General, which representative body had not met since 1614. Upon hearing of their veto, the infuriated king exiled the parlement, but reinstated them briefly in November 1787.

With the process of tax collection disintegrating and the loyalty of the army slipping, Louis XVI suspended the parlements in May 1788, created 47 new courts. Emboldened by an aroused public opinion and drawing on the support of the Church and the nobility, the parlements openly resisted this royal move, and riots broke out in many provincial capitals. In the face of this nationwide upheaval, the king bowed and agreed to convene the Estates General for May 1, 1789. The parlements were again restored to power; and on September 23, 1788 the returning Parlement of Paris was greeted like conquering kings. Two days later, however, the declaration convoking the assembly stipulated that it should meet and vote as it had in 1614. If this did indeed occur, the first two estates, clergy and nobility, could overturn the will of the Third Estate. Suddenly the parlement's championing of rights was revealed as supporting only their own wishes and not the "general will of the nation."

At this point, with the preparation to convene the Estates General, polarization between the nobility and the bourgeoisie started to solidify. By tradition, each estate met locally to draw up lists of grievances. In the highly charged atmosphere of 1788 (and with the rate of literacy much higher than it had been 150 years earlier), this tradition became an opportunity for political education and mobilization. The number of pamphlets published in France soared from 217 in 1787 to 819 in 1788 and 3,305 in 1789 and 3,121 in 1790. This proliferation was nothing compared to the explosion of newspapers: 184 appeared in 1789, and another 335 in 1790. Over the course of the decade, 1789–1799, more than 1,300 newspapers were published.[2] In addition, the number of associations and clubs also escalated: 1,100 were created between 1789 and 1791 and this number skyrocketed to over 5,500 by 1794.[3] In short, a new political culture developed, based on discussion, organization, and petition.

Public opinion quickly splintered: the nobility and clergy worried about their privileges, and the Third Estate, now embracing the notion that they constituted the nation, worried about the people. By driving a sharp wedge between noble and commoner, the calling of the Estates General also created a schism between those who had complete nobility and could pass their titles on to their heirs, and those whose heirs had to purchase nobility in turn for one or two generations before the family was fully noble. The latter were considered members of the Third Estate (commoners) for the purpose of the elections to the Estates General.

The most famous of the era's pamphlets, *What Is the Third Estate?* written by Abbé Emmanuel Sieyès, expressed the growing self-awareness and confidence of the Third Estate. The power of its message derived from its simplicity: What was the Third Estate in French society? Everything. What was it in terms of political power? Nothing. What did it wish to be? Something. Sieyès based these answers on the belief that members of the Third Estate performed all the important work of society and that the aristocracy merely reaped the benefits.

The first goal of the Third Estate was to achieve double representation, so as to have the same number of delegates as the first two estates. The crown granted this right in late December 1788 but left undecided the matter of voting by estate or by head. If the former, the Third Estate would surely have its will constantly frustrated; if the latter, they could at least occasionally create a tie.

Between February and May 1789, the three estates met to elect their representatives and draw up their grievances (*cahiers de doléances*). All males above the age of 25 were eligible to vote. Among the clergy, parish priests dominated numerically, holding two-thirds of the positions. In general, these local clerics came from poor backgrounds and chafed under the rule of the upper classes who held the high posts of the Church. Among the nobility, superior numbers likewise gave the poor rural nobility a two-thirds majority. The remaining third, however, comprised liberals dedicated to making fundamental changes. Among the Third Estate, the selection process did not follow demographics but rather literacy and education. Thus lawyers and government officials were chosen over the laboring poor. Despite the diversity of the delegates, demands across all three estates indicated a remarkable uniformity: trust in the monarch and desire for moderate reform.

Meantime the economy continued to deteriorate. In normal times anything between a third and a half of an urban worker's wage went for his daily bread; for landless agricultural laborers the figure might be higher. As prices climbed over the spring of 1789 the proportion rose to two-thirds for the most affluent and possibly as high as nine-tenths for the poorest. A severe winter, in which ice and snow froze or paralyzed rivers, roads, workshops, and mills, exacerbated the misery. "The wretchedness of the poor people during this inclement season," wrote the Duke of Dorset from Paris on January 8, 1789, "surpasses all description."[4]

When the Estates General met, on May 4, 1789, the monarchy, through insensitivity and lack of leadership, compounded the differences among these estates. Royal protocol dictated that the Third-Estate delegates clearly defer, by dress and gesture, to the "superior" estates. The king, in his opening address and during the subsequent month, was dignified but indecisive: the three estates were to decide separately which topics they should consider and how to vote. Members of the Third Estate, at first from Brittany, and then from other regions, met in a Versailles café to discuss their political options. Their gathering quickly became known as the Breton Club. The Third Estate called on the other two to meet with them and form a national assembly. Weeks passed until the king finally sided with his clergy and nobility and, to intimidate the Third Estate, on June 20 he had their meeting hall locked. Undaunted members of the Third Estate gathered instead at a nearby tennis court and swore (the famous tennis court oath) not to separate until they had written a constitution. In the face of such resolution, the king again retreated and allowed the three estates to meet as the National Assembly. Once assembled, the delegates quickly declared themselves the Constituent Assembly, thus signaling their intention to write a constitution. At the same time, nobles began to leave the country and to plot the downfall of the Constituent Assembly, signaling their intention to start a counterrevolution.

Although Louis had granted the wishes of the Third Estate, he feared its growing power and massed troops outside Paris and dismissed the popular Necker. At this moment, first in Paris and then in the country, the people decisively intervened. News of Necker's ouster reached Paris on Sunday morning, July 12, 1789. As this was the traditional day of rest, crowds gathered to hear and discuss the news. As had been the case throughout the 1780s, the largest crowds gathered in the Palais Royal. This colonnaded arcade had become the favorite site in Paris for recreation and agitation because—being the property of a member of the royal family, the duke of Orléans—it was not subject to overt police surveillance. The most famous of the speakers that Sunday was a young journalist, Camille Desmoulins, who, after climbing on top of a café table, called the citizens to arms in order to end their "bondage." This and similar speeches led Parisians over the following days to amass as many muskets, cannons, powder, and shot as possible to stop any royal repression of the revolution. Their search for firepower led the Parisian crowds, on Tuesday, July 14, 1789, to storm the infamous royal prison and fortress on the eastern side of the city, the Bastille.

The fall of the Bastille netted the revolutionaries little in the way of tangible, but much in the way of symbolic, results. The fortress was lightly defended—by 30 Swiss Guards and 80 retired soldiers—and contained only seven prisoners still being held in its depths and only nominal amounts of cannons, powder, and muskets. Initially the revolutionaries hoped the royal commander would surrender without a fight, but negotiations stalled, the royal troops panicked, and shooting erupted. Angered at what seemed monarchal duplicity, the crowd, now at around 80,000 on that hot summer day in July, brought up cannon and smashed the most tangible—with 10-foot-thick walls and eight towers of over 100 feet—monument to royal power in Paris. In the process, almost 100 artisans and journeymen, who predominated in the crowd, fell as martyrs to the revolution. After victory, the enraged crowd cut off the heads of the Bastille's commander and some royal officials and marched the severed heads around Paris on pikes. The following day, the Marquis de Lafayette, a liberal nobleman and American Revolutionary War hero, was named head of the National Guard. This police force, composed of middle-class citizens wealthy enough to buy their own weapons and uniforms, assumed the duties of maintaining order. The rest of the royal administration of Paris was also replaced with one loyal to the National Assembly. Lafayette created a potent new symbol when he created the tricolor by joining the white flag of the Bourbon Dynasty to the red and blue colors of Paris. On July 17, Louis XVI came to Paris and put on a cockade with the new colors of the tricolor. For the moment, it appeared that the revolution had triumphed and that the king had given the spontaneous popular revolt his blessing. The fall of the Bastille thus gave birth to one of the central myths of the French Revolution: the unstoppable power of an aroused citizenry. The fall of the Bastille quickly resonated throughout France, then Europe, then the world.

French peasants stormed their own bastilles, the châteaus of the noble landlords. Even nature seemed to intervene when a freak hailstorm on July 13, 1788 laid waste to hundreds of square miles of crops on the eve of the harvest. On July 14, 1789, grain prices in Paris jumped to their highest level during Louis XVI's reign. The momentous political events in Paris and the catastrophic agrarian crisis in the countryside gave birth to a conspiracy theory in the overheated and undernourished minds of the peasantry. From village to village, the rumor spread that the nobility had hired gangs of brigands to destroy the harvest and frustrate any hope of reform. Reacting to this "Great Fear," the peasants gathered whatever weapons they could find and went into direct action against their seigneurs, attacking châteaus, harassing estate managers, burning feudal records, seizing forests, and reclaiming common lands.

Fearing the peasants would destroy all sense of property, the National Assembly formally abolished what they considered to be feudalism during a long night session on August 4, 1789. The term covered all obligations (such as labor services) that went beyond the simple payment of rent. Led by enthusiastic liberal nobles like Lafayette, the assembly also extended the term feudalism to a wide range of ancien régime practices, including the Church tithe and venal offices. To reassure holders of these traditional rights, the National Assembly agreed to allow compensation. These changes mark one of the primary social and economic consequences of the revolution.

Three weeks later, on August 26, the National Assembly enunciated a positive set of principles: the Declaration of the Rights of Man and Citizen, the most famous and important document of the revolution. Couched in the rational and universal language of the Enlightenment and inspired by the example of the American Revolution and the Declaration of Independence, the 1789 articles enumerate the freedom and equality of all men, the aim of every political association to be the conservation of that liberty, and the source of sovereignty to reside in the nation. Liberty is defined as the right to do anything that does not harm others, and law is described as the expression of the general will, including the right to fair and speedy justice. The document guarantees the freedoms of religion and speech, as well as representation in government, equal obligation to be taxed, and, finally, the "inviolable and sacred" right of property. The rule of law, hallmark of the Declaration, is directly noted in 9 of the 17 articles. The expressed right of all citizens to pursue whatever vocation they so choose, based on their abilities, introduced the notion of careers open to talents.

These historic measures, however idealistic, did not put bread in people's mouths. The price of bread, after a brief decline in late July and August, climbed again after a poor harvest. On September 14, 1789, the king summoned the loyal Flanders Regiment to the royal palace at Versailles. He then felt secure enough to denounce the abolition of feudalism and to express reservations about the Declaration of the Rights of Man and Citizen. Less than a month later, at a reception the royal family gave for the Flanders Regiment at Versailles, the tricolor cockade was trampled on the ground. Upon hearing of this desecration of the new national symbol and already enraged at the continuing high price of bread in the markets, the women of Paris rose in revolt. On October 5, the women marched, with Lafayette and the National Guard following to maintain order, to Versailles—12 miles away—to bring the "baker, the baker's wife, and the baker's son" (their terms for the royal family) back to Paris. Thus women played a decisive role in the Revolution from the start. The Constituent Assembly shortly followed. The Breton club found a place to meet not far from the hall where the National Assembly met in the convent of the Jacobins. Henceforth this venue for debate and discussion

would become known as the Jacobin Club. In Paris the club's membership had swelled from 200 to 1,000 by the end of December 1789. Affil-
iates of the Jacobin Club soon opened up across the towns and cities of
France, totaling over 1,000 clubs by September 1791. The Jacobin Club
played a central role in formulating revolutionary ideas in Paris and
disseminating them throughout the country. The king was now back in
Paris, the royal family now resided at the Tuileries palace near the
present-day Louvre museum, and they were no longer insulated at Versailles. Henceforth, the populace would play a decisive role in the
revolution through 1794.

After these dramatic "October Days" of 1789, the revolution achieved
a period of equilibrium that lasted over a year. In November and December the National Assembly extricated itself from imminent bankruptcy by nationalizing Church property (from 6 to 10 percent of arable
land). To facilitate an orderly sale of the land, the National Assembly
printed notes called *assignats*, secured by the land's value, which could
be cashed when the land was sold. Although momentarily averting a
crisis, these notes would eventually become a de facto and unstable national currency, for the reckless government printed too many. Principal
purchasers of this property were members of the urban bourgeoisie and
prosperous peasants. This measure won the revolution some powerful
allies in town and country, the harvest improved the following year, and
the resulting decline in the price of bread quieted the general populace.

The mood of national reconciliation reached its high point with the
Festival of the Federation on July 14, 1790, the first anniversary of the
fall of the Bastille. Through a downpour, 300,000 spectators watched a
military review of 50,000 of the National Guard on the Champ de Mars
(now the site of the Eiffel Tower). But by the time Lafayette had administered the oath of allegiance to the National Guard, to the National
Assembly, and to Louis XVI and his queen Marie Antoinette, the sun
had broken through. The nation read rapturous newspaper reports about
this festival, which, with the sudden appearance of the sun, seemed to
have been given heavenly sanction.

During this period of relative tranquility, the National Assembly created a liberal constitutional monarchy, and the reforms they initiated
between 1789 and 1791 laid the foundations of modern French government. Grounded in the Enlightenment notions of rationality, efficiency,
and humanity, the legislators tried to rid France of the peculiarities and
privileges of the monarchy. Although Louis XVI was to remain king, his
power was strictly limited. For example, legislators provided for only a

"suspensive" rather than a permanent veto—the king could only delay (that is, suspend) rather than permanently cancel acts of the legislature. The National Assembly abolished the nobility as a legal order, the guilds, the provinces, the parlements, and the systems of taxes, tolls, weights, and measures. In place of all these, the planners created a uniform body of citizens, a network of 83 administrative departments relatively the same size, and, by 1793, a uniform system of weights and measures known as the metric system that would eventually become nearly universal. The laws of August 16–24, 1790 set up a new French national legal and court system, including local justices of the peace, police courts, correctional tribunals, assize courts, and a supreme court of appeals, the court of cassation, a rough equivalent of the U.S. Supreme Court. The laws of March 2–17, 1791, removed the guild restraints listed above and instituted freedom of commerce. Voters could elect not only their representatives but also their clergy and judiciary. Religious tolerance was extended not only to Protestants but also, unprecedentedly, to Jews. The National Assembly also confirmed habeas corpus (the requirement that anyone detained by the police be quickly brought to court) and upheld the freedom of speech and the freedom of the press.

The liberalism of the National Assembly, however, had definite limits. Fear of the lower classes in city and country led the legislators, following the lead of Abbé Sieyes, to create two types of citizenship. Active citizens were those who paid a specified amount in taxes—a direct tax equal to the value of three days of work annually. They were eligible to vote. Passive citizens—those who paid little or no taxes—were denied the vote. In addition, while any aspiring entrepreneur could open a business, any attempt at organizing a union by employees was prevented by the Le Chapelier law of June 14, 1791, which banned workers' combinations. Moreover, the rights of the poor to subsistence or the unemployed to work were not seriously considered. On all these points, the future would hold much dissension and conflict.

The sense of national unity was quickly fractured not only by class distinctions but also, and even more immediately and importantly, by religious matters. In the same month as the Festival of the Federation, July 1790, the National Assembly passed the Civil Constitution of the Clergy, a measure that sharply divided the nation. This act, seen as a logical step after the nationalization of Church properties, turned Catholic priests into civil servants and required them to swear an oath of allegiance to the nation. About half of France's priests, believing such an oath compromised their religious vows, refused to take the oath. Regions

with the loudest protests—most notably the west and north—would remain clerical and conservative through the 1950s: the areas whose priests
accepted the oath tended to be, and to remain, anti-clerical and republican. Within a year (April 1791), a papal bull would condemn the Civil
Constitution of the Clergy and, in essence, excommunicate the revolutionaries.

Growing religious fissures spurred Louis XVI to try to flee the country.
On the night of June 20–21, 1791, this deeply religious king, shocked by
these latest measures and fortified by appeals from emigrés and foreign
monarchs, fled Paris by coach. His capture 124 miles outside of Paris and
the ensuing trip back to Paris under the hostile gaze of the crowd set
the stage for the radicalization of the revolution. On the left, radical
journalists and agitators demanded the abolition of the monarchy. These
radicals gathered at the Cordeliers Club, a more radical and inclusive
club than the Jacobin Club. On the right, monarchists frequented the
Club de Valois in Paris.

Despite the king's flight, the National Assembly concentrated on fin-
ishing its work: creating a constitutional monarchy. Since Louis XVI was
essential for the operation of its constitution, the assembly propagated
the convenient fiction that the king had been abducted by aristocrats. In
September 1791 the king dutifully signed the constitution into law. The
constitution of 1791, which codified all the laws previously noted, was
the culmination of the "liberal" phase of the revolution. The Constitution
of September 1791 established a limited monarchy complemented by a
Legislative Assembly to rule over a nation of legally, but not politically,
equal citizens. Although now all citizens were subject to the same laws,
only active citizens had the right to vote. After the constitution had been
promulgated, the National Assembly dissolved itself. In an idealistic gesture, the assembly passed a self-denying ordinance stipulating that none
of its members could run for election to its successor, the Legislative
Assembly. Voter turnout was low but in fervent support of the revolution: fewer than 40 representatives from the clergy or nobility were in
the new 745-member assembly. The rest were members of the Third Estate, again primarily lawyers and local government officials.

In the fall of 1791, this inexperienced Legislative Assembly confronted
an ever-growing number of problems. Economic discontent mounted after the middle of 1791. To the depression of another bad harvest was
added the disintegration of the colonial economy, a major source of
France's prosperity throughout the century. Radical journalists and political militants demanded political power and economic security for the

passive citizens. In October 1791 Paris learned that enslaved Africans in Saint Domingue, inspired by the Revolution and the Declaration of the Rights of Man and Citizen, had risen against their masters. The resulting drop in colonial products, especially sugar, sparked riots in Paris and other cities. Within this same year, a self-taught dramatist with the stage name of Olympe de Gouges, in her *Declaration of the Rights of Women* posed the same questions for her gender that the enslaved Africans had asked regarding race. She made her declaration even more provocative by dedicating it to Marie Antoinette. Hers was by no means a lone voice; women were actively participating in demonstrations, organizing clubs, and publishing revolutionary tracts. All of this agitation helped shape modern feminism.

The Legislative Assembly did take some positive steps to deal with these challenges. In response to the revolution in Saint Domingue, the Assembly sent commissioners to mediate rather than an army to repress. Although certainly not in direct response to Olympe de Gouges, the assembly did lessen familial restraints by legalizing divorce and granting women equal access to divorce not only for adultery, or brutality, but also for incompatibility. The assembly, however, fully adhering to the liberal individualism of the age, contemplated no government action to aid the poor.

Rather than searching for solutions to France's worsening economic situation, the Legislative Assembly searched for scapegoats and looked to war as a possible solution to their problems. Counterrevolutionary nobles and "refractory" priests were deemed prime suspects. Laws were passed carrying the death penalty or confiscation of aristocratic lands, but were promptly vetoed by Louis XVI. The king's continued intransigence and the growing belligerence of the crowned heads of Europe made the leaders of the Legislative Assembly contemplate war as a means of crushing not only internal but also external enemies. Louis XVI, for his part, also became an advocate of war, but for exactly opposite motives: he hoped a conflict would nullify the revolution and restore his monarchy.

The primary advocate of war in the Legislative Assembly was journalist and Jacobin Club member Jacques-Pierre Brissot. He felt that war would secure national unity, expose the traitors, and carry the revolution to the rest of Europe. He was certain that the peoples of Europe would rise up against their oppressive monarchs just as the French had: "Volcanoes are everywhere in readiness . . . only a spark is needed to bring about a universal explosion."[5]

The revolutionaries lighted this spark on April 20, 1792 by declaring war on Austria. The ensuing conflict, which would endure in one fashion or another until 1815, transformed the French Revolution in ways neither its proponents nor even its opponents could ever have imagined. Indeed the political climate would be so different from the first three years of the revolution that historians called the period from 1792 to 1794 the Second Revolution.

Initially the war went badly because of the confused state of the French army, which was neither a royal nor a national army. In battle, officers from the nobility frequently argued with recently incorporated National Guard units and in many cases defected. As a result, the combined Austro-Prussian army scored a series of victories and advanced on Paris. On July 28, the duke of Brunswick, leader of the Austro-Prussian armies, trying to intimidate the revolutionaries and protect the royal family, issued a proclamation promising Paris would face "exemplary and forever memorable vengeance" if any harm came to the king and his family.[6]

This Brunswick Manifesto had results totally contrary to its intentions. A new social movement was emerging in Paris, made up of shopkeepers and craftsmen, the nucleus of the crowds that had taken the Bastille, who had become increasingly politicized since that summer of 1789. Now three years later, they had gained control over the 48 political assemblies, called sections, and National Guard units that Paris had been granted in 1790. The new element radicalized the sections by turning them into centers of agitation and mobilization of the passive citizens. These *sans-culottes*—so-called because they wore the long trousers of the working class rather than the short knee breeches of the wealthy—first caught public attention when they stormed the royal palace on June 20, 1792, and demanded that the king withdraw the vetoes which, by causing delays, they felt were crippling the war effort. On August 10, two weeks after the Brunswick Manifesto, the *sans-culottes* attacked the king's palace. They were aided and abetted by revolutionaries from south, who sang a song written by Claude Rouget de Lisle, a song which quickly became known as the "Marseillaise." Although Louis XVI and his family escaped from their residence at the Tuileries palace, the Legislative Assembly suspended him as monarch and put him and his family in jail at the Temple (the former palace of the Templar Knights of the Crusades). The assembly also called for new elections to choose a National Convention to determine the fate of the monarchy and to write a new constitution. The deputies also abolished the distinction between active and passive citizens and allowed all males to vote. On August 19, little more than a week after the king's fall, Lafayette fled France. The liberal revolution had become a democratic, even a radical, revolution.

Between the dissolution of the Legislative Assembly in early August and the convening of the National Convention of France in late September, France and Europe had an introduction to the creativity, energy, and brutality that a popular government could generate. The country, including its capital city, was in the hands of, respectively, an executive council and the commune of Paris. Georges Danton, a member of the radical Cordeliers Club, became minister of justice in the executive council and used his powerful oratory to energize Paris and the provinces to the defense of the homeland. On August 17, the council formed an emergency Revolutionary Tribunal that operated with few legal restrictions. Those condemned by this court faced a new type of execution pioneered by a legislator, one Dr. Joseph Guillotin, who had wished to mitigate the suffering of capital punishment. His machine, the guillotine, was designed to make beheading faster and more accurate. Other extraordinary decrees banished "refractory" priests and sent commissioners to the provinces to ensure a unified war effort. When the strategic Verdun fortifications fell on September 2, Parisian militants stormed into local prisons and killed roughly 1,300 prisoners whom they suspected of counterrevolution. Despite these bloodthirsty acts, the popular government did succeed in turning back the Austro-Prussian invader. On September 20, at Valmy, a valiant citizen army defeated the duke of Brunswick's professional troops. French citizen armies won an even more impressive victory on November 19 at Jemappes, Belgium, and occupied that country for a brief period.

With the revolution momentarily secure, the newly elected National Convention met for the first time on September 21, 1792. The 749 elected deputies came from the same socioeconomic and professional backgrounds as the previous two parliaments. Many had already served, since no self-denying ordinance applied in either the National or the Legislative Assembly. Although deeply committed to the revolution, these solid, middle-class lawyers and government officials believed in due process and distrusted the Parisian sans-culottes and their call for direct democracy. Once the threat of immediate invasion had passed, these different conceptions of revolution proved to be a source of tension between the government and the population of Paris.

In September 1792 the sans-culottes seemed a minor distraction compared to the problems of the monarchy, the defeat of internal counterrevolution, and external invasion. At its second meeting the newly seated deputies abolished the monarchy. In November they declared that French armies would assist all peoples wishing to be free. In the following two months they tried and then executed the king. Louis XVI was guillotined in front of a massive crowd on the Place de la Concorde on January 21, 1793; his wife, often called by radicals the scythe of the revolution, followed him to the guillotine the following October.

From February to August 1793, the revolution faced its darkest hour and responded by instituting what has become known as the Reign of Terror. In rapid succession, France faced another severe subsistence crisis, a war with England then Spain, a royalist revolt in the northwest (the Vendée), the loss of Belgium and the treason of its leading general Dumouriez, the revolt of Lyon and other cities, and the fall of the Mediterranean port of Toulon to the English. During this crisis a number of fault lines developed—notably over religion, social radicalism, and political centralization—which divided the nation well into the twentieth century.

To meet these multiple threats, the Convention issued 12,000 decrees and raised 14 armies. The Convention implemented a wide range of radical measures that anticipated the welfare and warfare states of the twentieth century. To provide coherence and unity to the war effort, the Convention created the Committee of Public Safety in April 1793. Its most famous member, Maximilien Robespierre, joined the committee on July 13, 1793. To sustain popular support in Paris and the provinces, the Convention fixed the maximum prices of wheat, flour, and a long list of other goods deemed essential for subsistence. To deter infractions, speculation in grain was made a capital offense. These measures became known under the title of the first law of the Maximum (May 1793).

In June 1793, after the most radical members of the Convention had gained control, the Montagnards (so called because they sat at the summit, the mountaintop, of the Convention) drafted a new and more radical constitution. It defined a "right of subsistence" and stated that all children should receive a free public education. The Convention also eliminated the final elements of feudalism, abolished slavery, confirmed divorce, instituted the metric system, and devised and implemented a new Republican calendar which was a composite of decimal (weeks), doudecimal (12 months), and solar (year) based on the decimal system. A national conscription—the *levée en masse*—was introduced in August 1793, a precursor to the mass warfare of the twentieth century. To regain control over the country, the Convention sent out representatives on missions to enforce its will in the provinces. Revolutionary tribunals were made permanent, and revolutionary armies were established. Staffed largely by the *sans-culottes*, these armies not only collected food for the military and the cities but also engaged in a zealous program of dechristianization. Churches were closed down or demolished and religious statues, relics, and books were destroyed.

In September 1793 the Convention passed a "law against suspects" and officially made terror the order of the day. During the Reign of Terror, under 3,000 individuals were executed in Paris; several hundreds of thousands were put to death in the provinces. Upwards of half a million "suspects"—those judged to be threats to the revolution, that is, counterrevolutionaries—were imprisoned, and an additional 130,000 to 150,000 persons emigrated.[7] Although nobles and priests were targeted initially, the majority of later victims came from the lower classes. In March 1794 the tribunals turned their attention to leaders of the *sans-culotte* movement, judged them to be too "extreme," and executed the Hebertists (the followers of the radical journalist Jacques Hébert). In the following month, the courts eliminated those they considered too "moderate," including the once-popular hero Danton.

The instrument of the National Convention's will was the Committee of Public Safety, created in April 1793 and given near dictatorial powers. The Committee included some of the most famous and effective leaders of the revolution: the "incorruptible" Robespierre, the "organizer of victory" Lazare Carnot, and the precocious Louis Antoine de Saint-Just, not yet 25 when he joined the Committee. By the summer of 1794 the Committee had succeeded both in repressing interior rebellion and counter-revolution and in repulsing invasion.

The very success of the Committee of Public Safety undermined its power. Robespierre, as an antidote to the anarchy and atheism that he felt *sans-culotte* dechristianization represented, staged a Festival of the Supreme Being on June 8, 1794. Members of the Convention began to worry that he was setting himself up as some new emperor. When, later in the month, French armies reconquered Belgium and ended the most pressing threat to France's security, Robespierre's enemies in the Convention felt they could dispense with him and also with the entire apparatus of emergency government.

By the end of July 1793, an anti-Robespierre faction had gained a majority in the Convention. The conspirators included not only moderate and conservative deputies who dreaded Robespierre's revolutionary zeal but also radicals, such as Joseph Fouché, who feared Robespierre's moral purity would expose their rapacity and brutality, in Fouché's case as a representative on mission suppressing the Lyon revolt. On July 27, 1794, during a speech in which he was critical of the revolution's excesses and his own faults, Robespierre and his allies were denounced as tyrants and arrested by the Convention. Almost immediately, however, Robespierre and a few followers escaped to the Hôtel de Ville (city hall), where they appealed to the Parisian popular militants to save them. With much of the popular leadership already executed or intimidated, the Parisian people could no longer change the destiny of the revolution. Robespierre's little group was quickly captured and guillotined on July 28, 1794 (in the month of Thermidor in the revolutionary calendar then in use). The vanquishers of Robespierre immediately acquired the name of the Thermidorians and promptly stepped into the leadership void. Moderate Thermidorian deputies now dominated the Convention; the *sans-culotte* militants were stripped of power in the Paris sections, the price-fixing measures were abolished, and in November the Jacobin Club was closed.

The fall of the Committee of Public Safety ended the most innovative period of the revolution. The Thermidorian Convention lacked any clear-cut vision other than its own survival and the prevention of another recurrence of the Reign of Terror. When the Abbé Sieyès reappeared in 1795, he was asked what he had done during the Terror. Tradition holds that he simply said, "J'ai vécu—I lived."[8] Perhaps the most characteristic leader of the period between the execution of Robespierre and the elevation of Napoleon Bonaparte was Paul Barras. This manipulative, mercenary, and unscrupulous member of the Thermidorian Convention was a member of all the succeeding five-man directories that ruled France.

The Thermidorians tried to rule from the political center but quickly found that no such center existed. The Thermidorian Convention applied itself the task of writing a new constitution. This new batch of framers tried diligently to prevent the reemergence of another Robespierre. They divided leadership among five "directors," who were put under the close supervision of a bicameral legislature composed of a Council of 500 and a Council of Elders, restricted to deputies over the age of forty. Voting and office-holding restrictions were also reimposed, as were indirect elections. About one million men, 20 percent of the electorate, were eligible for election to departmental assemblies. The 30,000 members of these assemblies ultimately chose the deputies. "We shall be governed by the best and the best are those best educated and most interested in upholding the laws. With very few exceptions you will only find such men among those who, possessing property are attached to the country containing it and the laws which protect it," declared the chief writer of the Constitution, the moderate François Boissy d'Anglas.[9] Rather than listing the "social rights" of the poor, the Constitution enumerated a "declaration of duties" including the requirement to honor private property and the law.

In an attempt, first, to prevent the radicals from either left or right from gaining power and, second, to avoid the problems that followed the Constituent Assembly's self-denying ordinance, the Convention decreed that two-thirds of the members of the new councils had to be chosen from among the members of the outgoing assembly. This stipulation provoked great anger in the Paris sections, now composed of the militant young rich—the Gilded Youth (*Jeunesse dorée*)—who had suppressed the *sans-culottes*. These sections marched on the Convention on October 5, 1795 (13 Vendémiaire according to the revolutionary calendar). The troops that scattered the militants were led by Paul Barras; one of his artillery commanders was the young general Napoleon Bonaparte. The Vendémiaire episode taught the new Directory two harsh lessons: first, the new regime could not trust the middle-class landowners, businessmen, and professionals whom it tried to reach, and, second, until the regime had a secure political base, it must rely on the military to maintain order.

Lacking a solid center, the Directory strove to remain above politics over the course of its four-year rule. The attempt failed miserably. Between its inception in November 1795 through its dissolution exactly four years later, the Directory had to strike alternately against the royalists and the neo-Jacobins. This balance-beam policy multiplied the regime's enemies without creating a viable middle.

Despite such manifest political ineffectiveness, historians have recently concluded that several achievements did take place during the Directory era. The regime benefited from a favorable economic climate, thanks to a series of good harvests. The Directory returned to a metallic currency (based on gold and silver) in 1797, ending the rampant inflation that had occurred under the Thermidorians. The public debt was "consolidated" by writing off two-thirds of it in a partial bankruptcy, a move that freed up government revenue but enraged bondholders who thus lost two-thirds of their investment. The Directory also provided for a secure tax base by regularizing the collection of taxes, both direct and indirect, on land, business activity, and luxury items, and even on doors and windows—another measure that alienated much of the population. The Directory's most substantial achievements, however, were made in the field of education: new medical schools, an institute for the philosophic and scientific elite, the *école normale* to train teachers, the *école polytechnique* to train engineers, and the expansion of the Museum of Natural History. An entire network of new academies and schools created a new bourgeois intellectual elite based on merit and recruited on a national scale. As a result, Paris became, for many decades, the world center in science and medicine.

One of the most striking achievements of the Thermidorian and Directory periods (the creation of the best army in Europe) would lead not to stability but to further political turmoil. Almost continuous warfare since 1792 had transformed the raw but energetic citizen-soldiers into a well-trained, experienced army and created promising young generals whose rise was based not on aristocratic privilege but instead on individual talent.

Napoleon Bonaparte was the most illustrious and skilled general created by this dynamic and innovative military. Only the complete shakeup of the French army during the revolution could have allowed a man of Napoleon's background to emerge as master of France and of Europe. Although born into a noble family, Napoleon came from the poor peripheral island of Corsica which had been become French only a year before his birth in 1769. A royal scholarship allowed him to attend the military school at Brienne and to become a sublieutenant in the artillery at the age of 16. At the start of the revolution, Napoleon wrote, "Men of genius are meteors destined to be consumed in illuminating their century."[10] Although famous for his below-average height, it was the power of his "hypnotic" gray-blue eyes and the range of his "near-photographic memory" that commanded the allegiance of virtually all who served with or under him.

Napoleon quickly proved his genius first as an artillery commander in the recapture of the Mediterranean port of Toulon. Although promoted to brigadier general, Napoleon had to exercise great discretion after the fall of Robespierre. When Barras became one of the Directors he raised Napoleon to general on the Italian front. In his campaigns in northern Italy, Napoleon proved to be not only a master general but also a statesman and adept at setting up sister republics in the regions he conquered.

Sensing a threat from this young general, whose victories in Italy had made him a popular hero, the Directory sent Napoleon on an expedition to Egypt in May 1798. While Napoleon tried to threaten the British Empire in the east, the Directory continued to suffer instability, then military reversals. When neo-Jacobins made impressive gains in the April 1798 elections, the Directory overturned the results with a coup. But within a year this Directory unraveled as a result of an economic downturn, and its armies were pushed back to the French frontiers by a new allied coalition that included not only Britain and Austria but now also Russia. Following new elections in the spring of 1799, the deputies turned the tables on the Directory and purged it.

One of the new Directors appointed in June was the Abbé Sieyès. His years in exile and obscurity had convinced Sieyès that France needed a strong government with a stern and steady leader. Reversing his earlier position, Sieyès now believed that only an authoritarian government could end the continuing instability, and he started to organize a coup. Recognizing his own lack of charisma, Sieyès searched for a military hero who could act as his puppet in his new constitutional system.

At this moment, in the fall of 1799, Bonaparte returned from Egypt. He seemed to Sieyès the perfect candidate. The conspirators then hatched and implemented their plot: claiming the Jacobins were preparing to depose the legislature, Sieyès moved the body to suburban Saint Cloud. Even though the Parisian populace had become quiescent, Sieyès and Napoleon still feared their intervention might wreck their plans. In Saint Cloud, however, Napoleon easily and discretely surrounded the building in which the legislators met with loyal troops. He then entered and asserted the claims of a Jacobin conspiracy. Dubious and shrewd, much of the legislative body felt the real conspirator was Napoleon and called for his arrest. At this supreme moment the future master of Europe hesitated and was saved by the fast action of his brother Lucien who sent in the troops and scattered the recalcitrant legislators. Napoleon quickly regained his composure and rounded up a sufficient number of parliamentarians to vote him and Sieyès full power. This seizure of power has become known to history as the *coup d'état* of 18 Brumaire Year VIII, after the revolutionary calendar (November 9, 1799).

After a decade of revolution, counterrevolution, war, and disorder, the nation greeted the new consulate government with widespread apathy. Sieyès rapidly learned who was the puppeteer and who the puppet. Napoleon concentrated a virtually dictatorial power in his position as first consul and retired Sieyès to a country estate. He also legitimated his consulate and constitution by holding a plebiscite in which intimidation, abstention, and voter fraud resulted in over 99 percent of the voters approving.[11]

Napoleon both ended and consolidated the revolution. He asserted simultaneously, "I am the Revolution," and "The Revolution is over."[12] He became first consul for life in May 1802, and then, two years later, again in May (1804), he proclaimed himself emperor. As in the time of Charlemagne the pope blessed the event; however, as befitting a son of the Enlightenment and the revolution, Napoleon had the pope come to Paris (rather than go to Rome) and crowned himself (rather than having it done by the pope). Napoleon was able to achieve such dominance because the traditional restraints on powerful rulers in the past had been swept away during the revolution.

Through his administrative reforms and innovations, Napoleon created the modern French government and state. By means of his military victories, he spread the ideals and institutions of the revolution across Europe. He gutted without fully abolishing the legislative institutions and turned his primary attention to perfecting the "administrative grid" that the revolution had put in place over all of France. The result would be the most far-reaching centralized state in world history to that point. During his fifteen-year regime, Napoleon was personally responsible for 80,000 letters and decrees covering every aspect of civil, criminal, and military administration.

Napoleon kept the department as the basic unit of government but endowed it with his own authoritarian impetus. In 1800 he created a corps of prefects to administer the departments. The central government appointed prefects as well as their deputies, the subprefects. Napoleon's first minister of the interior, his brother Lucien, spelled out their capacious powers, "Your powers embrace everything that relates to the public fortune, national prosperity, and tranquility of the people over whom you are charged with the administration."[13] Among other myriad powers, these junior Napoleons could appoint mayors. To monitor the bureaucracy Napoleon created a Council of State and set up a special branch of auditors charged with educating future prefects and upper functionaries.

Napoleon also completed the work of codifying a legal system. His most impressive achievement, the Civil Code—also known as the Code Napoleon and imposed or adopted in much of Europe—synthesized revolutionary rationalism and idealism with his own authoritarianism. Issued in 1804, the Civil Code confirmed the end of feudal obligations and the abolition of guilds, instituted unambiguous contractual ownership of property, equal treatment under law, freedom of religion, and careers open to talents. At the same time, however, the family law of the revolutionary decade, which had made important steps toward egalitarianism and gender neutrality, was dropped. Instead, Roman law, stressing parental authority, turned women into virtual children in terms of legal status. For example, women could no longer be a witness to a legal act such as a wedding or baptism; they could no longer file a lawsuit or own property in their own right. Napoleon also amended the divorce law, making it much harder for wives to charge their husbands with battery, desertion, or adultery. Charity for widows and unwed mothers was also curtailed or abolished. The one concession toward equality that Napoleon retained was equal inheritance. His less famous but still highly influential criminal code extended his authoritarianism by limiting defendants' rights and the jury's role but providing prosecutors with wide powers.

The long-standing struggle between the revolution and the Catholic Church was also resolved. In April 1802 Napoleon and the pope agreed on a Concordat that reestablished the Church in French society. Although the document acknowledged that Catholicism was "the religion of the majority of Frenchmen," Protestants and Jews received state recognition. For Napoleon, religion was not a matter of sanctity but of social control. He demanded that the clergy, now salaried public officials (as first envisioned in the Civil Constitution of the Clergy), contain bishops functioning as "prefects in purple" and parish priests as "mayors in black."[14]

A second pillar of social control, in Napoleon's mind, was education. He created the Imperial University to administer the entire educational system. He focused most of his attention on the 44 high schools (lycées) devoted to training his administrative, military, and technical elite. Primary education was left primarily to individual localities, which in practice usually meant the Church.

If education and religion failed to dissuade revolutionaries, rebels, and criminals, then Napoleon was ready with his revamped and augmented police force. Under the former Terrorist and Thermidorian Joseph Fouché, Napoleon increased the centralization and efficiency of the police in both Paris and the provinces. An extensive system of secret police and close surveillance of theaters, cafés, and newspapers managed to blunt any effective political opposition up until the last years of the empire.

Napoleon furthered the financial recovery initiated by the Directory by establishing a national bank, the Bank of France, in 1803 as well as simplifying and increasing the efficiency of the tax code. He was also able, until his last years, to maintain a low tax rate because his conquests kept the treasury full. This booty economy, not seen since the days of Charlemagne, kept France out of debt. In essence, Napoleon forced Europe to pay for French glory and prosperity.

The First Empire was able to restore a great deal of the social harmony lost during the revolutionary decade. Napoleon strove for and, in a large measure, achieved a fusion of the old regime aristocracy with the new bourgeoisie into a ruling elite of notables. He recruited his administration from those of either status whom he deemed most competent. He permitted nobles who swore allegiance to him to return to France. The day of the king's execution, January 21, was dropped as a national holiday, and the oath of hatred for royalty was replaced by an oath of loyalty to the empire.

But while Napoleon's rule brought stability, it also led to artistic and intellectual stagnation. The intellectual dynamism and social ferment of the previous decade ended under the weight of rigorous censorship. Between 1789 and 1799, over 1,300 new newspapers had appeared; by 1811 in Paris only four had full governmental authorization and each department was allowed only one.[15] Napoleon felt his control over the French press was so complete that he did not need to hear what the newspapers said. "Skip it, skip it," Napoleon would tell his secretary who was reading the paper while he shaved in the morning, "They only say what I tell them to."[16] As his interior minister Jean Chaptal was later to remark, "He wanted valets, not advisers."[17]

Napoleon's regime rested on a clever but precarious balance of domestic stability and military victory. Although he did not invent a new military strategy, he brilliantly combined the technological advances in artillery, the field in which he had been trained, with the ideological passion of a citizen army fighting for its national and personal freedom. The mercenary royal armies of Europe that opposed him, at least until his last battles, proved to be no match. Napoleon's basic strategy centered on the concepts of penetration, central position, and envelopment. Penetration stemmed from his maxim "You engage, and then you wait and see."[18] Central position entailed attaining a place from which to divide the opposing army. Then, through envelopment, Napoleon broke the adversary's supply and communication lines. In battle Napoleon's armies fused maneuver, battle, and pursuit all in one coherent whole. The Napoleonic imperium reached its zenith in December 1805 with his most brilliant victory at Austerlitz in which he demolished the combined armies of Prussia and Austria. He had become the master of Continental Europe. Even recalcitrant Russia became his ally.

To Napoleon's chagrin, the French navy never proved the equal of England's and thus his attempts to re-create a French overseas empire foundered. His navy and an army failed to reconquer the island of Haiti, and he sold the extensive Louisiana territory, which had been won from Spain, to the United States to aid his war efforts in Europe. Realizing that he lacked the naval power necessary to invade England, Napoleon turned to economic warfare as the best means to bring his last enemy, England, to heel, and to stimulate France's economy. A series of decrees, promulgated in Berlin in 1806 and in Milan in 1807, excluded all British commerce from the European Continent. These measures became known as the Continental System. Soon, however, it became apparent that the nation of shopkeepers, Napoleon's description of England, was not being ruined. Smuggling and open opposition to his system would prevent the blockade from being effective.

Napoleon's dream of dominating Europe, by 1807, was alienating not only the peoples of Europe but also many of his supporters. In 1807 Napoleon's long-standing and brilliant foreign minister, Talleyrand, resigned. This adept and astute diplomat believed that Napoleon's insatiable ambition would lead to the collapse of his empire. In the following year, 1808, a guerilla war that erupted in Spain would prove to be a constant drain. The following year, 1809, Napoleon's dispute with the pope, resulting in the annexation of the papal states and the imprisonment of Pius VII, alienated Catholics. Meanwhile, Russia's czar disregarded the Continental System and distanced himself from his alliance with Napoleon. Thus in 1812 Napoleon determined to conquer Russia, the last European country that defied him. The debacle amidst the harsh Russian winter not only cost him 300,000 men but also inspired Prussia and Austria to renew their coalition effort against him.[19]

In 1813 Napoleon's good fortune began to run out. At the moment when he had to rely upon French manpower and economic resources to replenish his depleted ranks, an economic crisis erupted, bringing business failures, unemployment, and a sharp rise in bread prices. As a result, his army was simply not the well-honed military machine it had been previously. Even though he conducted some of his most brilliant campaigns in 1812 and 1813, he could not overcome a united Europe. "His lament proved correct: 'Your sovereigns born on the throne can let themselves be beaten twenty times and return to their capitals. I cannot do this because I am an upstart soldier. My domination will not survive the day when I cease to be strong and therefore feared.' "[20]

On April 6, 1814, with the Parisians in particular and the French in general unwilling to defend the empire to the death, Napoleon abdicated in favor of his young son. The allies, however, did not accept even an infant of Bonaparte's on the throne and, instead, opted to restore the brother of Louis XVI, who called himself Louis XVIII in deference to his dead brother and nephew.

After the events of the past twenty-five years, from 1789 to 1814, the crowned heads of Europe were determined to restore order when they met in Vienna in 1814. France naturally lost its Continental empire, but the diplomatic genius of Talleyrand ensured that France was not dismembered or subjected to an unduly harsh punishment. Napoleon was exiled to the tiny Mediterranean island of Elba. There he quickly set to work transforming the island's government and biding his time.

At the end of a quarter century of revolution and war, what had France become? It was a much more centralized and liberal society. The rulers in Paris faced few restrictions, and businessmen enjoyed virtual freedom of commerce. Urban workers and poor peasants, in contrast, could mount only feeble protest against their employers. Although the nobility had been stripped of its privileges and some of its land, the class system had not been eliminated; over the next fifty years the nobility would fuse with the upper bourgeoisie to create a new ruling class: the notables. The Church had lost its central role in society, yet it still remained a powerful force under the Concordat. Despite undoubted gains in administrative and legal rationalization, the French economy had weakened. A British blockade during most of the Revolutionary and Napoleonic periods had crippled the once-thriving Atlantic colonial economy, although European markets opened up by military conquest did somewhat compensate for this loss. During these twenty-five years, England had opened up a dramatic lead in industrialization over the French economy.

Perhaps the most momentous social change—although hardly noticed at the time—was the fall in the French birthrate. Equally impressive, but with consequences that were less dramatic, was the fall in the death rate. Historians are still uncertain exactly why the birthrate fell. Some scholars believe that the Napoleonic code's stipulation that all children must inherit land equally (as opposed to prior law which permitted a parent to leave the bulk of land to one child) inhibited peasants from having large numbers of children out of fear of having to split up their land into economically unviable plots upon their death. In any case, this was not a problem Napoleon had to face. Like Charlemagne and Louis XIV before him, Napoleon had been able to dominate Europe because of France's large population. By 1870 this was no longer possible because France had by far the lowest birthrate among major European nations. In the 1640s France still had the largest population in Europe; in the late seventeenth century, Russia surged ahead of France, and in the late nineteenth century so did Germany.

Despite this relative diminution in political status, France remained at the center of European political, social, cultural, and even economic life. In the final analysis, the French Revolution inspired much creative ferment in France—indeed, in all of Europe—throughout the nineteenth century. Following the revolution a large number of words entered the political vocabulary, including "revolution," "left," "right," "Terror," "bureaucrat," "conscription," "vandalism," and "centralize."

The bourgeoisie had been forged by the Revolutionary era into a true middle class. On its right stood a nobility and clergy who wished to erase the revolution; on its left stood a new breed of revolutionaries who felt 1789 was only the start of a humanities march to equality, liberty, and prosperity. Across the nineteenth century first the French, and then the rest of the European middle classes, would have to navigate these turbulent new political waters.

NOTES

1. Gordon Wright, *France in Modern Times*, 5th ed. (New York: W. W. Norton, 1995), p. 23.

2. Antoine De Baecque, "Pamphlets: Libel and Political Mythology," in *Revolution in Print: The Press in France, 1775–1800*, Robert Darnton and Daniel Roche, eds. (Berkeley: University of California Press in collaboration with the New York Public Library, 1989), p. 165, and Jeremy D. Popkin, "Journals: The New Face of News," in *Revolution in Print*, p. 150, and Jeremy D. Popkin, *Revolutionary News: The Press in France, 1789–1799* (Durham, NC: Duke University Press, 1990), pp. 9–10.

3. Patrice Gueniffey and Ron Halévi, "Clubs and Popular Societies," in *A Critical Dictionary of the French Revolution*, François Furet and Mona Ozouf, eds., Arthur Goldhammer, trans. (Cambridge, MA: Belknap Press of Harvard University Press, 1989), pp. 463, 458.

4. William Doyle, *The Oxford History of the French Revolution* (Oxford: Clarendon Press, 1989), p. 87.

5. Paul Beik, ed., *The French Revolution* (New York: Harper and Row, 1970), p. 201. Thanks to Professor Jeremy D. Popkin for this reference.

6. Doyle, *The Oxford History of the French Revolution*, p. 188.

7. Colin Jones, *The Cambridge Illustrated History of France* (Cambridge: Cambridge University Press, 1994), p. 191.

8. William H. Sewell Jr., *A Rhetoric of Bourgeois Revolution: The Abbé Sieyès and What Is the Third Estate?* (Durham, NC: Duke University Press, 1994), p. 19.

9. Doyle, *The Oxford History of the French Revolution*, p. 318.

10. David G. Chandler, *The Illustrated Napoleon* (New York: Henry Holt, 1990), pp. 62–63.

11. Frank McLynn, *Napoleon: A Biography* (London: Pimlico, 1998), pp. 224–225.

12. Jones, *The Cambridge Illustrated History of France*, p. 194.

13. Louis Bergeron, *France Under Napoleon*, trans. R. R. Palmer (Princeton, NJ: Princeton University Press, 1981), p. 27.

14. Jones, *The Cambridge Illustrated History of France*, p. 198.

15. Popkin, *Revolutionary News*, pp. 9–10 and 177.

16. Felix Markham, *Napoleon* (New York: Mentor, New American Library, 1963), p. 100.

17. Jones, *The Cambridge Illustrated History of France*, p. 196.

18. Owen Connelly, *Blundering to Glory: Napoleon's Military Campaigns* (Wilmington, DE: SR Books, 1987), p. 1.

19. Chandler, *The Illustrated Napoleon*, pp. 128–129.

20. Markham, *Napoleon*, p. 202.

7

An Unstable Era (1815–1870): Monarchies, Republic, and Empire

The restoration that followed Napoleon's abdication brought respite but not resolution to the ferment unleashed by the French Revolution. Indeed, the years between 1814 and 1870 saw a series of dramatic political ruptures: the first Bourbon Restoration under Louis XVIII (1814–1815); Napoleon's brief return in the Hundred Days (1815); the second Bourbon Restoration (1815–1830); the Revolution of 1830, followed by the July Monarchy of the citizen-king Louis-Philippe (1830–1848); the 1848 Revolution, succeeded by the Second Republic (1848–1851)—named "second" in honor of the revolutionary republic that emerged after the guillotining of the king and that fell with the rise of Napoleon; the Second Empire of Napoleon III (1852–1870); the collapse of the Second Empire during the Franco-Prussian war of 1870; and finally, the establishment of a Third Republic in the same year. On first glance, this rapid succession of regimes seems to have produced only repetitions of the Revolution of 1789. On closer examination, however, the fertile upheavals produced innovations in political and intellectual life that are still powerful forces around the world. The seeds of modern socialism, feminism, bohemianism, social Catholicism, technocracy, and modernism in art and literature all flowered during this time.

Beneath the surface turbulence and ferment, French society remained remarkably stable after the revolution. Legal equality (embodied in "careers open to talents"), the new administrative system (established grid of departments administered by prefects), and the Bank of France (which maintained a stable currency) remained in place as regimes rose and fell. The classes that had most profited from the revolution, the bourgeoisie, the bureaucracy, and the wealthier peasants, made very sure that these gains would not be reversed.

Despite the remarkable growth of Paris, France was not undergoing the same rate of urbanization as England. Starting under the July Monarchy, whose liberal economic policies provided impetus, France's industrial revolution picked up impressive speed under the Second Empire, in which the government played a big role in the economy, but still lagged behind that of Britain. In one vital sector of social and economic behavior, however, the French were in the vanguard. The nation's fertility rate, even among the so-called backward peasants, began a dramatic fall as a result of the peasants' fear that large families would lead to the breakup of their farms. By the last decades of the nineteenth century, France had become the first nation in the modern world to reach a population equilibrium thus providing another underlying source of stability.

Louis XVIII and other returning émigré nobles had to come to terms with the revolution, and Louis did not try to reimpose the three estates, much less the distinctive privileges of the clergy and nobility. He was also unable and unwilling to purge the administration of revolutionary and Napoleonic officials.

In an effort to save face, Louis "granted" a Charter on June 14, 1814, six weeks after his return to Paris. In essence the Charter was a constitution, but Louis did not wish to use that term owing to its revolutionary connotations. The Charter reaffirmed the basic principles of the Declaration of the Rights of Man and Citizen. Additionally, Louis XVIII set up a parliament of two houses; as in Great Britain, the lower chamber was elected by an electoral college chosen by a narrow suffrage. The upper chamber was dominated not by the upper nobility of the old regime, but by the notables of the Napoleonic regime. Moreover, Article 14 of the Charter gave him virtually a blank check to choose his ministers without the consent of parliament and to make the changes he deemed necessary "for the execution of the laws and the security of the state."

Before his first year back in Paris was complete, Louis XVIII would again be an émigré. Within ten months, economic dislocation, military demobilization, and social polarization led to political unrest. The termination of large orders for military goods and services caused widespread unemployment as did the dismemberment of Napoleon's army. Landowners who had profited from the purchase of clerical or noble land feared their gains would revert to returning nobles or the Church, groups that, like Louis XVIII, it seemed "had learned nothing and forgotten nothing."[1]

Just off the Italian coast on the tiny Mediterranean island of Elba, Napoleon noted the rising groundswell of dissent. On March 1, 1815, when he judged the moment opportune, Napoleon escaped from the island and returned to France. His former general, Marshal Michel Ney, promised his new sovereign, Louis XVIII, that he would bring Napoleon back in an iron cage, a type of coach used to transport prisoners, but instead he joined his former commander. When the army switched its allegiance to its former emperor, Louis XVIII returned to exile.

Within twenty days of his landing, Napoleon was again master of France. To regain the people's support he promised to rule as a liberal rather than an autocratic emperor. One of the leading liberals of the era, Benjamin Constant, actually drew up a constitution and had a new set of democratic institutions approved by a plebiscite. When the allies at the Congress of Vienna, convened to restore monarchical order to Europe, heard of Napoleon's return, they declared him an outlaw and formed a seventh and final coalition to stop him. The English general, the Duke of Wellington, vanquisher of Napoleonic armies in Spain, and the Prussian general, Gebhard von Blücher, immediately left to command armies. Ever true to his tradition of audacity, Napoleon marched north to the French border hoping to defeat the two generals by dividing their armies and then cutting off their communications and scattering them before reinforcements arrived. The battle of Waterloo, however, showed that age and poor health had taken their toll on Napoleon's generalship and that his crack army, especially its corps of superb commanders, could not be quickly reassembled. After the battle on June 18, 1815, Napoleon fled and abdicated again. He tried to escape to America but was caught and shipped by the British to a rocky island in the Atlantic, Saint Helena, where he finished his days.

The brief Hundred Days is historically important because it helped create a Napoleonic legend. Napoleon elaborated eloquently on how he would have become a liberal and beneficent ruler in his exile on Saint Helena in his dictated memoirs. This legend steadily grew over the next thirty years and helped elect his nephew president in 1848.

The rapid collapse of his First Restoration government in the face of

Napoleon sapped Louis XVIII's Second Restoration (1815–1824) of strength and legitimacy.

Under the steady hand of Louis's prime minister Armand Richelieu, France quickly paid off the allied indemnity, lifted the occupation, and set the stage for a decade of economic prosperity. Some historians see the period from 1815 to 1830 as an "Indian summer of the aristocracy." During this time, the aristocracy retained a powerful land base, about 20 percent of the land. In the 1820s, 60 percent of the richest 670 families and 90 percent of the 500 richest landowners in France were *ancien régime* aristocrats.[2] Their power was strongest in isolated areas, such as Brittany and Languedoc, away from the influence of towns and cities. Royalist strongholds often remained, as they had been during the revolution, areas of popular anarchy, that is, poaching and tax and conscription evasion.

The Second Restoration sparked a religious revival, especially among women. Through education and charitable works, Catholicism provided a space for women outside the private sphere, and so the number of nuns rose almost tenfold between 1815 and the 1870s (from 15,000 to over 130,000) and by this latter decade held a 3 to 2 numerical advantage over male clergy.[3]

The end of the Revolutionary and Napoleonic wars produced an intellectual and artistic ferment that would continue throughout the nineteenth century. Royalism developed into a political ideology in the writings of Joseph de Maistre, Louis de Bonald, and Félicité de Lamennais. Another aristocrat, the Duc de Saint-Simon, in prophesying a future in which engineers and scientists would direct society, provided the foundations for both technocratic and socialistic theories that appeared later in the century. In art and literature France developed its own version of Romanticism, after the movement's start in the German states and England. Painters such as Théodore Géricault and Eugène Delacroix, with masterpieces such as *The Raft of the Medusa* and *The Massacres of Scio*, respectively, explored extreme and exotic subjects. At the end of the regime, in the late 1820s, the young Victor Hugo transformed French drama with his *Cromwell* (1827) and *Hernani* (1830). As Hugo's politics shifted from royalism to liberalism so did that of many other Romantics. In music Hector Berlioz pioneered a flamboyant and idiosyncratic Romanticism in his *Symphonie Fantastique* just a few months before the revolution in the summer of 1830.

The period of relative stability ended with the death of Louis XVIII in September 1824 and the succession of his younger brother, Charles X.

Overestimating the power of the religious revival, Charles X tried to turn back the clock. Whereas poor health (and perhaps astuteness) had prevented his brother from seeking a coronation at Reims, Charles X felt no such qualms about insisting on the traditional ceremony. Charles even tried to revive the ancient royal tradition known as the "king's touch"— that the king, by putting his hands on someone with a skin disease such as scrofula, could cure him. Liberal opinion felt threatened, and popular singers satirized his attempts to revive divine-right monarchy.

Charles X's government made conciliatory attempts to compensate the approximately 70,000 émigrés and their descendants for lands lost through annual annuities, a proposal that provoked fears among middle-class and peasant landholders who had benefited from the revolutionary land transfers. Fears of political reaction were aggravated after 1827 by economic discontent, as poor harvests and cold winters again created grain and bread shortages. The economic downturn was exacerbated by a banking crisis which led to bankruptcies and rising unemployment. In January 1828 a draconian law on the press (imposition of a high stamp duty on printed material) led to the fall of the prime minister, Villèle. In August 1829 Charles replaced Viellèle with an arch reactionary and royal favorite, Prince Jules Polignac.

The depth of the country's displeasure with Charles in this choice was exposed when the chamber voted "no confidence" in the Polignac ministry. Charles X then gambled that he could use Article 14 of the 1814 Charter (which gave him exceptional power in emergencies) to cow the chamber and come closer to the absolute rule of his ancestors. He kept his ministers but dissolved the chamber and called for new elections. The new liberal newspapers (e.g., *Le National*, backed by Talleyrand) touted the English Revolution of 1688 as the answer to the French constitutional impasse. Despite pressure, the number of opposition deputies increased from 221 to 274. Undismayed, Charles invoked Article 14 of the Charter and issued four ordinances on July 25, 1830. By calling for the suppression of the freedom of the press, dissolving the chamber again, restricting the electorate to 25,000, and fixing a date for new elections, Charles clearly intended to concentrate as much power in the crown as possible.

When the Parisian people heard about the ordinances, demonstrations erupted. Soon barricades went up and a revolutionary crowd comprising artisans, unemployed workers, and students routed the undermanned government forces. Within three days (subsequently known as the Three Glorious Days, "*Les Trois Glorieuses*," July 27–29, 1830), the capital fell to the revolutionaries. Rather than put up with another revolution, the king abdicated in favor of his grandson Henry, known as the "miracle child" because he was born seven months after his father, the Duc de Berry, had been assassinated in February 1820. Charles X hoped that his cousin Louis-Philippe would head a regency, but these hopes were quickly dashed when Louis-Philippe accepted the crown for himself instead. His regime quickly became known as the July Monarchy. As a result a new division appeared in French society—that between "legitimists," who favored the elder Bourbon line of Henry, and the "Orléanists," who sided with the younger line. This distinction would remain a vital part of French politics for forty years.

The liberal opposition, including such old stalwarts as Lafayette and Talleyrand along with young journalists and students, feared that the Parisian crowd—again a factor in politics—might demand a republic, so they turned to Louis-Philippe to ensure order and unity. The Marquis Gilbert du Motier de Lafayette (the hero of the American Revolution and a force in the French Revolution of 1789) believed that Louis Philippe would create "a popular and free" constitutional monarchy, and France would become a *"royal* [italics in the original] republic."[4] Louis-Philippe personified a middle course between, as he said, the "excesses of popular power" and the "abuses of royal power." He had fought with the revolutionary armies and had become an émigré only during the Reign of Terror.

He took the title the "king of the French" rather than "king of France" in order to demonstrate that he was indeed a citizen king. The fact that his monarchy was named after the month he assumed power, July, rather than after his lineage also democratized the regime. In the words of historian Colin Jones, "Charles X had tried to heal the sick like a saint: Louis-Philippe carried an umbrella."[5] The tricolor again became the national flag and the "Marseillaise"—the great marching song of the French Revolution—became the national anthem but, true to his views of moderation, Louis-Philippe rejected July 14, the anniversary of the storming of the Bastille, as a national holiday.

Louis-Philippe's primary supporters came from the upper bourgeoisie. Lawyers, financiers, stockbrokers, and substantial farmers now surrounded the king, and the court adopted the drab, dark colors of the business suit. Although this regime tried to follow its king and keep a low profile, opposition smoldered on every side. Ultraroyalists and legitimists retired to their country estates to nurse their rancor; their continued political presence was indicated by a few small insurrections in the conservative west. Conservative Catholics openly opposed the growing secularization of education under Louis-Philippe's minister François Guizot, and a new movement of liberal Catholics, led by Félicité de Lamennais (who like Hugo became more liberal after 1830), tried to orient the church toward the sufferings of the poor rather than toward the defense of tradition. The Vatican proscribed Lamennais's movement in 1834, but they did authorize the Society of Saint Vincent de Paul, which was engaged in charity, in 1833 and allowed the work of such nuns as Sister Rosalie Rendu in the slums of the rapidly growing capital. At least half of Paris lived in poverty; 80 percent left their heirs less than 500 francs; 81 percent were buried at public expense; 52.5 percent paid a rent of less than 150 francs, the index of indigence.[6]

Emboldened by the continuing myth of the good emperor, Bonapartists remained active. Their cause suffered a blow when Napoleon's son died at the age of 20 in Austria. One of Napoleon's nephews, Louis Napoleon Bonaparte, however, stepped into the void to become the pretender. At first his uncertain paternity (some claimed he was not a Bonaparte at all) and his conspiratorial methods seemed ineffectual. Louis Napoleon's attempt to foment a military revolt at the border garrison of Strasbourg fizzled in 1836 and he was jailed for a short period. Another attempt in 1840 at another border city, Lille, led to lifetime imprisonment. This harsh sentence, however, was soon commuted and Louis Napoleon went into exile. While in prison at Ham, Louis Napoleon developed a program aimed at gaining widespread popular appeal through a plan to abolish poverty. The July Monarchy hoped to gain popularity by bringing Napoleon's remains back to Paris, in December 1840, for burial at the military hospital, the Invalides. But such a move merely fanned the flames of Bonapartism and added little luster to the citizen king.

The regime correctly saw its most pressing challenge, however, as coming from the reemergence of popular political pressure. Parisian workers who had toppled Charles X believed that they had reaped no benefits. Paris remained in an agitated state, and the archbishop's palace was sacked in 1831. Three years later, at the news of the revolt of the Lyon silk workers, Parisian workers erected barricades in the eastern slums. The biggest revolts, however, which took place in Lyon in 1831 and 1834, were suppressed by military force. Subsequently, the government severely restricted the freedom of the people to form associations and to publish newspapers. Repression prompted the establishment of secret societies, the most famous of which was the Parisian Society of the Seasons. Led by the lifelong revolutionary conspirator, Auguste Blanqui, this society's attempted insurrection in May 1839 was quickly suppressed. Although Blanqui went to jail, he would be heard from again.

What made popular rebellion so ominous was the rise of modern socialism. Here again France would be at the forefront of European developments. During the 1830s and 1840s, writers and journalists from both middle and working classes speculated on the new industrial society that was taking shape in France. The pace of industrialization increased markedly during the July Monarchy. After the downturn of the late 1820s and early 1830s, the index of industrial production shot up: this index in 1846 was 50 percent higher than in 1831.[7] The invention of the railroad provided much of this stimulation by increasing the demand for coal and iron. Louis-Philippe's government provided a whole range of supports for French business. High tariffs, for instance, protected French business, especially the textile industry, from foreign competition. The Railway Law of 1842 provided for low taxes for railroads and a guaranteed return in land purchased. Bankruptcy laws were more lenient and, although associations of workers were further restricted, the ability of businessmen to form companies was made easier. The government also encouraged trade through an ambitious program of road and canal construction.

Although Louis-Philippe earned the confidence of the business class, he inspired little loyalty among the population in general. His drab personal appearance, so reassuring after the pretensions of Charles X, soon grated on people. One of Honoré Daumier's (one of the greatest nineteenth-century caricaturists) most effective caricatures emphasized the king's pear-shaped head. After two assassination attempts (1835 and 1840) and a secret-society plot (1839), the unpopular Louis-Philippe tried to ensure his survival through patronage. This, however, resulted in corruption, especially in parliament and in the election system. As long as the economy expanded, however, the July Monarchy remained secure.

By 1845 clouds appeared on the horizon. The economic crisis of 1845–1850 affirmed that the French economy, despite fifteen years of expansion and the arrival of railroads, remained primarily agricultural. As in the past, the problems of a poor harvest spread to the cities and devastated the lives of the lower classes. In Caen, a city northwest of Paris near the English Channel, the price of a hectoliter of wheat rose from 22 francs in May 1846 to 46 francs in May 1847.[8] In Paris, during the latter year, almost 400,000 out of the capital's total population of 945,000 subsisted on government-subsidized bread. In the southwest provincial cities of Toulouse and Bordeaux, the numbers of people needing subsidized bread stood in the following relation to the total population: 20,000 out of 94,000 (Toulouse) and 21,700 out of 126,000 (Bordeaux).[9]

During this same period, Republicans continued their agitation for an expansion of the electorate. To evade the restrictions on associations, they campaigned at banquets throughout France, planning to finish with a great banquet held in Paris on February 22, 1848. The king's prime minister prohibited this final banquet, however, and the people of Paris, again playing a decisive role in their own affairs, first protested then built barricades. After some initial fighting, neither the National Guard nor the king wished to continue a struggle that had already taken dozens of lives. On February 24, 1848, Louis-Philippe abdicated, hoping that the Chamber of Deputies would create a regency for his young grandson. Instead, revolutionaries, backed by the people of Paris, proclaimed a Second Republic, instituted universal manhood suffrage, and abolished slavery.

Once again we see a king toppled from office by the populace. The swift and seemingly effortless political transformation induced a festive and fraternal atmosphere throughout Paris and the provinces. The French, as in 1789, planted liberty trees, created clubs, and opened newspapers. After he was released from prison, Auguste Blanqui quickly became an influential force in the Paris clubs. Soon 200 clubs and as many newspapers appeared in Paris and inspired similar developments in the provinces. Conspicuous in their reappearance were women's clubs and journals—the first burst of popular feminist activity since the 1790s.

Although the provisional French republican government, of this nascent Second Republic, had promised not to export revolution, the rest of Europe, 50 years after 1789, was ripe for change. Across central Europe a "springtime of peoples" seemed to dawn as the events in Paris were repeated in other capitals.

The idealism of the moment was perhaps best expressed by the new head of the provisional government, the romantic poet Alphonse de Lamartine, who proclaimed universal manhood suffrage and urged setting up elections for a Constituent Assembly. In addition, the government announced the total liberty of the press, freedom of assembly and association, the abolition of slavery in the French colonies, and the abolition of the death penalty in political cases. One of the most innovative rights declared was the right to work. The new socialist ideas found a strong voice in the new government with the theorist of socialism Louis Blanc.

The optimism of the first month promptly smashed upon the hard rock of economic dislocation. The revolution had not alleviated but rather exacerbated the economic situation. Banks closed, government securities fell, and the stock market closed. The unemployment rate climbed to 60 percent in Paris, as businesses failed and the unemployed from the provinces streamed in hoping for help from the new government.[10] To prevent bankruptcy, the Provisional Government increased direct land taxes by 45 percent.[11]

To stem the economic distress, the government reduced the working day by one hour and set up national workshops for the unemployed as part of a guaranteed right to work. The Luxembourg commission was set up and directed to explore other possible social reforms.

To oversee the April 1848 election, the Provisional Government put Alexandre-Auguste Ledru-Rollin, a "radical liberal" and veteran parliamentarian, in charge as minister of the interior. He sent commissioners for the republic to the provinces to spread the republican message for the upcoming elections. Continuing economic troubles and grumbling over the new taxes quickly made it apparent that the republicans might do poorly in the upcoming elections. Faced with the demands made by Blanqui's delegation, on March 17 the government accepted a postponement but only one of a derisory duration: rather than holding them on April 9 they were moved back to April 23.

The elections brought an amazing 84 percent of the electorate to the ballot box.[12] The fact that the elections were held on Easter Sunday, a day when High Mass had gathered together the entire village, may have contributed to the impressive turnout. The results saw radical republicans and socialists win only 100 out of 900 seats. Although Thiers lost for the right, the most prominent casualties were such radicals as François Raspail, Auguste Blanqui, and Etienne Cabet for the left. One of the most significant new members, Louis Napoleon Bonaparte, had recently returned from exile (after his imprisonment). A major reason for the peasants' vote against the republicans was their anger over the new tax and their objection to the special provisions for urban workers.

After the seating of the new Constituent Assembly, tension steadily increased between the deputies and the radicals in the city, especially in the clubs. On May 15, 1848, the radicals staged a demonstration that started as support for the Polish people in their attempt to win national self-determination from the Russians, Austrians, and Prussians and escalated to an invasion of the virtually unguarded Constituent Assembly, with loud demands for a true democratic and social republic. Although momentarily intimidated, the Assembly soon began to dismantle the Parisian radicalism, first by stopping additional unemployed people from joining the workshops and then, on June 21, dissolving the workshops altogether.

The Assembly's action sparked spontaneous revolt in the eastern part of Paris. In four days of brutal fighting the republican general Eugène Cavaignac systematically destroyed the barricades, killed between 1,500 and 3,000 insurgents, and arrested 15,000 suspects. Subsequently, 4,500 of these detainees were either imprisoned or deported to Algeria.[13] By the end of June, the hard-bitten realist General Cavaignac had replaced Lamartine as the leader of the government, and he passed laws restricting the freedom of the press and of assembly. He also closed political clubs, disbanded the Luxembourg commission, and tried to prevent women from engaging in politics. New prefects were sent out to the countryside to dismantle the republican networks that had emerged in imitation of those in Paris. The April elections and the June repressions revealed that the provinces no longer followed the lead of Paris. Henceforth, the largely conservative provinces would impose their will on the radical capital.

In this climate of repression, the Assembly did not postpone or suppress the coming election for president. Instead, Cavaignac ran, in an attempt to consolidate his rule. As the campaign picked up, however, Louis Napoleon Bonaparte became the obvious front-runner. Ledru Rollin was the primary candidate of the democratic socialists, and Lamartine ran as a moderate. The election results on December 10 revealed the depth to which the Napoleonic legend had penetrated the electorate. The nephew of Napoleon easily outdistanced Cavignac: 5,400,000 votes to 1,400,000. Following them in the vote were Ledru-Rollin who received fewer than 400,000 votes; Raspail, 37,000, and Lamartine, 8,000.[14] Louis Napoleon had not only had the charismatic Napoleonic name but also the good luck of improved economic times. After 1849 brought an abundant harvest, business confidence returned; and the discovery of gold in California gave the international economy a new stimulus for expansion.

The democratic social movement, although defeated in Paris, was far from dead. Rather, it showed a remarkable vitality in the supposedly conservative countryside, especially the south and center. Taking the name of Montagnards, after the radicals of the 1789 Revolution, these radical republicans found issues that drew the peasants: a progressive income tax, abolition of taxes on drink, free and mandatory primary education, and credit banks for peasants. The Montagnards spread their message to a still largely illiterate population through graphic and oral communication networks of markets, fairs, cafés with iconographic images (especially using the color red), lithographs, songs, and stories. In the legislative elections of May 13, 1849, this rural socialism made great headway, winning one-third of the seats in the National Assembly. Bolstered by these results, Ledru-Rollin attempted an ill-fated insurrection in June 1849. Despite this setback and mounting repression, the left won still more seats in the by-elections of 1850.

To stamp out the growing leftist threat, Louis Napoleon joined with the conservative "party of order" in a widespread and systematic campaign to crush political dissent. The singing of the "Marseillaise"—the marching song of the 1789 Revolution and the national anthem under the July Monarchy—became illegal, and the color red—whether in caps and belts or the color of cafés—was outlawed. Liberty trees were chopped down. More restrictions were placed on the rights of assembly and association; suspect national guard units were shut down; mayors and schoolteachers were dismissed or fired; and radical republican leaders were jailed or intimidated. Having already restored the pope to his domains around Rome, Louis Napoleon then promoted the Falloux Laws which allowed the Catholic clergy to open secondary schools and serve in the educational administration. The law of May 31, 1850 reduced the electoral body by almost one-third, from 9,600,000 to 6,800,000, disenfranchising a large number of itinerant urban workers.[15] Still not satisfied in the fall of 1851, Louis Napoleon declared martial law in many departments.

Many French people had come to suspect, however, that what worried Louis Napoleon most was not the radical red threat but the fact that the National Assembly had not rescinded the law permitting only one term for the president. Because the Legislative Assembly of July 1851 had failed to amend the constitution, Napoleon ensured his stay in office by staging a coup d'état on December 2, 1851. Although only a few barricades appeared in Paris, the Montagnard-led southern and central departments had maintained and now called on a network of secret societies. These societies, set up when overt forms of political participation had been banned, organized the largest insurrection in nineteenth-century France and the largest peasant rebellion in nineteenth-century

Europe. Comprising almost 100,000 insurgents from 30 departments, this widespread revolt met with swift and brutal repression: mixed commissions (composed of a prefect, public prosecutor, and a general) examined over 26,000 suspects and deported about 10,000.[16] The scale of this repression has led some historians to call Louis Napoleon's government a police state.[17] Although workers and peasants were generally quiescent during the first decade following the coup, Napoleon still faced three assassination attempts.

The December 2 coup reinstituted universal suffrage, and when Louis Napoleon staged a plebiscite on December 14 his measures were approved by a margin of 10 to 1. One year from the day of his coup, following the promulgation of a new constitution and plebiscite, Louis took the title of Napoleon III (in deference to Napoleon I's son who had died at the age of 20 in Austria). Amidst a surging stock market and a thriving economic climate, the Second Empire started its twenty-year run.

Napoleon III, a man of many facets, has been classified variously as a sphinx, a buffoon, and a modern dictator. Over the course of his reign we see him promote political repression and economic expansion in the 1850s, then become more liberal in politics and attentive to working-class demands in the 1860s. A December 29, 1851, decree led to the closing of 40,000 cafés, deemed dens of sedition, across France. In February 1852 all newspapers needed government permission to publish, and press censorship was the harshest it had been since the first Napoleon. In March 1852, the 1834 law on associations was extended to ordinary meetings; on December 30 theater censorship was reinstated; the powers of correctional tribunals were increased to cover all these cases. Louis Napoleon ruled without a cabinet, only a set of imperial agents, and he alone could initiate laws. His legislative body during his first decade of rule was virtually impotent. For eleven years (1852 to 1863) a small elite governed as ministers.

The resourceful Louis Napoleon achieved an innovative, if uneasy, synthesis of republicanism and royalism. For example, his reign combined both universal manhood suffrage and an authoritarian administration. Unlike virtually any other dictator, he liberalized his regime. Napoleon III's adaptability allowed him to remain in power longer than any leader since 1789. Only military disaster would topple him.

The Second Empire went beyond the July Monarchy's liberal laissez-faire notions of promoting economic expansion and tried instead to direct the economic growth and structural development of the economy.

In this quest, helped greatly by a worldwide economic expansion, Napoleon III achieved great success. Over the course of his reign, the value of industrial production doubled. Equally important as this quantitative increase was a major qualitative shift: the use of machine power in industry quintupled. The length of railway track also increased fivefold from 3,248 kilometers in 1851 to 16,465 in 1869. Trains carried one-half of the internal trade in 1870; in 1850, they had carried only one-tenth.[18] The rail boom stimulated the expansion of the coal and metallurgical industries as well as specialization in regional agriculture. Easy rail transit encouraged farmers to abandon self-sufficiency and produce for an emerging national market. The wine growers of lower Languedoc, for example, now took over the Parisian market; local and less productive vineyards declined. Table wine was for the first time within the reach of the ordinary working-class drinker.

This impressive economic performance was made possible by the modernization of the French banking system in which transformation Louis Napoleon played a vital role. While investment banks funneled money into railroad construction and urban renovation, savings banks tapped the wealth of ordinary individuals. Increasingly ordinary French people felt secure in shifting their savings from under the mattress to the local bank. The emergence of the small saver also heralded the issuing of banknotes in small denominations. Overall, the circulation of paper currency increased fivefold.[19]

Napoleon III also promoted major urban renewal projects in Paris and other major cities. Under Baron Georges Haussmann, prefect of the Seine, the capital expanded in size, annexed its immediate suburbs, and increased in population from 1,227,000 in 1846 to 1,970,000 in 1870.[20] Haussmann drew on resources of the investment bank Credit Foncier to create broad boulevards, luxurious apartments, spacious department stores, ornate theaters, and an opera house, and pretentious government offices. He also added modern sanitation, transportation, and water systems. On his wide boulevards appeared a new type of commerce—modern department stores such as the Galeries Lafayette. Their vast galaxy of goods was advertised in innovative ways, with posters in Paris and catalogs circulating in the provinces. Similar modernization, although on a smaller scale, occurred in such provincial towns as Cherbourg, Le Havre, Rouen, Blois, and Besançon; Lyon flourished under Prefect Claude Vaisse, who rivaled Haussmann. Many of these provincial cities also experienced a comparable population growth: from 1851 to 1866, Saint Étienne grew from 50,000 to 96,000; Lyon, from 177,000 to 301,000; and

Marseilles, from 195,000 to 300,000. Even nonindustrial towns grew during these years: Bordeaux from 131,000 to 194,000 and Toulouse from 93,000 to more than 130,000.[21] Until after World War I, Haussmann's renewal of Paris set the world standard for urban renovation.

The transformation of Paris, however, only redistributed the problems of urban growth; it did not resolve them. As rents skyrocketed in the redeveloped areas, the poor had to move to the outlying periphery, where few of the amenities of central Paris were available. As a result, poverty was merely displaced rather than eradicated. The persistence of urban poverty revealed the fallacy of Napoleon III's hope that economic development could eradicate poverty, the subject of one of his youthful pamphlets, and secure the loyalty of the lower classes.

Moreover, during the 1860s, the French economy suffered a series of setbacks that exacerbated class conflict. Crises hit the cotton trade because of the American Civil War, and the silk and wine industries suffered from plant diseases. The new banking system underwent a crisis in 1867 with the downfall of the Pereire brothers of the investment bank Credit Mobilier at the hands of the more conservative banking houses, such as the Rothschilds. By the end of Haussmann's tenure as prefect of Paris in 1869, the debts of the city had reached 2,500 million francs, and France experienced a wave of strikes not only in Paris but also in the provinces.[22]

From 1858 on, however, the emperor tried to address these problems in his reign by creating a "liberal empire." As in all else he did, his motives were mixed and complex and his actions lacked overall coherence. His quest for liberty, which took many forms, alienated some of his previous allies and gained him some additional enemies. For example, in 1859, he lost popularity among Catholics and businessmen and gained support among liberals when he sent diplomatic and military aid for Italian independence and, to win British acquiescence on this matter, signed a free-trade treaty with England. To increase liberal and working-class support in later years, he gradually gave more power to the legislature to debate and propose laws. In 1864 he permitted strikes; in 1866 he tolerated trade unions; and in succeeding years he loosened restraints on the freedom of press, assembly, and meetings. During the legislative elections of 1857, 1863, and 1869, the Republican opposition steadily increased in its number of votes, from 665,000 in 1857 to 3.3 million in 1869.[23] But the opposition was far from united, and Napoleon was able to win over one of the most prominent Republicans, Émile Ollivier, to form a government in January 1870. Ollivier persuaded Napoleon III to adopt constitutional changes that would give the legislative body more power and return the country to a situation similar to that under the 1814 Charter, with the addition of universal male suffrage. Despite growing political protests and an increasing number of strikes, a plebiscite held in May 1870 overwhelmingly approved these changes: 7,350,000 to 1,538,000.[24]

Despite the Second Empire's repressive and gaudy atmosphere, it saw significant artistic and literary achievement. In general the Romantic styles of the first half of the century evolved into realism, symbolism, and Impressionism. A concern to detail the nature of daily life, among the middle or lower classes, united novelists such Gustave Flaubert and Émile Zola and the dramatist Alexandre Dumas the younger. The poetry of Charles Baudelaire made the sights, sounds, and smells of the modern city the subject of a new modernist poetry. At the end of the empire, Arthur Rimbaud and Paul Verlaine elaborated on Baudelaire's approach, helping to produce the subsequent symbolist style of poetry. Realism also found champions among painters, particularly Gustave Courbet and Jean-François Millet, who depicted the travails of peasants and workers. Again, as in literature, the later years of the empire brought further innovation. Edouard Manet, often considered the first modern painter, and Camille Pissarro opened up painting in both style and subject matter for a younger generation of painters, including Claude Monet, Auguste Renoir, and Alfred Sisley, later grouped in the school of the Impressionists. These radical innovations brought prosecution for pornography against Flaubert and Baudelaire and exclusion from the salon of the French Academy of Painting for Manet, Pissarro, and the Impressionists. Louis Napoleon rectified this slight by letting the artists display their work at the famous Salon of the Refused (*Salon des Refusés*).

The empire's internal economic, political, and cultural vigor was never equaled by its diplomatic and military endeavors. Although France under Napoleon III asserted itself around the world in a fashion not seen since the old regime, his moves often ended in failure. His participation, with England, in the Crimean War during the mid-1850s halted Russian expansion to the Mediterranean but gained France nothing else. Napoleon's support of Italian unification, during the 1850s and 1860s, resulted in a grateful Italy ceding the provinces of Nice and Savoy to France (the only territorial acquisitions of the nineteenth century) but alienated French Catholic opinion as a result of the pope's loss of control over the papal states. Napoleon III suffered a worse setback when he intervened in Mexico during the American Civil War. He went into Mexico, in 1862, along with Great Britain and Spain, because Mexico had not paid its foreign debt. French forces stayed after their allies left and made Austrian archduke Maximilian emperor of Mexico in 1864. (Napoleon hoped that such a move would strengthen Franco-Austrian relations.) After the American Civil War ended, the United States reasserted the Monroe Doctrine and forced the French to leave in February 1867. Without French support, Maximilian quickly fell and was executed by a new Mexican government.

Napoleon III had more success expanding France's colonial empire and foreign investment. In northern Africa control over Algeria was consolidated; in west Africa the port of Dakar in Senegal was founded; and in east Africa a naval and administrative base was established in Djibouti. To the Near East Napoleon dispatched an expeditionary force to protect the Maronite Christians in present-day Lebanon and reasserted the traditional French prerogative, since the Crusades, to protect Christians and Christian churches in the Holy Land. In Southeast Asia, the French detached present-day Vietnam, Cambodia, and Laos from China and created the nucleus for the future colony of Cochin China. In the South Pacific, finally, the island of New Caledonia became part of the new French colonial empire. During the Second Empire, too, the new credit banks invested French capital in the construction of railroads, bridges, and canals around the world. The Suez Canal, built under the direction of French engineer Ferdinand de Lesseps, is the most famous of these investments.

Napoleon, however, was unable to modernize the army or integrate its strategy because of France's inadequate railway system. Consequently, military disaster occurred in the summer of 1870. Prussian Chancellor Otto von Bismarck, having maneuvered Napoleon into neutrality during Prussia's war with Austria in 1866, provoked military action in July 1870. To maintain France's honor in the face of an apparent Prussian snub over succession to the Spanish throne, Napoleon III declared war. Unhappily, the faster and more efficient Prussian army, with railroad lines all the way to the front in eastern France, moved quickly against Napoleon's forces. Lacking rail lines to the German border, the French army found itself encircled. By September 2, 1870, Napoleon III and some 84,000 of his troops surrendered following the battle at Sedan.[25] With the French army in disarray, Republicans in Paris proclaimed the end of the empire and the creation of a Third Republic.

NOTES

1. René Rémond, *The Right Wing in France: From 1815 to de Gaulle*, 2nd American ed., trans. James M. Laux (Philadelphia: University of Pennsylvania Press, 1969), p. 57.

2. Colin Jones, *The Cambridge Illustrated History of France* (Cambridge: Cambridge University Press, 1994), p. 201.

3. Robert Tombs, *France, 1814–1914* (London: Longman, 1996), pp. 167 and 243.

4. Lloyd Kramer, *Lafayette in Two Worlds: Public Cultures & Personal Identities in an Age of Revolution* (Chapel Hill: University of North Carolina Press, 1996), p. 241.

5. Jones, *Cambridge Illustrated History of France*, p. 203.

6. André Jardin and André-Jean Tudesq, *Restoration & Reaction, 1815–1848*, trans. Elborg Forster (Cambridge and Paris: Cambridge University Press and Editions de la Maison des Sciences de l'Homme, 1983), p. 379.

7. G. de Bertier de Sauvigny and David H. Pinkney, *History of France* Revised and Enlarged Edition, French text trans. Jams Friguglietti (Arlington Heights, IL: Forum Press, 1983), p. 271.

8. Jardin and Tudesq, *Restoration & Reaction, 1815–1848*, p. 192.

9. Roger Price, *A Social History of Nineteenth-Century France* (New York: Holmes & Meier, 1987), p. 51 and William B. Cohen, *Urban Government and the Rise of the French City: Five Municipalities in the Nineteenth Century* (New York: St. Martin's Press, 1998), p. 19.

10. Roger Magraw, *France 1815–1914: The Bourgeois Century* (Oxford: Fontana, 1983), p. 125, and Gordon Wright, *France in Modern Times*, 5th ed. (New York: W. W. Norton, 1995), p. 186.

11. Price, *A Social History of Nineteenth-Century France*, p. 186.

12. Roger Price, *A Concise History of France* (Cambridge: Cambridge University Press, 1997), p. 172.

13. Peter McPhee, *A Social History of France, 1780–1880* (London: Routledge, 1992), p. 179.

14. Maurice Agulhon, *The Republican Experiment, 1848–1852*, trans. Janet Lloyd (Cambridge and Paris: Cambridge University Press and Editions de la Maison des Sciences de l'Homme, 1983), p. 72.

15. Ibid., p. 126.

16. Ted W. Margadant, *French Peasants in Revolt: The Insurrection of 1851* (Princeton: Princeton University Press, 1979), pp. 8–12 and 302.

17. Howard C. Payne, *The Police State of Louis Napoleon Bonaparte, 1851–1860* (Seattle: University of Washington Press, 1966), passim.

18. Jones, *The Cambridge Illustrated History of France*, pp. 212–213.

19. Ibid., p. 213.

20. David H. Pinkney, *Napoleon II and the Rebuilding of Paris* (Princeton, NJ: Princeton University Press, 1958), p. 152.

21. William B. Cohen, *Urban Government and the Rise of the French City*, p. 19.

22. Alain Plessis, *The Rise & Fall of the Second Empire, 1852–1870*, trans. Jonathan Mandelbaum (Cambridge and Paris: Cambridge University Press and Editions de la Maison des Sciences de l'Homme, 1987), p. 121.

23. Plessis, *The Rise & Fall of the Second Empire, 1852–1870*, p. 158.

24. Ibid., p. 166.

25. James F. McMillan, *Napoleon III* (London: Longman, 1991), pp. 163–164.

8

The Consolidation of the Third Republic in Peace and War (1870–1918)

Emerging from military defeat, class conflict, economic deterioration, and demographic decline, the Third Republic appeared the least likely postrevolutionary regime to succeed. Indeed, events in May 1870 and May 1871 resulted in that time in French history being known as "the terrible year." Yet, the years between the proclamation of the Republic in September 1870 and its consolidation with the election of Jules Grévey as president in January 1879 marked a truly decisive decade. In this nearly ten-year period, the French finally chose the republican form of government and achieved the moderate consensus that had eluded all governments since the French Revolution of 1789. Royalism and Bonapartism had made their last serious bids for power during the 1870s and 1880s. Once securely in power, the Republicans turned to building a republic through a variety of measures that had profound economic, educational, military, recreational, and religious ramifications.

The Republic may have been proclaimed in the spring of 1870 but its supporters disagreed as to its nature. Three distinct strains of republicanism surfaced following defeat at Sedan in May 1870. First, a moderate strain focusing on national defense emerged when the young legislator Léon Gambetta tried to rally the nation to expel the Prussian army, which surrounded Paris. Gambetta escaped from the besieged city by balloon and set up a command post at Tours. Over the following months he raised 600,000 soldiers and organized them into three armies to try and lift the siege of Paris. Fervid mass patriotism this time, however, did not work its wonders against the Prussians, who were equally fired by a nationalist objective, the unification of Germany.

By January 1871, much of France had concluded that continued war would be fruitless. At this moment the second strain surfaced: conservative Republicans such as the elder statesman Louis Adolphe Thiers. Conservatives wished to make peace immediately with Prussia to prevent the war from becoming a class conflict. They were especially worried that the armed national guard in Paris might try to mount another revolution. On January 28, 1871, the government signed an armistice with Prussia and set up elections for a National Assembly which would be authorized to sign a peace treaty. The February 8, 1871, elections revealed the continued power, lacking any Republican leadership from Paris, of local large landowners who were primarily conservative (if not royalist) and who had no desire to continue what seemed to them a hopeless war. Thus Gambetta and other Republicans had little influence and obtained only 200 seats in the new 630-seat Assembly. In contrast, the various factions of royalism gained more than 400 seats. Because they did not wish for a king to be saddled with a humiliating peace treaty, the Assembly voted Adolphe Thiers as "chief of the executive power of the French Republic . . . until the institutions of France have been established." The Assembly then accepted the humiliating peace treaty with the Prussians: France ceded virtually all of Alsace and Lorraine, agreed to pay a war indemnity of five billion francs, and accepted German military occupation until the sum was paid.

The peace treaty sparked the third strain, radical Republicanism, in Paris. The besieged people of Paris, having now suffered five months of encirclement, bombardment, and malnourishment, became enraged upon learning what they believed was the government's capitulation. This rage turned white hot when the Assembly discontinued paying the salary of National Guardsmen and ended the moratorium on payment of rents and debts. The spark that ignited the Paris Commune was Thiers's order to seize 200 cannons that the Parisian National Guard had amassed on Montmartre. Fearing a government attempt to disarm them, local National Guardsmen and citizens disarmed Thiers's contingent and in the process killed the general sent to oversee the operation. Fearing a repeat of the June Days of 1848 and wishing to crush the Paris revolutionary milieu once and for all, Thiers ordered the government out of Paris.

Into this vacuum stepped the recently formed Central Committee of the National Guard. The Central Committee called for municipal elections for a commune, established a municipal government, and invited the other cities of France to do the same. Similar stirrings occurred in Lyon, Toulouse, Narbonne, and especially Marseilles, but only in Paris did a real countervailing power to the national government emerge. The Parisian elections put a diverse set of revolutionaries and radicals into power: self-called "Jacobins," who wished to follow the model of the Committee of Public Safety; Blanquists, followers of the great professional revolutionary (who, after being freed briefly, was now back in jail); federalists wishing to decentralize France; and various shades of social revolutionaries, notably members of Karl Marx's Socialist International. Having so recently developed, these groups had not yet formulated any specific ideology. Indeed, they would not be given time. The Commune lasted a mere six weeks, from its proclamation on March 28 to its suppression amidst the fire and fighting of the "bloody week" of May 21–28. Within the short span of seven days, the Army of Versailles killed 10,000 people they believed were Communards, and they took an additional 40,000 prisoners.[1]

While relatively insignificant as a political event, the Commune quickly became a potent political myth. Karl Marx, author of the Communist Manifesto and founder of the First Workers' International, was at first reticent about the Commune's chances for success, but he quickly embraced it when he saw that the middle-class world blamed him and his International for the attempted revolution. He proclaimed the Commune the first proletarian revolution because it tried to smash the bourgeois state and create a workers' government.

Ironically, the man who had just crushed the Commune, Adolphe Thiers, then proved instrumental in establishing the Republic. Perhaps because he had proven to be such a relentless foe of radical republicanism, the conservatives felt they could trust him. Indeed, Thiers was vested with joint powers of both president and premier. Not only did Thiers restore order to the government, he also engineered the first of the loan drives that paid off the indemnity 18 months ahead of schedule. He further endeared himself to conservatives by scuttling attempts to impose an income tax and by moving away from Napoleon III's free trade policies.

Perhaps most important for the monarchists, Thiers promised not to stand in the way of a restoration of the Bourbon monarchy. The way thus seemed clear for the return of the Bourbon pretender, the Comte de Chambord, the now aging and childless "miracle baby" of the Duchess de Berry. Amidst the burning embers of Paris, Chambord returned to France in July 1871 with little sense of what century he lived in. He had spent most of his life in an Austrian castle surrounded by admirers and had imbibed a mystically religious rather than a politically realistic view of the throne. A manifesto announced that he would accept the throne only on his own terms: these stressed a government in the mold of Charles X, resting on decentralization and the restoration of provincial liberties. He insisted that France accept the flag and symbols of the Bourbons: "I will not let the standard of Henry IV, of Francis I, of Jeanne d'Arc be torn from my hands."[2] Although he also promised parliamentary government and universal male suffrage, his fixation on the royal flag finished his chances for all but the most diehard monarchists.

Moderate monarchists, however, still hoped that in the following years some compromise would eventually be worked out and that the aging comte would sit on the throne briefly and then, upon his death, give it to the Orléans branch of the family. The Orléanists looked to the young and vigorous Orléanist count of Paris as a viable modern monarch. He had toured the world, had investigated trade unionism in England, and had fought in and written about the American Civil War. Their hopes were realized when in August 1873 the count of Paris made a pilgrimage to Chambord's residence in Austria and secured this assurance. Notwithstanding, Chambord remained adamant on the issue of the tricolor.

While still president, Thiers had come to a fateful decision. By the end of 1872, with a decision that changed the history of France, this former minister of monarchs, this conservative who had determinedly crushed the Commune, publicly endorsed a conservative republic as the government that "would divide Frenchmen the least." Monarchists quickly took their first opportunity to remove Thiers and forced him to resign in May 1873. They replaced him with Marshal Edmé Patrice Maurice Mac-Mahon the Bonapartist general with monarchist sympathies who had led the army against the Commune. But they divested the president's office of much of the power that Theirs had wielded and gave it to the prime minister, the Orléanist duc de Broglie. From this point forward, the Third Republic of France had a weak president and a strong parliament. Wishing to prolong the possibility of restoration and postpone the inauguration of a republic, de Broglie and the Orléanists set up a seven-year presidency, the *septerninat*, in November 1873, with Mac-Mahon as president.

Although not particularly astute politically, even Mac-Mahon realized, when Chambord made a secret visit to France in 1874, that a restoration epitomized by the fleur-de-lis instead of the tricolor was untenable. Unable to consolidate their rule through a king, the Monarchists turned to the Catholic Church to cement their government of "moral order." Toward this end Republican mayors were dismissed, newspapers censored, cafés closed, and the celebration of Bastille Day prohibited.

Such repressive measures, however, could not stem a groundswell of support not only for Republicans but also for Bonapartists in the by-elections held between 1871 and 1873. In fear of a possible return of either the empire or a republic, many moderate Orléanists and Republicans were drawn to the idea of creating a republic to preempt more radical measures should they lose power. The Wallon Amendment, which set the process in motion in January 1875, passed by merely one vote. But the Constitutional laws of 1875, which eventually emerged from the moderates' fears and compromises, proved to be much more durable than anyone had anticipated.

The Constitution of the Third Republic worked because it cleverly satisfied, and inadvertently reconciled, the Republican and Conservative tendencies of the majority of French people. On the one hand, Republicans had a strong parliament—the Chamber of Deputies—elected by universal manhood suffrage and a weak executive, thus forestalling some powerful new Napoleon or royalist from taking power. On the other hand, the constitution calmed Conservatives with the institution of an upper house, a 300-member Senate. The National Assembly appointed the first 75 senators for life, then decreed that the rest had to be at least 40 years of age and were to be chosen by departmental electoral colleges composed of local notables. This system, embodying both popular and conservative impulses, would be a major reason why the Third Republic, although often called a stalemate society, was yet able to survive for 70 years. In short, this complex and ambiguous constitution provided the flexibility that the fractious French polity needed to end the cycle of revolutions that had spanned the period from 1789 to 1871.

Before the Republic fully emerged, however, it faced one final period of turbulence. After completing its constitutional work in December 1875, the National Assembly retired and awaited the results of the elections of January–March 1876. Led by Gambetta, the Republicans scored an impressive victory, winning 340 out of 553 seats in the Chamber and making significant inroads in the Senate (which nevertheless remained royalist). The division between the houses permitted Mac-Mahon to bypass members of the Republican majority in his choice of prime minister. He carefully selected conservative Republicans who had served under Thiers, first Armand Dufaure, then Jules Simon. This compromise government quickly foundered over the conflict between clericalism and anticlericalism. On May 16, 1877 Mac-Mahon dismissed Simon and recalled de Broglie, who formed a government dominated by Orléanists and Bonapartists. With the support of the Senate, Mac-Mahon subsequently dissolved the Chamber and called for new elections. He exerted maximum pressure on his prefects and the priests to produce a victory for the moral order and, in turn, the Republicans rallied to Gambetta's slogan, "Clericalism, that is the enemy."[3]

The elections of October 1877 firmly established the Republicans in power. Despite immense pressure, the Conservatives were able to gain only 40 new seats, leaving Republicans still in the majority. The following year, in the municipal elections, the Republicans' victory was so great it became known as the "town-hall revolution." This victory ensured that Republicans could now dominate the electoral colleges that chose the Senate. In the Senate elections of January 1879, the Republicans achieved a majority in this Conservative bastion as well. Having lost all significant sources of power, Mac-Mahon resigned at the end of January, and the National Assembly, consisting of the Chamber of Deputies and the Senate, subsequently elected as president a mellowed 1848 Republican, Jules Grévy. The May 16 Crisis, as it came to be known, decisively confirmed parliamentary democracy. No subsequent Third Republic president tried either to dissolve the Chamber of Deputies or to appoint the prime minister who lacked the support of the majority of the Chamber. Whichever party achieved a parliamentary majority would henceforth rule under the Third Republic.

The triumph over legitimists, Orléanists, and Bonapartists, however, did not result either in the solidification of a Republican party or in parliamentary stability. If anything, this victory over foes to the right permitted the various fault lines among Republicans to become accentuated. A fundamental chasm opened up between "opportunist" and "radical" Republicans. "Opportunists," on the one hand, tended to be more upper class and conservative and stressed enlarging the sphere of freedom and opportunity in French society. Reform should come at "opportune" moments, hence their name. "Radicals," on the other hand, felt that the 1875 Constitution was not fully Republican; they pressed for substantial amendments such as the abolition of the Senate, separation of church and state, an income tax, nationalization of the railway companies, and elections to the Chamber of Deputies by departmental lists rather than by individual member districts.

Parliamentary rule under the Third Republic was a complicated blend of stability and flux. Although France had 50 governments between 1879 and 1918—with the longest one lasting three years—these governments tended to be simple rearrangements of the same parliamentarians. A minister might be prime minister under one government, for instance, and minister of education under the next. Indeed, during the 1880s, the same seven deputies were in almost every government, and over the course of the entire Third Republic (1870–1940) virtually two-thirds of the deputies sat in parliament for an average of fourteen years.

Until the 1890s, Opportunist Republicans dominated these various governments. Following the consolidation of the Republic in 1879, they passed a rapid succession of laws ensuring freedom of assembly, freedom of the press, and freedom to form unions. They also granted municipal councils the right to elect their own mayors, except in Paris, which they still deemed was too dangerous. They also established Bastille Day, July 14, as a national holiday and the "Marseillaise" as the national anthem. The town halls of France were equipped with busts of Marianne (an allegorical female figure that had come to stand for the Republic in the minds of much of the population) often modeled after the statue unveiled in the Place de la Republique in Paris in 1883.

The Opportunists focused especially on education and achieved some of their most important and lasting results in this area. Higher education was taken out of the hands of the Church and placed back under the care of the state. Between 1881 and 1886, under the leadership of Minister of Education Jules Ferry, a series of laws was passed to establish a universal, secular system of primary education for children between 6 and 13 years of age. These Ferry laws intended to ensure the Republic's survival by creating a nation of literate and secular citizens. In 1865 approximately a quarter of the people residing in France could not speak French and in 1870 30 percent of men entering the army were illiterate; by 1906 only 5 percent of military conscripts were illiterate and 97.1 percent of men and 94.8 percent of women could sign their marriage contracts.[4]

Opportunist governments also enacted some of the legislative agenda of the radicals. Life tenure in the Senate was revoked in 1884, the vote by list in departments (*scrutin de liste*) was reinstituted in 1885, and labor

exchanges (*bourses du travail*) were set up in cities in 1887 for the organization, education, and assistance of the workers. The vote by list was
especially prized by the Radicals because it gave them a great chance of
winning parliamentary seats. Under this electoral system, candidates
competed not to win specific districts but to be among the leading vote
getters at the department level. Such a system of proportional representation usually favored less-established parties such as the radicals.

At the same time the Opportunists were planting the seeds of a republican system and trying to mollify the Radicals, they were also bat-
tling the effects of a worldwide economic depression. To overcome the
effects of this great depression (which lasted roughly from 1873 to 1897
and was called the "great" depression until the economic collapse of
1929–1939), the Opportunists resorted to a combination of protectionism
and public works. To preserve its electoral base in the peasantry and to
guarantee the continued allegiance of large manufacturers (especially
iron and steel), the Opportunists imposed tariffs to prevent the growing
worldwide competition in steel and agriculture from undercutting
French producers. The process of protectionism reached its culmination
in the tariff system of Jules Méline, which passed in 1892 and succeeded
in reconciling these diverse interests. To enable French producers to ex-
ploit the home market more easily, the "Freycinet Plan," started in 1878,
authorized the construction of new canals and roads and more than doubled the amount of railroad track (from 24,000 in 1881 to over 64,000
kilometers in 1914).[5] These secondary rail lines connected almost every
commune in France to the national market. Under this system, the French
economy grew at about 1.25 percent a year between 1879 and 1904.[6]

This growth rate, however, was below that of both the United States
and Germany; by 1900, France had slipped from the world's second to
fourth largest economy. As a result of protectionism, a higher percentage
of the French population was still engaged in agriculture than either the
English or German. Nevertheless, the modest growth combined with an
essentially stagnant population ensured that the living standard of the
French population was higher than that of its rival across the Rhine.

Although the Opportunists thus tried to win over radical republicans
as well as the urban and the rural poor, these groups still felt margin-
alized in the face of the continuing economic downturn. The Radicals felt frustrated that the parliament would not abolish the Napoleonic
Concordat (separating Church and state) or return to free trade (to supply urban workers with cheap foreign food). As a result, they were prey
to any movements from the right or the left that promised sweeping

change. The Opportunist grip on the Chamber of Deputies weakened after the October 1885 elections, forcing them to ally with the Radicals against a resurgence of royalists and Bonapartists. As a reward for this alliance, the radicals were allowed to appoint the ministers of education and war.

The new minister of war, General Georges Boulanger, soon became the champion of the discontented on both the right and the left. His earlier, sympathetic handling of the striking miners at the southern town of Decazeville in 1886 had won him the favor of the workers, and his threat of war to regain the lost provinces of Alsace and Lorraine gained the applause of nationalists. Royalists soon concluded that here was a charismatic hero who might overthrow the Republic and restore the monarchy. Backed by royalist funding, Boulanger ran for a seat in the Chamber of Deputies and, thanks to the first truly mass-marketed electoral campaign in France—with widespread distribution of posters, photographs, pamphlets, busts, and souvenirs—won in many districts, gaining large numbers of peasant and working-class voters. Ironically, the general could not sit in the Chamber after his victory because soldiers were ineligible to serve. The Opportunist government tried to cool the public ardor for him by assigning him to a provincial post, but a scandal involving the son-in-law of President Jules Grévey forced the resignation of the president and kept Boulanger in the center of national attention. When the Opportunists retired, General Boulanger was eligible to run for the Chamber again. His stunning victory in Paris on January 27, 1889, brought out a large, tumultuous crowd which might have carried the general to the presidential palace. This man of action, however, failed to act, and four months later, fearing that the government could convict him of treason, he fled to Belgium and committed suicide on the grave of his mistress. In subsequent elections, the Opportunists shifted back to single-member constituencies and prohibited any candidate from running for more than one office. The October 1889 elections returned 366 Republicans and a combined total of only 210 Monarchists, Bonapartists, and Boulangists.

Although the Boulangist movement dissipated after its hero's suicide, a new synthesis of conservatism, populism, and nationalism was set in motion that would play a decisive role in French history for the next 50 years. A scandal broke in November 1892 when a number of prominent deputies, including the Radical Georges Clemenceau, were exposed in the corruption and bankruptcy of a scheme to construct a Panama canal. At this juncture, another vital piece of the new right fell into place: anti-

Semitism. Anti-Semitic journalists, writers, and organizers Édouard Drumont and Paul Déroulède pounced on the fact that a few of the directors of the bankrupt company had been Jewish, and they propagated their theory of the Jewish exploitation of France.

A climate of anti-Semitism was thus already in place in 1894 when a Jewish army officer, Alfred Dreyfus, was charged as a German spy, convicted, and deported to Devil's Island, the French penal colony in Guyana. Believing that the army had framed him, his family and friends, various journalists, and a growing number of politicians were drawn to his case. The newly emerging Socialist party, under the leadership of Jean Jaurès, also joined the Dreyfus supporters. These "pro-Dreyfusard" writers became known as "intellectuals"; indeed, during the crisis, the word gained its modern denotation of writers turned activists in the cause of public morality.

What turned the Dreyfus affair into a crisis that threatened to divide the nation and destroy the Republic was the power of the press. Mass-circulation procedures had developed after 1870, both in Paris and in the provinces, and the press had experienced explosive growth. From total daily newspaper sales of 235,000 copies in 1858, the number had jumped to one million in 1870, two million in 1880, and almost five million in 1910. Technological innovations such as the rotary press (1860s) and the linotype (1880s) put daily papers in the hands of literally millions of French people.[7]

The most famous newspaper article of the Dreyfus affair was Émile Zola's 1898 open letter to the president of the Republic, known as "J'accuse" (I accuse). Published in the radical newspaper L'Aurore in an edition of 300,000 copies, the letter put the affair at the center of French life for several years. Zola was able, in part, to generate such controversy because he had become one of the most famous, widely read novelists in the world. In addition, his letter contained explosive charges: French army officers, whom he named, had conspired to frame Dreyfus and then tried to cover it up. Zola's charges led to his being prosecuted and convicted for defamation of the army. His actions also inspired the creation of the League of the Rights of Man. This organization, dedicated to championing the rights of the individual against militarism, clericalism, and nationalism, quickly became a powerful nationwide organization. Along with Zola, the League was instrumental in obtaining Dreyfus's return from Devil's Island and a new trial.

The new right, which had germinated under Boulanger, flowered during the Dreyfus affair. Royalists, Bonapartists, and the Catholic Church rose to defend the honor of the army against an alleged conspiracy of Jews and Freemasons. Freemasons, part of the masonic movement, had been popular in France since the mid-eighteenth century. Masonic lodges attracted a large number of Republican leaders due to Masonry's secular and rationalistic philosophy and its commitment to social improvement. Conservative Catholics and royalists feared such rational secularism, which they believed Jews also advocated, would destroy France. This potent blend of conservatism, Catholicism, anti-Semitism, and nationalism found embodiment in such organizations as the Young Royalists, the Anti-Semitic League, the League of Patriots, and the League of the French Nation—all of which engaged in propaganda, agitation, and street fighting. Another right-wing anti-Semitic organization, the Action Française, founded in July 1899, became highly influential over the next four decades.

Fearing that the right might try to seize power, René Waldeck-Rousseau, a former labor lawyer and radical parliamentary deputy, formed a government of "republican defense" in June 1899. This government brought the radicals to power and saw the eclipse of the Opportunists. Drawing on the help of Jaurès and on the backing of their faithful followers among the lesser bourgeoisie—shopkeepers, clerks, schoolteachers, and the rank and file of the civil service—the radicals gained the support of the emerging Socialist party. This government would remain in power, with only one change of prime minister, until 1905 and would essentially settle the Dreyfus affair.

Three months after the formation of the government of republican defense, Dreyfus was brought back to France and retried. Although he was again found guilty of treason, the finding of "extenuating circumstances" permitted Waldeck-Rousseau to pardon the former officer. In 1906 France's highest *cour de cassation*, the Supreme Court of Appeals, overturned the military court-martial and confirmed his innocence.

In the meantime, the government, dominated by Radicals and fired up by the passions of the Dreyfus affair, achieved a long-standing goal: the separation of the Catholic Church from the republican state. A general law on associations, passed on July 1, 1901, granted both chambers of the French parliament the right to authorize religious orders. The next year, strengthened by electoral gains and following the zealous direction of the vigorous anticlerical Emile Combes, few authorizations were granted. On the contrary, 135 Catholic orders were exiled from France, including two of the most anti-Dreyfusard, the Jesuits and the Assumptionists. Moreover, Catholic property was seized and schools were closed; in 1904, members of religious orders were prohibited from teaching in either Church or state schools. Although Catholic schools lost upward of one-third of their enrollment, they were not physically destroyed.

In 1905 Combes had readied a law abolishing the Concordat of 1801, thereby providing for a final separation of Church and state, when he was forced to resign due to parliamentary intrigue. His replacement, Maurice Rouvier, carried out a more moderate separation, permitting the Church to retain its property, for example. The intransigence of the pope, who wanted a blanket rejection of the separation, resulted in the state's continued control of the properties. Over the following decades, however, hostility subsided and the two sides compromised, allowing parish councils to lease churches from the state.

The decade following the end of the Dreyfus affair and the disestablishment of the Catholic Church saw social problems move to the center of French life: the conditions of the French working class. On this question the radicals proved far less resolute in their attempts to ameliorate the problems of French industrial workers.

Although France had seen some of the earliest proponents of revolutionary socialism and although Karl Marx had been inspired by the revolution of 1848 and the Commune, France's slower rate of industrialization and urbanization produced a smaller and less concentrated working class than that of either Germany or England. In 1911 France was still 56 percent rural, with 43 percent of its population employed in agriculture. In contrast, while the number of industrial workers had increased by over 1.3 million between 1896 and 1911, they still had not surpassed the number of peasants.[8] It is not surprising, therefore, that both Opportunists and radicals granted protectionist measures (tariffs) to its broad peasant constituency rather than passing laws regulating labor in workshops and factories. Although the government had legalized trade unions in 1884, Republicans of both tendencies downplayed the problems specific to the emerging working class in their attempt to create an all-embracing Republican ideology. Although many Republicans, especially radicals, had worked for the amnesty of the Communards (finally accomplished in 1879 and 1880), the specter of the Commune still disturbed many moderate and conservative Republicans.

As a result of Republican indifference and fear of the Commune, French socialism and the labor movement developed on the periphery of French politics during the early decades of the Third Republic. Already fractious before and during the Commune, French socialism remained fragmented. The main division separated "possible" and "impossible" socialists. "Possibilists," epitomized by the faction led by Jean Allemane, rejected the call for a new revolution, believing that social reforms and socialism could triumph through the institutions of the Third Republic. Their first tangible goal was to win municipal elections and run towns and cities, but "municipal socialism" had little autonomy because of the centralized French state.

Allemane and his followers dubbed as "impossibilists" those socialists who continued to be inspired by the French revolutionary tradition, as exemplified by the 1871 Commune. The foremost advocate of revolution and of Marxist socialism in France was Jules Guesde, who founded the French Workers' party. An austere purist, he had earlier broken away from the Federation of the Socialist Workers' Party, which he had also led, when he believed it had become too reformist. Although small, this party was highly disciplined and had achieved a degree of organizational sophistication (in the northern industrial regions, it relied on a network of café owners) lacking in the more diffuse opportunist and radical republican movements. In short, the French Workers' party was the first modern political party in France. Although Guesde supported the general socialist reforms, such as the eight-hour workday, he viewed elections primarily as a means to expand and consolidate a revolutionary movement that might someday be able to seize power. Consequently, Guesde opposed the entry of reform socialist Alexander Millerand into the government of republican defense in 1899 on the grounds that socialists should undermine rather than sustain the bourgeois republic.

French socialism finally achieved unity in 1905, thanks to the political acumen and personal magnetism of the philosopher and Republican Jean Jaurès. Jaurès's ability to synthesize the conflicting elements in socialism and republicanism paid handsome dividends when he overcame the differences between the various belligerent socialist factions and was also able to attract a substantial number of shopkeepers, peasants, and white-collar workers to his view. The united Socialist party that emerged from Jaurès's efforts (officially named the French Section of the Working-Class International, or SFIO) made steady progress in the elections. In 1906 the SFIO obtained almost a million votes and elected 51 deputies; by the April and May elections of 1914, these figures rose to 1,398,777 votes and 101 deputies, virtually a fifth of the members of the Chamber of Deputies.[9]

The effectiveness of French socialism, however, was hampered through the 1880s and 1900s because the labor movement became attracted to ideologies, such as anarchism and syndicalism, which stressed direct action rather than political organization. The first philosopher ever to call himself an anarchist had been the largely self-taught Pierre Joseph Proudhon. His philosophy, that all government potentially, if not actually, oppressed individual liberty, had inspired most of the French members of Marx's First International and had had a substantial following among the Communards in 1871. Anarchism (the belief that all forms of government are oppressive and must be overthrown), which continued to develop throughout the 1870s and 1880s, became increasingly radical. Many anarchists, such as François Ravachol, now believed that through individual acts of defiance or violence against governmental authority, from insulting police officers to killing presidents, they could inspire the people to rise in revolt to create a truly free society. This notion of propaganda by the deed, in the early 1890s, erupted into infamy with a series of bombings in restaurants and in the Chamber of Deputies, as well as a series of murders and assassinations, including the president of the Republic, Sadi Carnot, in June 1894. Repressive laws were quickly passed and soon ended the anarchist attempt to put their theory of "philosophy by deed" into action.

Nevertheless, anarchist philosophy had filtered into the labor movement and helped spawn the revolutionary syndicalism that the General Federation of Labor (CGT) adopted at its inception in 1895. Often also known as anarcho-syndicalism, this philosophy asserted that only workers could free themselves—that they could not rely on the government or on political parties to help them. Labor unions, however, were acceptable as long as they were run by and for the workers. This philosophy inspired the CGT, the largest French union, to refuse partnership with any socialist party. Instead, it advocated the general strike—a visionary syndicalist theory holding that bourgeois society would collapse if all workers went out on strike at once. In short, it was a variation on the theme of propaganda by deed.

Following the Dreyfus affair, syndicalism briefly moved to the center of French life by inspiring the biggest wave of strikes France had ever known. Between 1906 and 1909, Georges Clemenceau, the radical prime minister, mercilessly repressed these strikes. His harsh reaction demonstrated the limits of his party's commitment to radicalism, as the workers understood the term. This anticlerical Dreyfusard lost all sympathy for the oppressed when workers by the thousands went out on strike. Indeed, he proudly appropriated as a complimentary title—the epithet the workers used for him—France's top cop.

The notion of social justice held by the radicals clearly did not include ameliorating the lot of the working class through state intervention. Clemenceau and others remained steadfastly committed to the laissez-faire doctrine of no government intervention in the economy, at least in terms of helping workers. By 1914 Great Britain and Germany had passed far more social reform legislation than France. The French measures that were passed included a law on factory sanitation (1894), employer responsibility for safe working conditions (1898), a ten-hour workday for women and children (1900), eight-hour shifts in the mines (1905), and a compulsory day of rest each week (1906). Not until 1910 were workers able to obtain the various forms of insurance that were already widely used in Germany. French workers, as they had since the 1840s, consequently relied on mutual aid societies. By 1914 over 3 million workers participated in these self-help institutions.[10] Not surprisingly, French workers in general suffered higher rates of disease and death than their counterparts in England and Germany.

Despite the rise in strikes and the government's relative reluctance concerning social reform, French workers did experience some improvements during the Third Republic. The average worker's real wages (i.e., after inflation) rose by 50 percent between 1895 and 1914.[11] Moreover, the length of the workday, in general, declined from 12 hours during the 1860s to 10 hours by 1910. Although mechanization and increased division of labor meant that fewer workers attained the skills of the traditional artisan, there were more opportunities to become white-collar workers. The percentage of workers who filled various clerical functions increased from one-fifth during the 1850s to one-third by 1914.

During this beautiful era, the French economy showed renewed vigor, especially between 1905 and 1914. After an average growth rate of only 2 percent a year between 1873 and 1896, this rate subsequently increased between 1905 and 1914 to nearly 5 percent annually. Growth was especially impressive in those sectors representing the so-called second industrial revolution: steel, chemicals, and automobiles. Under the banner of such names as Renault, Citroën, and Michelin, France's auto industry rivaled that of America. The French fully embraced the telephone and the airplane. For example, the number of telephones in France exploded from 12,000 in 1889 to 300,000 in 1913.[12] In addition, the French invented the film industry; the Lumière brothers showed the first film at the Grand Café in Paris in December 1895.

Modern consumerism and mass leisure emerged during this era. By 1900 the Bon Marché department store in Paris was the world's biggest, and in 1916 the Parisian newspaper *Le Petit Parisien* was the world's largest-selling paper, with 2,183,000 copies daily.[13] Mail-order catalogs extended the reach of Parisian department stores into the provinces. The Belle Époque was also the golden age of the French theater and music hall. National and international tours ensured that actors, actresses (such as Sarah Bernhardt), and singers brought the latest hits to the countryside and to the world. The bicycle became one of the most widely diffused consumer items; in 1898, the French people were pedaling 395,000 bicycles, and by 1914 that number had jumped to 3.5 million.[14] Contemporary reports noted that by 1910 the peasantry were wearing ready-to-wear clothes and riding bicycles to music halls in nearby towns. The 1889 and 1900 international expositions of the era commemorated the centennial of the French Revolution, the Republic, and modern science and technology, and helped to develop an international tourist industry and to democratize leisure activities.

Paris sparkled as the capital of pleasure and as a center of culture. Between 1870 and 1914, the City of Light witnessed the flowering, successively, of a plethora of artistic and literary movements that formed the basis of modern art: Impressionism, Fauvism, and Cubism. Indeed, the notion of an artistic avant-garde was born in Paris during this era. This constellation of creativity included poets such as Arthur Rimbaud and Paul Verlaine, in their later years, and Stéphane Mallarmé and Guillaume Appolinaire; novelists such as the mature Émile Zola, Romain Rolland, André Gide, and Marcel Proust; the French master of the short story, Guy de Maupassant; painters and sculptors such as Édouard Manet, Pierre Auguste Renoir, Claude Monet, Edgar Degas, and Camille Pissarro, who elaborated on Impressionism, and a younger generation including Auguste Rodin, Paul Cézanne, Henri Matisse, Georges Braque, and the Spaniard Pablo Picasso; and, finally, such composers as Claude Debussy, Erik Satie, Maurice Ravel, and the Russian Igor Stravinsky. In the world of science, French luminaries included biologist Louis Pasteur and physicists Pierre and Marie Curie.

While the historical image may be one of elation, the era itself felt haunted by specters of decline and degeneration. Although French industrial output tripled and national income doubled, between 1870 and 1914 France fell from second place (behind Britain) to fourth (behind the United States, Germany, and Britain) among industrial powers.[15] This decline was not rooted in productivity—on a per capita basis the French worker was as efficient as any other—but in demography. While her rivals proliferated dramatically between 1870 and 1914, French population stagnated. In that half century, on the one hand, Germany increased from 41.1 million to over 65 million, England from 26 million to 41 million, and the United States from 39.8 million to over 92 million; on the other hand, France's population during that period inched up from 36.1 to 39.6 million.[16]

As a consequence, the French political and intellectual elite became obsessed with the decline of the French birthrate, and France became a pioneer in the modern science of demography. The birthrate did, indeed, fall from 26.1 per thousand in the 1860s to 18.8 per thousand in 1914; Germany's, by contrast, remained at 30 per thousand.[17] A flood of publications harped on a standard litany of causes: alcoholism, venereal diseases, crime, prostitution, suicide. Moralists and reformers across the political spectrum anxiously noted the virtual doubling of alcohol consumption between 1843 and 1907 and the fact that France, by 1914, had over 480,000 cafés and bars, more per capita than any other nation in the world.[18]

Many elite males attributed the falling birthrate to lower class women working and middle-class women becoming feminists. Since at least the time of Jules Simon's 1867 study *The Woman Worker*, reformers and moralists had worried that lower-class women being at work were responsible for the low birthrate. While France did indeed have a higher rate of female employment than any other European country, these writers merely lamented this fact rather than trying to improve the lives of these women[19] and their families. By the time of the Belle Epoque, there was concern as well about middle-class women fleeing the domestic sphere. Educational opportunities for women had expanded dramatically with the Ferry education laws of the 1880s, and women flocked to the teacher-training schools. By 1900 women were also establishing their presence in universities; by 1914, they constituted 10 percent of the national student body. In particular, women made their presence felt in the field of medicine; by 1914, 3 percent of France's doctors were women.

Many of these advances, however, provided signs of future liberation rather than delivering immediate emancipation. For many writers and journalists, the "new woman" was symbolized by the female bicycle rider or the fashionable woman who now wore the freer new styles of Paul Poiret and Coco Chanel instead of the old-fashioned corset. However, the restrictions on women's freedom as defined in the Napoleonic Civil Code were but slowly overcome: only in 1897 did married women win the right to control their own incomes.

An important reason why French women would win the vote only after World War II (rather than after World War I as in most other countries) was the Republican fear that women were still deeply under the influence of Catholicism and would vote according to the Church's dictates. Men more often congregated in the cafés with the local mayor and male teachers. Even some female Republicans feared that giving the vote to their sisters might be a threat to the Republic.

To overcome their deteriorating military position, due to low population growth French politicians and reformers undertook a wide variety of measures. To many educators, sports and physical education seemed crucial to improve the physical condition, if France was to regain its lost provinces of Alsace and Lorraine; thus, school curriculums after 1870 often added gymnastics and drilling. At the end of the century, the aristocrat Pierre de Coubertin succeeded in renewing the Olympic Games as a means not only of promoting international comity but also of regenerating French manhood.

To blunt the growing power of the German economy and military and to regain French prestige, the Republican leaders also embarked on an ambitious expansion of the colonial empire. Indeed, the Third Republic would create an overseas empire larger than under the monarchical or imperial regimes. France's expansion into Asia and Africa between 1880 and 1914 was also part of the broader European-wide "new imperialism" of the age.

In Africa, France's colonial expansion fanned out from the already secure colonies of Algeria, in the north, and Senegal, in west Africa. In 1881 the country to the east of Algeria, Tunisia, became a French colony. Morocco, to the west of Algeria, was incorporated much more slowly, due to inter-European rivalries. Even in 1913 Morocco was still merely a protectorate rather than a colony. In west Africa, from Senegal, the French pushed north, east, and west. Guinea was incorporated in the 1880s, Dahomey in the 1890s, and Mauritania and the Ivory Coast only on the eve and then during World War I. Farther south, below the English colony of Nigeria, soldiers, administrators, and priests established what became known as French Equatorial Africa, comprising Gabon and the French Congo. On the eastern coast of Africa, France consolidated its control over the port of Obock during the early 1880s; this area subsequently became French Somaliland. Located on the Gulf of Aden, it served as a coal depot for French steamers headed to French possessions in Southeast Asia, the South Pacific, and Madagascar. Madagascar, the fourth largest island in the world, subject to French influence since the seventeenth century, became a formal French colony in 1896.

France was also busy in Southeast Asia and the Pacific. Control over Indochina was consolidated in 1884 after Jules Ferry sent 30,000 soldiers to quell the last vestiges of Vietnamese resistance. Three years later, Annam (present-day Cambodia), Tonkin, and Cochin China formally became the Union of Indochina. In 1893 Laos was added. In the South Pacific, Tahiti was formally annexed in 1880 and the Austral archipelagoes in the late 1880s. Together, France's South Pacific holdings became the colony of Oceania.

By 1914 the French empire, including 50 million people and 3,000,000 square miles, ranked second only to the British. Like its European competitors, France believed colonies could supply new, and secure, sources of raw materials, outlets for French capital investment, and markets for French goods. By 1905 French generals saw colonial populations as a potential source of manpower, important because of France's low birthrate, in case of a new war.

While Republicans expanded the French imperial grasp, they did not transform the nature of the colonial process. Although politicians and administrators debated throughout the 1880s, 1890s, and 1900s about the merits of assimilating colonial peoples fully into French civilization or merely have them be "associated" with the metropole, much of this talk was academic. Old regime mercantilism, rather than republican liberalism, dominated colonial economic policy. Monarchical centralization rather than democratic participation motivated French colonial administrators. The rudimentary representative institutions set up for the indigenous peoples had little real power. Moreover, the system of universal free secular education the Republicans created for France was denied to its colonies. It is ironic that Jules Ferry, the main inspiration for the educational reforms, was also instrumental in the launching of imperial expansion in the Third Republic. In short, in much of Africa, association rather than assimilation was the rule.

Nevertheless, the Republic did continue the tradition of granting French citizenship to its older colonies. Thus the Caribbean island populations of Guadeloupe, Martinique, and Guyana and the coastal areas of Senegal received French citizenship and had representatives in parliament. Here the precepts of assimilation were essentially put in practice. In the case of Algeria, however, citizenship was extended only to the European population and indigenous Jews, not to the Muslim majority. This move, popular with the European population, had momentous implications for the future.

Such vigorous and extensive expansion was bound to result in conflict with other colonial powers. The most important conflicts occurred in 1898 with Great Britain over Fashoda (an oasis in present-day Sudan) and in 1905 and 1912 with Germany over Morocco. The conflict over Fashoda arose when the British and French both raced to link their African colonies into one continuous geographical unit (Britain, north and south; France, west and east) area. The two imperial powers collided at Fashoda. Realizing that they could not simultaneously outmaneuver Great Britain in the colonies and recover from Germany the lost territories of Alsace and Lorraine on the Continent, French diplomats recognized British control over the Sudan in a March 1899 settlement. This proved to be Théophile Delcassé's (minister of foreign affairs, 1898–1905) first master stroke in his plan to achieve an Anglo-French rapprochement.

In 1905 the German Kaiser William II forced an international conference—known as the Algeciras conference for the place in Morocco at which it was held—to be convened over the status of Morocco. Although the conference, including all the European powers, acknowledged France's right to be in Morocco, this decision did not inhibit the kaiser from provoking another crisis over Morocco in 1912 after France had expanded its power beyond the boundaries outlined at Algeciras. International negotiations again settled the conflict, but this time France had to cede an extensive amount of its territory in the French Congo to Germany (who incorporated it into its colony of Cameroon) in return for control of Morocco. These two affairs, coming within a decade of each other, convinced many French people that Germany was an implacable enemy and that France must prepare for war.

After 1890 French diplomats began to prepare for war by creating an alliance system against Germany. Powerful allies, to the east and west of Germany, could also offset, in short, French military weakness vis-à-vis a growing Germany. Until the dismissal of Otto von Bismarck as German chancellor in 1890, France had not been able to break out of the diplomatic isolation that had followed the defeat in 1870. After 1891, however, due to the ineptness and belligerence of German diplomacy under the young Kaiser William II and the brilliance of French diplomacy, especially that of Théophile Delcassé, France succeeded in forming two alliances, one with Russia and one with England. In 1905 the Triple Entente including France, England, and Russia was as solid as the Triple Alliance among Germany, Austria-Hungary, and Italy. Both sets of alliances had secret treaties—hidden from their populace—with their allies that bound each other to mutual support in the event of a crisis and that promised to divide the enemy's territories and colonies among themselves in the event of victory.

The preparations for war gathered momentum when former Prime Minister Raymond Poincaré won the presidency in January 1913. A native of Lorraine whose family left the province when it was annexed by Germany in 1871, he was a conservative Republican long associated with a hard-line stance toward the rival across the Rhine. As president, Poincaré reached military agreements with Great Britain, including how their navies would be used in time of war (Great Britain's navy was to defend the English Channel and France's to secure the Mediterranean). When Germany, in 1913, expanded its army by 200,000, Poincaré helped secure an amendment to France's conscription laws that required draftees to serve three rather than two years. This change kept the French army at the same strength as Germany's.

The military and diplomatic achievements of the Third Republic returned France to the first rank of the European powers by 1914, but it also made the nation vulnerable to any crisis that might affect an ally. Such a crisis struck in the Balkans during the early part of what everyone considered the exceptionally beautiful summer of 1914. Following the assassination in 1914 of the Austrian archduke Francis Ferdinand, first in line to the crown of Austria-Hungary, by Bosnian nationalists, Austria issued a harsh and unacceptable ultimatum to Serbia. France was drawn into crisis when its ally Russia came to the aid of its "Slav brothers" in Serbia, and then Germany backed its ally Austria. In the following month of July, the two sets of allies engaged in a complicated process first of diplomatic negotiation and then military mobilization. Germany, as it turned out, would declare war first—on Russia (August 1) and then on France (August 3).

When war finally erupted in August 1914, France found that the Third Republic's nation building had been successful. Despite the divisions and tensions of the prewar decades, peasants and workers willingly, if not enthusiastically, went to war. The military and the police had anticipated a desertion or evasion rate as high as 10 percent, but it was in fact less than 1 percent.[20] President Poincaré solemnized national unity by calling on all parties, including the Socialists, to participate in a government of "Sacred Union." What was not anticipated was a long, drawn-out war of stalemate and attrition. French strategy had been premised on the élan of attack rather than on the caution of defense.

The initial German strategy of a "swinging door" that would outflank the French army and capture Paris—the Schlieffen plan—failed because the German high command did not provide sufficient troops. German troops were stationed to defend Alsace and Lorraine or sent to guard the eastern front from a Russian army that had mobilized and moved faster than anticipated. Making good use of air technology, a French reconnaissance pilot noted a gap in the German army as it neared Paris. A French counterattack on September 5, 1914, stopped the German advance at the Marne River; this dramatic victory was quickly dubbed the "miracle on the Marne." The German, French, and the newly arrived English armies then engaged in a "race to the sea" to try to outflank each other.

By the end of November, the war of movement had become a war of attrition. Numerous lines of trenches (fortified with barbed wire, machine guns, and artillery in the rear areas) formed a dense and interlocking network from the English Channel to the Swiss border. Although under 500 miles as a bird flies, the dense grid of trenches covered an astounding 25,000 miles. French troops were deployed along 6,250 of these miles.[21] As the war settled into a stalemate, orders for shells skyrocketed from 84,000 a week to 700,000.[22] By the end of 1914, after only five months, fighting on the western front had killed 300,000 and wounded 600,000 on all sides. Battlefields in this new age of warfare no longer resembled the "field of honor" of nineteenth-century patriotic painters but rather the lunar-like landscape subsequently depicted by surrealist artists.

The enormous scale of men killed and firepower expended led to the reorganization of all French life into the "home front," one of many terms coined during the war. Production for the war effort in factories and shops became as important as fighting in the trenches. France quickly learned just how indispensable were its factory workers: by the end of 1915, a half-million workers who had initially been sent to the trenches were back at their machines, their places at the front now taken by peasants. To meet the ever-growing need for labor, women streamed into war production and took over thousands of jobs once held by men; by 1918, nearly 30 percent of all munitions workers in the vital Paris region were women.[23] In addition, the French recruited laborers from their colonies, as well as foreign European workers. To a degree unthinkable before the war, the French government stepped in to organize and direct the French economy. The laissez-faire policy of nonintervention gave way to government control over war production. Public opinion also became a province of government supervision. Propaganda, especially through the press and the newly emerging world of the cinema, became an all-pervasive, valuable tool for maintaining morale.

With the home front and the trenches in place for the long haul, the war slowly ground on. What made the war especially devastating for France was that most of the western front was on French soil and thus most of the battles on the western front occurred on their own soil. The year 1915 brought battles in the Champagne region in February, around Artois in May and June, and then back to Champagne in the fall. Poison gas was used for the first time. By the end of the year, 600,000 French soldiers lay dead with little to show for their sacrifice. The epic slaughter and stalemate battle of Verdun lasted from February through July 1916. The Germans gloated over "bleeding the French white" and inflicted over 300,000 casualties, but German troops lost about the same number and still did not take the strategic fortress. Henri Philippe Pétain emerged from the Verdun campaign as a rising star among French commanders; this anti-Dreyfusard of peasant stock broke with the former strategy of taking the offensive and instead stressed the simple yet overlooked truism that "gunfire kills." Later in the year the French commander in chief, General Joseph Joffre, launched an offensive at the Somme which lasted from July through November. The four-month offensive brought an advance of only seven miles and Joffre's transfer to a position in the war ministry.

Some decisive events occurred in 1917 but not a victory. Joffre's replacement, General Robert Nivelle, launched another offensive in the spring but was dismissed within a month. Under his command, the new offensive had not only failed to end the stalemate, but had actually sparked mutinies among the troops, who were willing to defend their positions but not willing to go on the offensive. His replacement, Pétain, brought the mutinies under control with a calculated mixture of severity and mercy. The year also brought two Russian revolutions, a massive strike wave among munitions workers in France, and, finally, American entry into the war. American participation, more than the new invention of the tank or improvements in aircraft, was the decisive factor in ending the stalemate.

By the time Georges Clemenceau had formed a new government in November 1917, the country had already seen four wartime administrations and was almost exhausted. Clemenceau's entrance caused the disintegration of the "Sacred Union" because the Socialists pulled out in protest over the return to power of this adamant strike breaker. Clemenceau then established a twentieth-century version of a Committee of Public Safety, modeled on his youthful friend Léon Gambetta's efforts in 1870–1871. "The Tiger," as Clemenceau became known, clamped down on dissent and installed an interallied command with French General Ferdinand Foch as supreme allied commander. The Tiger's ferocity galvanized France for the final effort—the successful defense against the German offensive of March–July 1918, followed by Foch's counteroffensive, the German collapse, and the armistice on November 9, 1918.

At the end of the war, the prewar French ambassador to Berlin, Jules Cambon, summed up France's position with a depressing lucidity that was lost amidst the celebration of victory and the end of the war: "France victorious must grow accustomed to being a lesser power than France vanquished."[24] The country least able to sustain large losses had suffered, proportionally, more than any other combatant: of the 8 million Frenchmen mobilized, 5 million had been killed or wounded. The more than 1.3 million dead alone represented over 10 percent of the active male population.[25] During the war the number of births fell precipitously from 709,800 in 1914 to 366,000 in 1916, then slowly rose to 475,500 in 1919, the year following the war. Only in 1920 did the number of births post an increase over 1914.[26] The four "hollow years" of 1914–1918 would haunt French society as another war loomed in the future.[27] Despite the creation of new factories for war material, especially around Paris, French industrial production had dropped 60 percent and agricultural production 45 percent during the war.[28] The franc, once a most stable currency, had now become one of the most unstable. France, formerly one of the great banker and creditor nations of the world, was now deeply in debt, especially to the United States. By 1918 the conflict was known in France as the Great War.

Where would France go from here?

NOTES

1. Robert Tombs, *The Paris Commune, 1871* (London: Longman, 1999), p. 180.

2. Alfred Cobban, *A History of Modern France, Vol. 3: 1871–1962* (Harmondsworth, Middlesex, England: Penguin Books, 1965), p. 12.

3. J.P.T. Bury, *France 1814–1940*, 5th ed. (London: Methuen, 1985), p. 157.

4. Eugen Weber, *Peasants into Frenchmen: The Modernization of Rural France, 1870–1914* (Stanford, CA: Stanford University Press, 1976), p. 67 and Gordon Wright, *France in Modern Times*, 5th ed. (New York: W. W.

Norton, 1995), p. 167, and François Furet and Jacques Ozouf, *Reading and Writing: Literacy in France from Calvin to Jules Ferry*, trans. not listed (Cambridge and Paris: Cambridge University Press and Editions de la Maison des Sciences de l'Homme, 1982), p. 46.

5. Colin Jones, *The Cambridge Illustrated History of France* (Cambridge: Cambridge University Press, 1994), p. 228.

6. Colin Heywood, *The Development of the French Economy, 1750–1914* (Cambridge: Cambridge University Press, 1992), pp. 7–8.

7. Jones, *The Cambridge Illustrated History of France*, p. 228 and Roger Price, *A Social History of Nineteenth-Century France* (New York: Holmes & Meier, 1987), p. 354.

8. Annie Moulin, *Peasantry and Society in France Since 1789*, trans. M. C. and M. F. Cleary (Cambridge and Paris: Cambridge University Press and Editions de la Maison des Sciences de l'Homme, 1991), p. 101 and Jeremy D. Popkin, *A History of Modern France* (Englewood Cliffs, NJ: Prentice Hall, 1994), p. 201.

9. Aaron Noland, *The Founding of the French Socialist Party (1893–1905)*. (1956; rept.: New York: Howard Fertig, 1970), p. 204.

10. Theodore Zeldin, *France 1848–1945, Vol. 1: Ambition, Love and Politics* (Oxford: Clarendon Press, 1973), pp. 660–661.

11. Jones, *The Cambridge Illustrated History of France*, p. 229.

12. Ibid., p. 228.

13. Zeldin, *France 1848–1945*, p. 529.

14. Eugen Weber, *France Fin de Siècle* (Cambridge, MA: Belknap Press of Harvard University Press, 1986), p. 200.

15. Jones, *The Cambridge Illustrated History of France*, p. 227.

16. Ibid., p. 231.

17. Joseph J. Spengler, *France Faces Depopulation. Postlude Edition 1936–1976* (Durham, NC: Duke University Press, 1979), p. 53.

18. Patricia E. Prestwich, *Drink and the Politics of Social Reform: Antialcoholism in France Since 1870* (Palo Alto, CA: Society for the Promotion of Science and Scholarship, 1988), p. 24 and Christophe Charle, *A Social History of France in the Nineteenth Century* trans. Miriam Kochan (Oxford: Berg, 1994), p. 142.

19. Jones, *The Cambridge Illustrated History of France*, p. 241 and James F. McMillan, *Twentieth-Century France: Politics and Society, 1898–1991* (London: Edward Arnold, 1992), p. 58.

20. Jones, *The Cambridge Illustrated History of France*, p. 243.

21. Paul Fussell, *The Great War and Modern Memory* (London: Oxford University Press, 1975), pp. 36–37.

22. Laura Lee Downs, *Manufacturing Inequality: Gender Division in the French and British Metalworking Industries, 1914–1939* (Ithaca, NY: Cornell University Press, 1995), p. 21.

23. Laura Lee Downs, "Women's Strikes and the Politics of Popular Egalitarianism in France, 1916–18" in *Rethinking Labor History*, Lenard R. Berlanstein, ed. (Urbana: University of Illinois Press, 1993), p. 119.

24. Wright, *France in Modern Times*, p. 331.

25. Ibid., 306 and Philippe Bernard and Henri Dubief, *The Decline of the Third Republic, 1914–1938*, trans. Anthony Forster (Cambridge and Paris: Cambridge University Press and Editions de la Maison des Sciences de l'Homme, 1985), p. 78.

26. Jacques Dupâquier et al., *Histoire de la population française, Vol. 4, de 1914 à nos jours* (Paris: Presses Universitaires de France, 1988), p. 73.

27. Eugen Weber, *The Hollow Years: France in the 1930s* (New York: W. W. Norton, 1994), pp. 11–18.

28. Wright, *France in Modern Times*, p. 306 and Roger Price, *A Concise History of France* (Cambridge: Cambridge University Press, 1997), p. 219.

9

Decline and Degradation: Interwar and Vichy

After the fighting stopped in 1918, France discovered just how costly victory had been, in material loss as well as in a crushing population loss. Almost one million buildings had been destroyed. In the heavily shelled combat areas, about 11,000 square miles had been devastated, including the destruction of residences, railways, roads, and bridges and the loss of hundreds of thousands of horses and other farm animals. In addition to the wartime ravages of human life and materiel, France lost 166,000 people in 1919 from a worldwide epidemic of Spanish influenza. With a generation decimated, a weak currency, high debts to the United States, and staggering material losses, the French people promptly adopted the slogan, "Germany will pay." But how and when?

In the heady months following victory, these questions did not appear to present major problems. Paris, as host to the peace conference, was once again at the center of world events, and Georges Clemenceau was one of the "Big Four" leaders who would decide the fate of the world. From the defeated empires France gained new colonies (in the interwar period known as mandates) from Germany, Cameroun and Togo in Africa, and from the Ottoman Empire, Syria and Lebanon.

On the questions of territorial security on the Rhine and German reparations, however, France quickly became frustrated. Clemenceau had hoped to annex the Rhineland, or have it, at least, declared neutral. At the peace conference he encountered American and British intransigence on this point, but did receive an Anglo-American guarantee of assistance if France were attacked. This pledge soon evaporated when the U.S. Senate rejected the Versailles Treaty and the attendant guarantees to the French. On the matter of reparations that Germany would pay the victorious allies, the conference set up an Inter-Allied Commission. American experts estimated damages at between $15 and $25 billion, but all parties were dissatisfied. The French, not surprisingly, when the final decision of the commission was made in 1921, found the amount too low; the Germans and the British thought it was too high.

French workers and peasants faced their own frustrations of a devastated economy and a society in the grip of inflation. While Clemenceau and the bourgeoisie waited for Germany's payments, militant workers felt the fortunes of the rich should finance reconstruction. The Bolshevik revolution in Russia, the westward movement of revolution into central Europe, and the overwhelming deprivations of the war all helped to inspire a wave of strikes in 1917 and 1918. The prevailing mood caused an unprecedented upsurge in membership in the Socialist party, or SFIO (from 36,000 in December 1918 to 133,000 by the following December) and a dramatic growth in the General Confederation of Labor (CGT)— from under 700,000 in 1914 to over one million in 1919.[1]

To calm the wave of working-class unrest, the Chamber of Deputies passed some social legislation: a law on collective bargaining (March 25, 1919) and a law promulgating an eight-hour day (April 23, 1919). These measures, however, did not prevent protest and revolt. Violent clashes occurred on May Day 1919 in Paris, for example, and there was much talk about a general strike.

By the end of 1919, however, the revolutionary wave had crested. Léon Jouhaux, the moderate prewar leader of the CGT, vanquished the revolutionary majority at the general trade congress held in Lyon on September 15–21, 1919. The SFIO also declared itself unready to follow the Bolsheviks by creating a revolution and decided as well against any alliance with a bourgeois political party for the 1919 elections. As a result, although the Socialists gained in votes—1,700,000 versus 1,400,000 in 1914—the party lost seats (down from 102 to 68) in the new Chamber of Deputies because of a change in the electoral laws.[2]

This new electoral law—a compromise between voting by list and voting by district—allowed the party with the most votes in any given department to get all the seats. It also rewarded parties that wished to form alliances. Frightened by the Bolshevik revolution, the Radical party moved to the right. Portraying Clemenceau as the "father of victory" and the Socialists as insane anarchists with knives-between-their-teeth murderers, the parties of the right swept the November 1919 elections. The parties of the right, the National Block, won 450 out of the total 616 in the Chamber of Deputies.[3]

This chamber was called the Blue Horizon Chamber, after the color of the military uniforms, due to the high proportion of ex-soldiers elected. It was also the first chamber in Third Republic history in which the majority were practicing Catholics. The belief was widespread among these parliamentarians (who often still wore their sky-blue uniforms) that prewar anticlericalism was dead. Diplomatic relations with the Vatican were resumed, and the Concordat was retained in the newly restored Alsace and Lorraine. Joan of Arc was sanctified by the Church in 1920 and her day was made a national festival.

In an attempt to stem and reverse France's low birthrate, the chamber, in July 1920, passed a law severely punishing the distribution of information on birth control methods and products for women. No restriction was placed on the use of the sheath, the main tool of contraception used by men and regarded as protection against venereal disease. Although the law proved ineffective, it did show the new reapprochement between Catholicism and nationalism.

This pious religious cast is one reason why the National Assembly did not elect Clemenceau in January 1920 as the new president of the republic: the uncompromising, old, anticlerical Jacobin had simply made too many enemies on his way to victory. Following this political defeat, "The Tiger" retired from public life for the remaining decade of his life. Republicanism had moved to the right, and the right had moved a bit toward the center: in that, clericalism lost some of its power to nationalism.

Despite electoral defeat, revolutionary workers continued trying to foment a revolution. In 1920, 1.3 million workers went on strike; the most dramatic strikes occurred among railroad workers and miners in the north. Fresh new railroad union members, in the Fédération des Cheminots, shut down much of the rail traffic in February and then launched a general strike on May 1, 1920. They requested support from the CGT, which Jouhaux skeptically granted, in the hopes of creating mass walkouts. But barely half of the railroad workers went out and even fewer in other fields. The strike was over by the end of May. The railroad bosses quickly took their revenge by dismissing 18,000 workers—some

5 percent of their labor force. Defeat quickly led to division within the CGT and the loss of half its membership. The union movement did not recover until after the onset of the Great Depression in 1931.

At this moment of defeat for the French proletariat, the shining example of Bolshevik Russia seemed even more alluring. The revolutionary wave had not finished in central Europe, and it could move west if only the proper organization were applied, or so it seemed to many on the left. With sentiments like these swirling about them, the Socialists, still loyal to the Second International, held a party congress at Tours in December 1920. The debates at this meeting provided some of the classic statements of the differences between socialism and communism. Those who wished to turn the SFIO into a disciplined vanguard party on V. I. Lenin's model were fully prepared to accept the 21 points of the Bolshevik Third International in Moscow. A sizable majority at Tours—3,247 to 1,398—adopted the Bolshevik conditions, and the French Communist party (PCF) was born.[4] Hopes were bright that the revolutionary current would propel France and the world into a new age of freedom and abundance as soon as the revolution had overthrown capitalism. Surely the antiwar protests and strikes of the previous few years were just a prelude to future triumphs.

The main opposition to the Bolshevization of the party came from Léon Blum, the son of a solid Parisian bourgeois. A Dreyfusard, a literary critic, a civil servant, a party member, and a great admirer of the socialist Jean Jaurès, Blum argued for a continuation of the French tradition of democratic socialism. The revolution must not forsake liberty, he urged; there was no such thing as a good dictatorship. Although Blum convinced the old stalwart Jules Guesde, and most of the parliamentary members, he nevertheless lost the majority of the delegates and Jaurès's paper *l'humanité* as well, which was now run by the new French Communist party. During the 1920s, while the Socialist party broadened its base with an infusion of government functionaries and schoolteachers, the Communists concentrated on factory workers and created a small, highly disciplined party leadership.

A similar split occurred in the labor movement. In July 1921 the CGT lost much of its membership to the new Communist-inspired Unified General Confederation of Labor (CGTU). Unlike the CGT, which had stayed aloof from party politics, the CGTU became the conduit (the phrase used was "transmission belt") of Communist ideology and strategy of labor unions.

While the Socialist party made a quick recovery, the new Communist party quickly fell into sectarian squabbles. In the parliamentary elections of 1924, the Socialists won 100 seats compared to 30 for the Communists. PCF influence was further limited by its aloofness from the leftist government, the *Cartel des gauches*. In 1927 the Communists, at the behest of the Third International, placed themselves even more in a self-imposed ghetto with a "class versus class" strategy which viewed the Socialists as little better than fascists. During the 1928 elections, the PCF gained over a million votes, but because it did not ally with or step aside for other left-wing parties in the second round of the elections, the right won the election. Although its quest for ideological purity prevented the Communist party from becoming broad based, it did secure a strong base in a few selected regions: the Paris suburbs (known as the red belt), the departments of Cher and Lot-et-Garonne, and the "red crescent" of the Massif Central. Most of these areas remained Communist strongholds through the 1980s.

Conflict between the Socialists and Communists on the left helped ensure that moderate and conservative Republican parties held power throughout most of the 1920s and early 1930s. Raymond Poincaré, a conservative Republican and former president, and Aristide Briand, a former socialist then flexible moderate, dominated these governments. Briand, as prime minister between January 1921 and 1922, created the little entente (a replacement for the Russian alliance) among the Eastern Europeans (Czechoslovakia, Romania, Yugoslavia, and Poland). As foreign minister between 1926 and 1932, he tried to achieve peace and reconciliation. For his faith in the League of Nations and his attempts with the Locarno Treaties, the Kellogg-Briand Pact, and the European Federal Union to achieve mutual security and disarmament, Briand became known as the "apostle of peace." Poincaré, on the contrary, as he did during his wartime tenure as president, took a hard line toward Germany and later vigorously fought to stabilize the French currency, the franc.

Currency instability was the cause of much of the governmental instability of the 1920s.[5] After being stable throughout the nineteenth century, the French franc lost one-fifth of its value during the war and then, after the government lifted currency controls, the franc lost 50 percent of its value in 1919, four-fifths of its value by 1920, and continued to depreciate through the early 1920s. Indebtedness abroad caused inflation at home and brought economic questions to the forefront of French political life in a fashion unknown during the Belle Époque. Economic troubles also made France much more insistent on the question of German reparations. Briand's government fell in January 1922 over his inability to obtain what were felt to be sufficient German payments. To force German compliance, Briand's successor, Poincaré, sent French troops to occupy Germany's vital Ruhr coal mines and factories in January 1923. By the end of the year, a new German government again started to pay reparations. Poincaré's get-tough policy, which raised taxes, did not help him with the voters in the 1924 parliamentary elections. However, his actions helped launch an international reparations conference at the end of the year which resulted in a new schedule of German payments, the Dawes Plan.

Religious and electoral factors were the primary causes for Poincaré's coalition losing the May 1924 elections. The partiality Briand and Poincaré had shown to the Church alienated the anticlerical Radicals and helped drive the party into an alliance with the Socialists. The resulting leftist coalition formulated resulted in a coherent electoral strategy and, unlike in 1919, a victory. The government, which became known as the Left Cartel (*Cartel des gauches*), included 139 Radicals and around 100 Socialists; it brought great hope on the Left and fear on the Right.[6] The Radical Édouard Herriot headed the cartel's first government. Although Herriot had Socialist support, the scrupulously legalistic Blum continued the prewar Socialist policy of not letting party members join the cabinet. The rich feared he would impose a tax on wealth to solve the currency problem. As it turned out, such anxiety proved groundless owing to a fundamental disagreement between the Radicals and the Socialists on economic policy. On the one hand, the Radicals, still faithful to their peasant and small shopkeeper electorate, remained committed to the laissez-faire doctrine of minimal government. On the other hand, the Socialists wished for greater government intervention. In short, economic issues quickly divided the new coalition. The chance of a Radical-Socialist compromise was diminished by the presence of the Communists, ever ready to accuse the Socialists of betraying the working class. While the left could achieve unity for an election, it could not retain it to govern.

The cartel also faced the unremitting hostility of the center and the right. During the election, President Alexander Millerand, who was attempting to strengthen the presidency, had broken with the tradition of presidential neutrality in parliamentary elections by advocating the cartel's defeat. After victory, the cartel forced him to resign. The moderates in parliament and the entire Senate then elected a conservative Radical, the current president of the Senate, Gaston Doumergue, who did his utmost to undermine the cartel.

The main reason for the cartel's disintegration, however, was economic. Fear of the cartel's nationalizing banks or industries led to international financiers and the wealthy taking their investments, that is, capital, out of the country and into the safety of Swiss or American banks and securities. In the spring of 1925, to counter this financial outflow, the cartel tried to print more money. The conservative Bank of France refused, however, citing the April 1919 law stipulating the amount of currency that could be in circulation. This setback forced Herriot's resignation in April 1925. Bitter, he complained that he had run into a "wall of money," a phrase that would gain popularity in the following years. A series of equally ineffective center-left governments followed in rapid succession. By July 1926 the franc was worth only 2 cents (whereas before 1914 it had been a quarter).[7] The cartel, in shambles, gave way to a broad coalition government.

In July 1926 Poincaré formed a new government, which represented all major parties except the Socialists. To short-circuit parliamentary intrigue and intransigence, Poincaré requested and received the power to promulgate decree laws on the economy. His authoritative handling of the crisis won the favor of British and American financiers and led to the Mellon-Béranger agreement of September 1926, which settled the war debts to the United States of America. Confidence returned and the franc rose so rapidly that the government now had to worry about the effect on French exports.

This new economic equilibrium brought about a right-wing victory in the April 1928 elections. Poincaré then moved decisively to end financial instability once and for all. The law of June 25, 1928, ended the obligatory acceptance of paper money (a wartime measure) and returned the franc to the gold standard, but only at one-fifth of the pre-1914 value. This devaluation enabled the treasury to pay off debts with highly debased currency. This solvency was achieved, however, at the cost of alienating thousands of bondholders—frugal bourgeois who had invested in the Republic. Although these investors suffered severe losses, they were not totally ruined as were their German counterparts during the hyperinflation of the early 1920s. The French investor, however, was receptive to extreme right-wing influence during the 1930s.

In the short term, stabilization allowed France to weather the initial international financial turbulence following the Wall Street crash of October 1929. Indeed, foreign capital took refuge in France, and the funds that poured in allowed the government to borrow on the money market on terms not seen since 1914. Poincaré's measures also compensated for the French failure to recover substantial German reparations. Regular payments, under the Dawes Plan, continued until 1931, by which time France had received the sum of 8 billion francs specie and 4 billion in goods and services (1913 value). This amount burdened Germany but did not satisfy the French, who claimed 62 billion, nor reimburse their losses.[8]

Despite an unstable currency and minimal reparations, the French economy boomed during the 1920s. During the early part of the decade it expanded more rapidly than did any of its major competitors, and reconstruction was 80 percent finished by 1924. To compensate for the wartime population losses, France recruited almost two million foreign laborers. Primarily drawn from Eastern and Southern Europe, these workers in general filled the low-paying, most menial jobs in the mines, factories, fields, and construction sites disdained by French workers. Their input was vital to France's 1920s expansion. New industries did especially well: iron and steel, rubber, autos, airplanes, petrochemicals, and electrical equipment. The production of electricity, for example, rose from 3.5 billion kilowatt-hours in 1920 to 15 billion in 1930.[9] Industrial companies grew larger and used more mechanization. Greater discipline was achieved through the "science of work" developed by Americans Frederick Winslow Taylor, the "efficiency expert," and Henry Ford, whose assembly-line techniques were known in Europe as "Fordism."[10] In 1929 industrial production was up 40 percent compared to 1913 and foreign trade spurted by 66 percent.[11] By 1930 industrial concentration was clearly on the rise; the number of companies with 500 workers doubled compared to 1900.[12]

Despite these sectors of economic dynamism, agriculture and retail distribution retarded economic development. Agricultural production could not meet the growth of the urban population. One quarter of France's food needs had to be met by imports.[13] Inefficiency in French farming stemmed, in part, from a continuing large sector of subsistence farming. The percentage of rural residents, although for the first time falling below 50 percent, declined more slowly than in other industrial nations. Rural residents still composed 48.8 percent of the population in 1931, and agricultural workers remained about 35 percent of the workforce in 1936.[14] In French towns and cities, small shops continued to predominate over mass-market retailers, in part, because of the tax system that favored small rather than large enterprises.[15]

When deteriorating health necessitated Poincaré's retirement in July 1929, the center-right coalition he had forged continued to dominate the nine governments that led up to the elections of June 1932. The major politician during the era between the decline of Poincaré and the 1932 elections was André Tardieu. A graduate of one of the most prestigious of France's elite schools, École Normale Superieure-ENS, he was also a journalist and had been a minister since 1926. Tardieu's actions and attitudes foreshadowed the antiparliamentarianism of the 1930s. He wished to transcend the traditional left-right split and replace this dichotomy with a strong state. He wished to woo the radicals from any temptation to ally with the Socialists (SFIO) or the Communists (PCF). He gave lip service to the two-party nonideologically polarized system found in the Anglo-American world. Ultimately he would fail, but from 1929 to 1932 he dominated and controlled governments as president of the council and minister of the interior, agriculture, and war.

Due to budget surpluses in the late 1920s and early 1930s, Tardieu was able to put into practice some of his ideas concerning activist government. For example, he created large public-works projects, abolished school fees for primary and secondary education, and set up a rudimentary social insurance plan. On the most famous of these measures, the Maginot Line of defensive fortifications built along the eastern border with Germany, he spent the sum of 5 billion francs. Tardieu's grand ideas became unacceptable to the right after 1932, however, because of the deepening of the depression due to increasing budget deficits.

The last real spark of optimism among the French elite occurred with the staging of the Colonial Exposition of 1931 in Paris. Indeed, this marked the last significant celebration of colonialism anywhere before its dramatic disintegration after World War II. At the lavish exposition held in Vincennes Park on the eastern border of Paris, each French colony had a pavilion in which to display its traditional "exotic" and unique culture. It became a showplace for the "France of one hundred million people" that politicians extolled (60 million colonials plus the 40 million within France itself).[16]

The exposition was also the last gasp of the "crazy years" (*les années folles*), French for the "Roaring Twenties." The French were experiencing jazz through such African-American expatriate entertainers and singers as Josephine Baker, who symbolized a new freedom not only for Africans and African Americans but also for women in general. Amidst this atmosphere Simone de Beauvoir, the pioneering postwar feminist, would come of age.

This era encouraged artistic experimentation, a spirit best summarized in the Dada and Surrealist movements. Both Dada and Surrealism tried to plumb the depths of the human psyche and its unconscious, after the fashion of Freudian psychology, in order to liberate the personality from the constraints of a culture that had produced such a horrific war. Only by reintegrating life and art, fantasy and reality, could life be made humane and whole again.

With a booming economy and a vital artistic and cultural life, France seemed to dominate Continental Europe between 1918 and 1932. France's paramount position, however, rested on foreign weakness rather than on internal strength: Germany was recovering from the war and the young Soviet Union was in the throes of modernization. While these nations recovered during the 1920s, France's crucial alliance with Great Britain deteriorated. Colonial conflicts and disagreements over reparations and security and over diplomatic moves in Eastern Europe sapped the wartime Entente Cordiale.

For almost two years after the Wall Street crash in October 1929, France seemed to be prosperous. By the autumn of 1931, however, France belatedly felt the effects of the crash. Although the economic downturn would never be as great as it was in the United States, Great Britain, and Germany, the depression in France lasted longer and recovery was slower. Even in 1938, as Great Britain and Germany were gearing up for war, French industrial production stagnated, and the country's share of international trade had shrunk from 11.2 percent in 1929 to 5.8 percent in 1937.[17]

The 1932 elections occurred during a quickening pace of bankruptcies and rising unemployment. Despite lavish infusions of campaign contributions from big business, voters punished Tardieu's right-wing coalition for the economic downturn. The left achieved its greatest electoral success since 1914, with 334 deputies—160 Radicals and 131 Socialists— as compared to 257 on the right. Although the Socialists had become the bigger party, in sheer number of ballots cast, Blum still was hesitant to participate in a government he could not control. As it turned out, this coalition was too divided and too timid in the face of ever-mounting problems. As in 1924, a parliament that started out on the left would move steadily to the right.

The 1930s proved to be a period of extreme political instability and economic futility. Following the 1932 elections, six cabinets tried fruit-lessly to cope with the growing crisis. Édouard Herriot reprised his 1924 role as premier. With depression sinking the German economy, U.S. President Herbert Hoover suspended reparations in June 1931 and ended them definitively a year later at the Lausanne Conference of July 1932. The great question for France then became: would it still have to pay its debt to the United States even if Germany had ended its reparations to France? Herriot believed that France should pay the debt, to maintain national credit and honor, but this stance caused his government to be toppled quickly, on December 14, 1932.

The Radicals now decided to fight the depression with the orthodox strategy of deflation. Frightened by the effects of their inflationary poli-cies in the *Cartel des gauches* of the 1920s, they could not settle on a consistent policy. Between 1932 and 1935, 11 governments produced 14 plans for economic recovery.[18] Deflationary measures tried at one point or another included slashing wages of government workers, cutting vet-erans' pensions, closing public works, and increasing taxes.[19] Such mea-sures only caused a further downward spiral in the economy and steady cuts in the military budget.

While bringing stagnation and inaction to France, the economic de-pression resulted in the dynamic and demonic Nazi Party coming to power. From the moment he assumed office as chancellor in January 1933, Adolf Hitler had started to prepare Germany for rearmament by embarking on a massive inflationary program of public works to end unemployment and speed economic recovery. At the same time, a sig-nificant transformation was taking place in France: the right, which had been nationalist and belligerent (especially toward Germany) during the 1920s, now shifted to an accommodationist, even pro-German, stance vis-à-vis its prime World War I enemy. A staple of right-wing journalism in the 1930s was the contrast between "fascist dynamism" and "parliamen-tary decadence."

The scandal that broke at the end of December 1933 was ready-made for right-wing exploitation. A swindler and confidence artist born in Rus-sia to Jewish parents, Serge Stavisky, had ties to the Radicals in the gov-ernment and was found dead during an investigation of his activities. Premier Camille Chautemps, indirectly implicated with Stavisky, was forced to resign.

As the revelations of the affair became public, *Action Française*, through its newspaper articles and the agitation of its newspaper sellers and street fighters (the king's vendors, or *Camelots du roi*), incessantly propagated antiparliamentary sentiment with the slogan, "Down with the Thieves!" The revelations also consolidated and catapulted into prominence other right-wing movements, many of which had their origins in the 1920s. One such was the Young Patriots (Jeunesse patriotes), a political party with its own street gang. Another was the Cross of Fire (Croix de feu), a veterans' organization.

The agitation had turned into street demonstrations by January 7, 1934, and it culminated on the night of February 6 when the various right-wing groups assembled on the periphery of the Chamber of Deputies on both the left and right banks in Paris. The resulting riot nearly toppled the Republic, despite its lack of coordination or strategy. The fracas resulted in 15 fatalities and more than 1,500 injured.[20]

The street, it now seemed, could dictate to the parliament: the right-wing street action had nullified the results of an election that had brought the left to power. Édouard Daladier, the Radical minister set to become prime minister replacing Chautemps, resigned, and conservatives formed a government of national union including former president Gaston Doumergue, along with Herriot and Tardieu, who had funneled money to the leagues that had staged the riots. As premier, Doumergue was given virtual freedom to govern via decree laws. In addition, a new constitutional amendment was proposed to augment the president's powers. The old warhorse Doumergue had no new ideas, however, and the sterility of his policies, in the face of the depression, caused his downfall in November 1934.

In the face of January's right-wing street action, which seemed to neutralize leftist electoral strength and open the way for a possible fascist coup, the left mobilized and strove to end internecine quarrels by creating a popular front. On the evening of February 9, the working-class east side of Paris was in a virtual state of siege as Communist-led demonstrators battled with the police. The CGT and the SFIO called a general strike for February 12, which the PCF joined. The left was rallying around the issue of antifascism, in a fashion not seen since the days of the Dreyfus affair. On March 3, a Vigilance Committee of Anti-Fascist Intellectuals emerged, and in July the SFIO and the PCF agreed on a pact for joint action.

Meanwhile, a group of "young Turks" in the Radical party—including the future Fourth Republic premier Pierre Mendès-France, future Popular Front education minister Jean Zay, and Pierre Cot, the future aviation minister in the Popular Front government—advocated that the party move away from the conservatives. After gaining the support of Daladier, the group largely succeeded in this effort, at least for the short term. Signs of growing strength and unity emerged in the leftist gains of the May 1935 municipal elections, and in March 1936 the Communist and Socialist trade unions merged. These measures of solidarity among intellectuals, politicians, and workers produced the euphoric, intense, but short period of social, economic, and political experimentation known as the Popular Front.

For the spring 1936 elections, the Popular Front campaigned under such banners as "Bar the way to fascism" and "Bread, peace, and freedom," broad slogans reflecting the considerable disagreement that Socialists, Communists, and Radicals still had over specific policies. The campaign conducted by the Popular Front's leader, Léon Blum, was notable for its deft use of the radio. Blum was also inspired by the New Deal of President Franklin Roosevelt in the United States; in short, moderate reform rather than revolution was desirable. Nationalization was urged only for the armaments industry, to rationalize weapons production, and for the Bank of France, to prevent conservative fiscal policy from hobbling economic reform.

In the initial round of the May elections, the Popular Front did fairly well, but rigorous discipline on the second round assured them a secure victory. The Popular Front, overall, won 378 seats as compared with 241 for the conservatives. The Socialists emerged as the largest party in the Chamber of Deputies with 146 deputies. The Radicals were the biggest losers, dropping 600,000 votes and 43 seats. The PCF emerged from its isolation to become a major force in French politics: its popular vote doubled, and the number of its representatives jumped from 10 to 72. In balance, the extreme-right deputies increased their number from 80 to 120.[21]

Moderate and defensive in intent, the Popular Front nevertheless inspired immoderate expectations. Within weeks of victory, over two million of the French working class spontaneously and unprecedentedly staged not only strikes but, even more creatively, factory occupations. Instead of revolutionary anger, however, the workers expressed a festive hope that their problems would finally be addressed. They sang, danced, ate, and drank, provisioned by their families, yet all the while taking care of their machines. But as a new hope flowered in working-class districts, a fear, bordering on panic, spread among the bosses and the bourgeoisie. Neither working class nor radical political parties—CGT, SFIO, or PCF—could control this movement any more than the managers could.

The strikes and factory occupations precipitated the greatest concern for social issues since the 1848 revolution. Once the workers started to take action, Blum moved swiftly to diffuse what could turn into a crisis situation. Representatives of business and labor met at the premier's residence, the Hotel Matignon, and worked out a series of measures that became known as the Matignon Accords. Its articles included a wage increase between 7 and 15 percent that was to be implemented immediately; collective bargaining; a 40-hour workweek; and the innovation for which the Popular Front would become most famous, two weeks of paid vacation. To implement these unanticipated reforms, Blum delivered on his promise to bring the Bank of France under greater government control and to nationalize the arms industries. In addition, to sustain support in the countryside, Blum established a governmental administration (office interprofessionnel du blé) to stabilize and then raise cereal prices. Other reforms included raising the age of mandatory education to 14, increasing the opportunities for the children of peasants and workers in secondary education, and the creation of a secretariat for sports and leisure.

The euphoria of the spring and the gains of the summer quickly dissipated. By June 1937 Blum had resigned and the heady days of the Popular Front were over. Internal dissension within the coalition, continuing economic deterioration, and new international crises caused Blum's fall. On his right, the Radicals feared that Blum was going beyond the boundaries of laissez-faire economics and was losing the confidence of employers. Trying to maintain business support, Blum refused to devalue or impose exchange control on the franc. Indeed, Blum's attachment to maintaining the franc's value vis-à-vis gold made it impossible for him to expand government borrowing to pay for his economic reforms. As a result, the wealthy sent substantial amounts of capital out of the country. In an attempt to restore business confidence and keep his radical allies in the government, Blum in January 1937 called for a "pause" in the implementation of Popular Front reforms. This proposal proved no more able to stem continued economic decline than did any of his other measures, and in fact it brought about sharp attacks by the Communists.

Equally dispiriting for Blum's government was the agony over the Spanish Civil War, which had erupted in 1936 shortly after he took office. Lacking support from England, the United States, and his own Radical allies, Blum believed that he did not have the mandate to intervene for the republic against General Francisco Franco, who had the support of Nazi Germany and fascist Italy. Instead he adopted a policy of neutrality, which further alienated much of his own Socialist party and the Communists.

In an ever more polarized France, indeed almost any domestic or foreign policy initiative seemed to cause dissension. The optimism of the workers following the heady summer of 1936 quickly turned sour as inflation rapidly wiped out wage increases, and the implementation of the 40-hour week (due in part to lack of employer compliance) disrupted industrial production. In desperation, on October 1, 1936, Blum painfully and belatedly reversed himself and devalued the franc; however, the downward spiral of industrial production negated the stimulative impact of the devaluation. Strikes reappeared in the summer of 1937, causing further unemployment and decreased production. On top of stubbornly high unemployment and lagging output, the flight of capital worsened the French trade deficit and sparked further flight. When Blum asked for emergency powers to cope with the extraordinary problems facing France, the Chamber of Deputies assented. The Senate, as it had during Herriot's premiership in 1925, flexed its conservative muscle and denied these powers. Blum had no alternative but resign. Once again, the Senate had assumed a central role in the declining Third Republic and nullified a left-wing victory.

The Popular Front mainly infuriated, rather than intimidated, the right. Right-wing journalists and politicians quickly adopted the slogan, "Better Hitler than Blum" and launched an intense campaign of invective and vilification against Blum and his government. He banned the Croix de feu and other right-wing leagues in June 1936, but these movements quickly re-formed into political parties. The Croix de feu became the French Social party (Parti Social Français) and attracted between 600,000 and 800,000 members. The once-Communist mayor of the Paris suburb of Saint Denis, Jacques Doriot, formed the French Popular party (Parti Populaire Français) which, at its height, comprised 200,000 members. In November 1937 a group of extremist army officers, known as the Secret Committee of Revolutionary Action (Comité secret d'action révolutionnaire), better known as the Cagoule, even planned a coup d'état. Although they were discovered before they could put their plan into action, the fact that retired marshals (including Henri Philippe Pétain, the victor of Verdun) almost certainly knew about the plot and did not inform the government indicated how divided political loyalties were during the

Popular Front. In a political culture where Pierre Laval and André Tardieu openly sympathized with fascist governments, however, such behavior did not seem especially noteworthy.

Blum was succeeded by the veterans Camille Chautemps and Édouard Daladier. Chautemps still governed with the Popular Front coalition, that is, with the support of the Communists and Socialists, but with Radicals in charge. Chautemps presided helplessly over a new strike wave, a worsening balance of trade payments, growing budget deficits owing to long-delayed increased military spending, and diminished tax revenues. In the face of Hitler's annexation of Austria in March 1938, he requested emergency decree powers, but he was turned down. Loss of Socialist support forced him out of office on March 10, 1938. Blum resumed the premiership on March 14. Although the chamber passed Blum's financial proposals, including exchange controls and a capital tax, the Senate rejected these measures. His government ended in less than a month.

Édouard Daladier then formed a coalition government from the center and right. Even if he had wished, which he did not, to continue focusing on the Popular Front's domestic reforms, foreign affairs would have prevented him from doing so. After annexing Austria, Hitler turned his covetous gaze on France's ally Czechoslovakia: in particular, the area near the German border with a German population, the Sudetenland. Initially France promised to fulfill its treaty agreement to defend its Central European partner, but Great Britain's prime minister Neville Chamberlain counseled what became an infamous doctrine of appeasement. Daladier followed the English lead in part because French public opinion also favored some type of settlement over the conflict. Thus Daladier joined Chamberlain, Hitler, and Benito Mussolini at the Munich conference which gave Hitler free reign to take the Sudetenland (and later the rest of Czechoslovakia).

Dissension over the Munich Agreements, bitterly denounced by the Communists, brought a formal end to the Popular Front. With the threat of Nazi Germany ever increasing, Daladier was granted the power to govern by emergency decree that had been denied to Blum and Chautemps. But his ineffective measures, rather than reflecting resolution, showed the disintegration of the parliamentary system. By the fall of 1938, economic recovery was finally achieved, but it was due less to Daladier's liberal economic policies than to the expanded military budgets that stimulated industrial production and the decree measures that increased employee confidence by outlawing strikes.

Hitler's occupation of the rest of Czechoslovakia in March 1939 caused a major shift in public opinion. The government thus gained the mandate to guarantee, along with England, the territorial integrity of Poland. The August 1939 Nazi-Soviet nonaggression pact, however, struck a mortal blow to French preparedness by nullifying the strong antifascist stance of the Communist party over the previous five years. Now the PCF became an outright opponent of war, and the party was quickly banned by Daladier.

Hitler invaded Poland on September 1, 1939, and two days later France and Britain declared war against Germany. However, few French people felt the sense of patriotic duty that their parents had on entering World War I 25 years earlier. In this war there would be no *union sacrée*, that is, the suspension of internal quarrels (such as between employers and workers or the right- and the left-wing parties) as had occurred in 1914. Due to the severe losses of World War I and the resulting demographic trough of 1914–1918 (known as the hollow years), veterans in their forties and fifties came out of retirement to man France's defenses.

The French general staff bet everything on the Maginot Line, the earlier strategy of defense rather than offense. This passive defensive strategy, inspired and directed by General Philippe Pétain, the French commander that had held Verdun against the Germans in World War I, during the interwar period, in the context of 1940, and the impressive showing of German lightning war (blitzkrieg) offensive in Poland, only added to the despair and defeatism felt by the French during the "phony war" between August 1939 and May 1940, in which neither they nor their German counterparts engaged in serious fighting.

This protracted period of waiting proved psychologically debilitating for France. While in wait for the German attack, the parliament overthrew Daladier's government on March 19, 1940, and replaced him with a leader deemed more effective and energetic: Paul Reynaud. Reynaud also was unable to end the personal rivalries and lack of clear objectives between ministers and military officers that bedeviled the French war effort. Rather than a straightforward attack, the French engaged in peripheral operations, such as attacking Soviet oil installations and Scandinavian iron ore deposits lest they fall into the hands of the Nazis. The French watched, with surprise, when Germany invaded Denmark and Norway in April.

On May 10, the day after yet another cabinet reshuffling, the Germans attacked France. Quickly they moved around the Maginot Line. Within a week, the Nazi blitzkrieg had divided and disorganized the French army and the British expeditionary force in Belgium. Two weeks later, on May 14, the Germans broke through at Sedan, the site of the disaster of the 1870 war, proving undeniably that the Ardennes forest was not impassable terrain for tanks. At roughly the same time, the great French theorist of mechanized warfare, Charles de Gaulle, headed a tank corps that held its own against the German panzers in the Laon region. A single example of tactical brilliance, however, could not cancel the strategic failures of a geriatric general staff.

Four days later, on May 18, in an attempt to recall and replay 1914's "miracle on the Marne," Reynaud brought in the 84-year-old Marshall Philippe Pétain to head the Ministry of War. Although Paris and the rest of the country did not learn immediately of the magnitude of the disaster, the military rout in the conquered northern departments set in motion a mass civilian exodus of six million people. Two weeks later, on June 19, the Nazi war machine reached Paris and caused 2 million Parisians to join the 8 million refugees fleeing the advancing enemy.[22] The government moved south, first to Tours, on June 10, and then to Bordeaux on June 15. Nearly ten million civilians, including two million Parisians, were on the move fleeing the invader. Within two days, Reynaud had resigned and Marshall Pétain formed a government fully beholden to, and ready to cooperate fully with, the Nazis. His call for an immediate armistice quickly gained a majority assent from the dispirited politicians.

Few were willing to try to carry on the struggle by moving the government across the Mediterranean to Algeria, or, as de Gaulle was about to do, by going to London. There, on June 18, de Gaulle broadcast his famous appeal for the war to be carried on. Against the seeming certainty of German victory, de Gaulle wagered that Britain could hold out and that the United States would eventually enter the war. He also countered Pétain's claim of legality with his own philosophy: the imperative of any state must be to survive to protect the liberties of the nation. This mission he believed Pétain had forfeited by surrendering to Hitler.

On June 22 Pétain signed an armistice with Nazi Germany at Rethondes in the same train car in which Germany had been forced to sign an armistice almost 22 years earlier. But Nazi vengeance went far beyond these symbolic terms. France was divided into a series of zones; Alsace and Lorraine were reannexed to Germany; and Italy gained territory in the southeast. Moreover, the Germans were to rule directly the northern and western maritime districts along with the northern industrial centers and Paris itself. All of these areas, including Paris, were put on Berlin time. The new French government being set up under Pétain retained control over the largely rural and underdeveloped central and eastern parts of France. Over 1,500,000 prisoners of war remained in Germany, and the Nazi war machine gained control over all French materiel.[23]

In the early summer of 1940, de Gaulle was virtually a solitary witness to the notion of a "Free France." Following a devastating defeat, public opinion was additionally enraged when the British, fearing that it might pass into the hands of the Nazis, sank the French fleet killing or wounding more than 1,600 on July 3 at Mérs-El-Kébir.[24] On July 9 and 10 the National Assembly, by a landslide, revised the 1875 constitution (624 to 4) and gave full powers to Pétain (569 to 80 with 18 abstentions).[25] On the following day, Pétain became head of the French "state," and he formally replaced the Republic and its trinity of "Liberty, Equality, and Fraternity" with "work, family, and country." At the heart of the regime was the governmental administration. Pétain and his entourage believed that France did not need another "corrupt" legislature. With the Germans controlling Paris, Pétain's new government chose the spa town of Vichy, in the center of the unoccupied zone, as the new capital. Along with its central location, the city's large number of hotels could house all the governmental ministries. Vichy France was unique among conquered nations under Nazi domination because it was the only government not put immediately and directly under Nazi administration.

Vichy blamed Republican "decadence," the freemasons, and especially the Jews for the defeat. Reform of education and a new emphasis on Catholicism were seen as antidotes to Republican moral turpitude. Vichy did not wait for their Nazi overlords to strike against the 330,000 Jews who resided in France in 1940. In part this derived from native French anti-Semitism, in part from Vichy wishing to ingratiate itself with the conquerors. Almost from the moment it came into existence, the Vichy government took anti-Jewish measures: Jews had to register with the police, they often lost their jobs, or they were immediately put in prison. On its own initiative in March 1941, Vichy created the General Office for Jewish Affairs to oversee this persecution. In July 1941 a systematic campaign of "Aryanization" commenced in which Jews were stripped of their businesses and homes. These measures proved to be the basis and rationale for deportations to Nazi death camps.

Blame for France's fall, in reality, should be placed especially on an uninspired military command. Lacking in imagination and vision, the generals (except for de Gaulle) learned nothing from the early Nazi blitzkrieg in Poland. French communications were so poor and so slow that messages from headquarters took up to 48 hours to reach the front. After

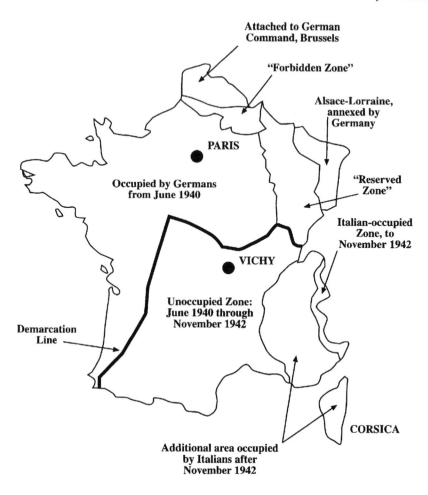

Attached to German
Command, Brussels

"Forbidden Zone"

Alsace-Lorraine,
annexed by
Germany

PARIS

Occupied by Germans
from June 1940

"Reserved
Zone"

Italian-occupied
Zone, to
November 1942

VICHY

Unoccupied Zone:
June 1940 through
November 1942

Demarcation
Line

CORSICA

Additional area occupied
by Italians after
November 1942

the initial devastating defeats, the generals, like their 1870 counterparts, became more concerned about preventing a possible social revolution by the Communists than about focusing on military victory.

For the next four years, the nation divided its loyalties among Pétain at Vichy, the fascist collaborators in Paris, and de Gaulle and the Free French who continued the war effort in London. Slowly an internal movement of resistance to Nazi rule developed in France.

Initially, in place of a legislature, the Pétain regime created a National Council and picked a selected group of "notables" from among clergy, nobility, military, and big business, as well as antiparlementarians on both the right and the left (such as the trade unionist André Belin). But this appointed body never found a role. To run the government, Pétain

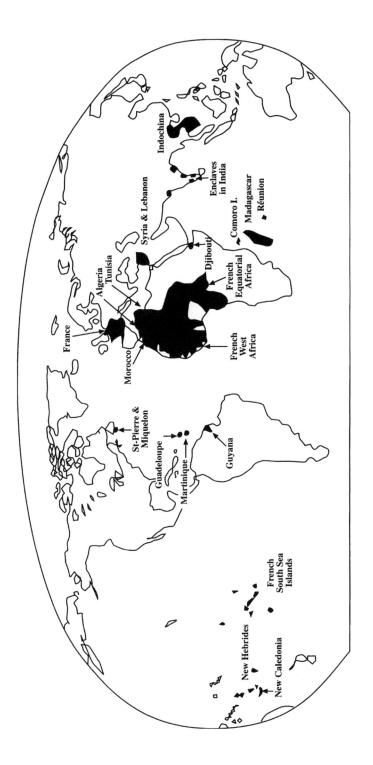

chose conservative intellectuals and sympathetic members of the administrative elite.

In addition to the political administration and the Catholic Church, the third pillar of Vichy France was the establishment of guild-like corporations. The edenic vision was that of a return to premodern corporations, where the differentiation between employers, employees, and apprentices is eradicated in one all-embracing community. Labor unions were abolished and strikes were prohibited. Instead, industrial workers, artisans, and peasants were now put into their own distinct corporations along with their employers. Special corporations were set up for children, adolescents of draft age, and veterans. The new elite would be trained at special leadership schools.

The imperatives of the Nazi war machine soon led to centralized economic planning under the administration of Jean Bichelonne, who was appointed minister of industrial production in 1942. Even though labor unions and strikes had been outlawed, employers were now required to set up committees so that their workers could have an input on production and thus contribute to promoting economic efficiency and rationalization. These measures, ironically continuing the Popular Front's quest for economic rationalization, did, indeed, facilitate technological innovation and had important long-term economic results.

Piérre Laval, a Third Republic official, returned to power in April 1942 as head of the government (to Pétain's head of state). With the Soviet Union and the United States now in the war and the subsequent German occupation of the entire country in November 1942, Vichy steadily lost its idealism and remaining popular support. Laval increasingly gathered the reins of day-to-day power in his own hands. Although later, at his postwar trial, he claimed to have mitigated Nazi depredations, there is little evidence to support this claim. Under the STO (Obligatory Labor Service, or Service du Travail Obligatoire), 600,000 laborers went to Germany, but only 100,000 prisoners of war (POWs) were returned. By 1943 Germany was taking 40 percent of the French industrial production and 15 percent of its agricultural output. Nearly one-third of the French labor force was employed in the Nazi war effort, and the Nazis were paying less than half market value for all the goods they took.[26]

Under Laval's auspices in 1942, Vichy participated in the Nazi extermination of the Jews (the Holocaust). By this year France was home to approximately 330,000 Jews, about 50 percent of them foreigners. Vichy had already, as noted earlier, started to restrict the rights of Jews and harass them in daily life. The first Nazi deportations of Jews occurred.

In 1942 the French police provided much help in rounding up and deporting 42,500 Jews. These deportations, as they included French citizens, caused some unease among the population and leadership. Some Catholics backed away from their full support of Vichy; the police often were not as zealous in enforcing anti-semitic laws or in rounding up Jews; even Laval balked at stripping French Jews of their French citizenship. These measures, however, were ineffectual at best. By August 1944 over 80,000 Jews in France had been sent to the Nazi death camps; more than 75,000 of them were killed. Although the figure of a quarter of the Jews in France being executed seems low, historians have found no evidence that Vichy tried to shield Jews, even French citizens, from the Holocaust. Overall, one-third of these Jews killed were French citizens.[27]

As the occupation continued, the population became increasingly poverty stricken. Industrial and agricultural production dropped even from the depressed levels of the 1930s. Gasoline for cars became almost nonexistent, coal and oil for heating were extremely scarce, and food was subject to strict rationing in urban areas. Standing in long lines outside the shops of butchers and bakers became a part of daily life. National nutritional levels plummeted; children and babies suffered from deprivation for years afterward.

To stem the growing dissatisfaction of the population, Vichy became more openly authoritarian and in the sphere of public order came close to being a fascist state. Arbitrary arrest and torture became standard practice. In August 1941 emergency courts were set up directly beholden to the state. In 1943 Vichy set up the *milice*, a special security force 35,000 strong, to follow up on an astronomical 3 to 5 million letters sent to Vichy officials informing on family, friends, neighbors, or strangers. At least 40,000 resisters and hostages were executed, and 60,000 were deported.

De Gaulle's initial struggles against Vichy in 1940 and 1941 met with little success. The support of British Prime Minister Winston Churchill and the British government initially seemed to be a liability after the British sank the French fleet at Mérs El-Kébir. The Free French government in London failed in its attempt to rally a revolt in Algeria, Senegal, or Syria. Free French forces helped but did not spearhead the defeat of Vichy forces in Syria. The Anglo-American allies considered de Gaulle's forces peripheral to their efforts. Thus the United States and Britain did not inform de Gaulle of their plan to invade North Africa and Algeria in the fall of 1942.

The Anglo-American allies made an abortive attempt to install their own leader of Free France, General Henri Giraud, a recent escapee from a German prisoner-of-war camp. Giraud showed little political acumen, and his star quickly waned when Admiral Darlan went over to the Allies and helped facilitate the liberation of North Africa. The subsequent assassination of Darlan provided de Gaulle with an opportunity to consolidate his control of the Free French movement. At the end of May 1943 he set up his headquarters in Algeria, and he and Giraud became co-chairmen of the Committee of National Liberation. While Giraud focused on setting up armed divisions to participate in the liberation, de Gaulle founded a Consultative Assembly, the nucleus for a new republic.

Significant resistance within France developed first in the Occupied Zone. The first incidents were often individual acts of defiance: insulting a German soldier in a café, assassinating an officer on the Paris streets, or printing or distributing clandestine literature. These acts continued throughout the war, but a second stage of resistance developed when networks emerged and intelligence began to be gathered and transmitted so that POWs, Jews, or downed fighter pilots could be shepherded out of the country. A third stage was reached when these networks acquired weapons for acts of sabotage or armed resistance. The southern zone, with large stretches of rural and mountainous terrain, provided the best hideouts for these groups of maquis. A still higher level of resistance was achieved when Nazi Germany invaded Soviet Russia in June 1941, thus freeing the Communist party to participate actively. Resistance continued to mount when the Nazis occupied all of France in November 1942, and again in 1943, when labor was conscripted for work in German factories.

To bring organization and coherence to the internal resistance, in January 1942 de Gaulle sent for Jean Moulin, a former prefect who had courageously escaped. By May 1943 the Resistance had developed sufficiently that representatives of the various groups met secretly in Paris to create the National Council of the Resistance (Conseil nationale de la résistance, or CNR). By November Allied planes were dropping large quantities of weapons to the various groups within the French Forces of the Interior (Forces françaises de l'intérieur, or FFI). The Communist forces, the French Partisan Snipers (Francs tireurs partisans français, or FTP), had a separate organization and, due to their ideology, did not receive the same level of support.

By the time the Allies landed on Normandy beaches on June 6, 1944, the Resistance was able to play a significant role. With de Gaulle having already set up a government in exile and with his ties to the internal resistance already in place, the Free French were able to take over from the retreating Germans with little discontinuity. The Vichy regime, of course, collapsed along with the Nazis. On Joseph Stalin's orders, the French Communist party did not stage an uprising, and consequently the Anglo-Americans did not set up a military administration in France. Indeed, the supreme allied commander, General Dwight David Eisenhower, allowed French General Jacques Philippe Leclerc to liberate Paris; again, the Resistance forces played a vital role within the city. French forces also played an integral part in the landing in southern France (Provence).

Following the expulsion of the Nazis from France, the French army, now bolstered by 100,000 volunteers from the FFI and the FTP, helped to defeat Nazism within Germany. Under the command of generals Philippe Leclerc, Jean de Lattre, and André Bethouart, French troops pushed deep into southern Germany. French military action warranted de Gaulle's participation in Germany's formal surrender, and France received an occupation zone in both Germany and Austria.

Thus the disasters and humiliations of the early and middle years of the war were partially offset by the war's-end contributions of the resistance movement and the French army. The material damage following this second war within a quarter century was more extensive than that following the first; virtually every area of the country had suffered. The loss in terms of human life, however, was much lower: some 600,000 French citizens, two-thirds of them civilians, had perished (as compared to over 1.5 million dead and almost 3 million debilitated to varying degrees in World War I). But massive rebuilding awaited in the postwar era: Over 2 million buildings had been destroyed or damaged, and inflation was rampant as the amount of paper money had increased from 142 billion francs in circulation in August 1939 to 632 billion francs in October 1944. Moreover, the purchasing power of the working class had dropped by at least 30 percent.[28] Although the nation was in ruins, the spirit of the people contained seeds of resilience and dynamism that would remake French society in unanticipated ways in the following three decades.

NOTES

1. Philippe Bernard and Henri Dubief, *The Decline of the Third Republic, 1914–1938*, trans. Anthony Forster (Cambridge and Paris: Cambridge

University Press and Editions de la Maison des Sciences de l'Homme, 1985), p. 87.

2. Ibid., p. 225.

3. Roger Price, *A Concise History of France* (Cambridge: Cambridge University Press, 1997), pp. 225–226.

4. Maurice Agulhon, *The French Republic, 1879–1992*, trans. Antonia Nevill (Oxford: Blackwell, 1993), p. 182.

5. Colin Jones, *The Cambridge Illustrated History of France* (Cambridge: Cambridge University Press, 1994), p. 248, and Maurice Agulhon, *The French Republic, 1879–1992*, pp. 202–203.

6. Bernard and Dubief, *The Decline of the Third Republic*, p. 163.

7. Price, *A Concise History of France*, p. 228.

8. G. de Bertier de Sauvigny and David H. Pinkney, *History of France* Revised and Enlarged Edition, French text trans. Jams Friguglietti (Arlington Heights, IL: Forum Press, 1983), p. 346.

9. Ibid., p. 340.

10. Jeremy D. Popkin, *A History of Modern France* (Englewood Cliffs, NJ: Prentice Hall, 1994), p. 252.

11. Jones, *The Cambridge Illustrated History of France*, p. 251.

12. de Sauvigny and Pinkney, *History of France*, p. 340.

13. Annie Moulin, *Peasantry and Society in France Since 1789*, trans. M. C. and M. F. Cleary (Cambridge and Paris: Cambridge University Press and Editions de la Maison des Sciences de l'Homme, 1991), p. 144.

14. Ibid., p. 141.

15. Popkin, *A History of Modern France*, p. 253.

16. Agulhon, *The French Republic, 1879–1992*, p. 204.

17. Price, *A Concise History of France*, 228, and John Merriman, *A History of Modern Europe: From the Renaissance* (New York: W. W. Norton, 1996), p. 1222.

18. Price, *A Concise History of France*, 234.

19. Alfred Cobban, *A History of Modern France, Vol. 3: 1871–1962* (Harmondsworth, Middlesex, England: Penguin Books, 1965), p. 138.

20. Gordon Wright, *France in Modern Times*, 5th ed. (New York: W. W. Norton, 1995), p. 359.

21. de Sauvigny and Pinkney, *History of France*, p. 348.

22. Jones, *The Cambridge Illustrated History of France*, p. 265.

23. Sarah Fishman, *We Will Wait: Wives of French Prisoners of War, 1940–1945* (New Haven: Yale University Press, 1991), p. XII.

24. W. A. Hoisington Jr., "Mérs-El-Kébir," *Historical Dictionary of World War II France: The Occupation, Vichy, and the Resistance, 1938–1946*, Bertram M. Gordon (ed.), (Westport, CT: Greenwood Press, 1998), p. 242.

25. Robert O. Paxton, *Vichy France: Old Guard and New Order* (New

York: W. W. Norton, 1972), p. 30, and Agulhon, *The French Republic, 1879–1992*, p. 268.

26. de Sauvigny and Pinkney, *History of France*, p. 361; and Price, *A Concise History of France*, pp. 255–56.

27. M. R. Marrus, "Holocaust," in *Historical Dictionary of World War II France: The Occupation, Vichy, and the Resistance, 1938–1946*, pp. 180–182, and J. Hellman, "Milice Française," in *Historical Dictionary of World War II France: The Occupation, Vichy, and the Resistance, 1938–1946*, pp. 243–244, and James F. McMillan, *Twentieth-Century France: Politics and Society, 1898–1991* (London: Edward Arnold, 1992), p. 137, and Price, *A Concise History of France*, p. 262.

28. de Sauvigny and Pinkney, *History of France*, 365–366; McMillan, *Twentieth-Century France*, p. 154; and Popkin, *A History of Modern France*, p. 300.

10

Renewal and Expansion: The Fourth Republic and de Gaulle's Fifth Republic

After all the horrors of the interwar and wartime years, France underwent an unprecedented economic, social, and cultural transformation in the thirty years following 1945. Indeed, during this "new French Revolution" of "thirty glorious years" of economic expansion, the nation would become as fully modern as any nation in the world, no longer a nation of peasants or small shopkeepers.

The initial euphoria of liberation in 1944 quickly turned to grim sobriety as the French surveyed the consequences of the Vichy government's collaboration with the Nazis and faced reconstruction in all sectors of economic, political, and social life. Following Vichy's fall, a populace that had largely sat on the sidelines while small cadres of resistance or collaboration battled over France's soul now had to deal with settling Vichy's accounts. About 10,000 Nazi collaborators were executed.[1] The high-profile trials of Pétain and Laval and 50,095 lesser cases came to the courts. Of these, 8,603 were acquitted, 4,397 were sentenced to death in absentia, and 2,640 received the death penalty, with 791 of these actually being executed. In short, most officials and businessmen who had collaborated escaped any meaningful punishment.

General Charles de Gaulle landed in France following the advancing troops. He immediately instituted a new government directed by commissioners of the Republic. In charge of local administration, their job was made easier by the widespread fear that excessive vengeance against collaborators might lead to a Communist takeover. Thus the commissioners promptly disarmed and disbanded the French Forces of the Interior (FFI). Moreover, the Resistance, of necessity, had had to keep much of the bureaucracy intact; even most of the judges who decided cases of collaboration had been holdovers from the Vichy administration. One most dramatic moment of the first two months of the liberation was de Gaulle's dramatic walk through the just liberated Paris on August 26, 1944.

De Gaulle was careful to choose a cabinet that reflected all the various political groups that had participated in the resistance and liberation, especially the Communists. By including the Communists, de Gaulle not only acknowledged their vital role in the resistance but also hoped to prevent a feared Communist bid to take over the government.

The horrors of the Holocaust were revealed when the Nazi death camps were liberated in the early months of 1945. The return of French prisoners of war, deportees, and laborers drove home the unmitigated horror of the Nazi regime. The political Far Right in France was discredited and for a generation would be prevented from gaining a mass following.

The leftward political shift of the French population was confirmed in the October 1945 general elections. In a dramatic break with past elections the Communist party, which emerged on top with 26.1 percent of the vote and 148 deputies, became the largest party in France. The runner-up was the *Mouvement Republicain Populaire* (MRP) or Popular Republican Movement, a new progressive Catholic movement (25.6 percent, 143 deputies) that emerged out of the small prewar liberal Catholic party. The socialists (SFIO) followed with 24.6 percent (almost the same as in 1936) and 135 deputies. The Radicals, however, obtained only 9.3 percent of the vote and merely 31 deputies.[2] The Communists participated in the government with the three other major parties, a system that quickly became known as "tripartism." Communist leader Maurice Thorez, after his return from Moscow, exhorted workers to "win the battle of production" and put France back on its feet.

De Gaulle's tripartite provisional government initially worked extremely well. De Gaulle, as was his desire, stood apart and above the parties and set the tone and the agenda for important political and economic innovations. His government did, indeed, achieve a fundamental restructuring of French government and society, quickly setting about to reestablish order and implement fundamental economic, political, and social reforms. Women were given the right to vote, in part, it seems, to blunt the power of the Communist party. DeGaulle nationalized coal, the electrical and gas industries, the airlines, the Renault automobile corporation (its founder was an especially flagrant collaborator), major insurance companies, and many of the largest banks. Labor unions were reborn, and workers were now placed on panels that monitored labor relations in companies with over 1,000 workers. An extensive social security system was also implemented.

In addition, a planning commission emerged to guide economic investment. This coordination was the inspiration of the former cognac maker and technocrat Jean Monnet. Inspired by America rather than the Soviet Union, Monnet also oversaw the creation of a National School of Administration (École National d'Administration, or ENA), which produced many of the most influential administrators and politicians of the next half-century. De Gaulle and Monnet felt France needed a trained technical elite to oversee economic reconstruction and expansion. The first Monnet-inspired plan, started in 1947 and lasting until 1952, placed its priorities on reconstruction; the second plan, from 1952 to 1958, focused on the industrial infrastructure. Emphasis was put on the production of coal, steel, cement, tractors, railroads, and heavy trucks. Agricultural modernization was a special priority in the 1950s.

In the late 1940s, the United States provided, partly because of its fear of a Communist takeover in Europe, vital assistance for French recovery. In June 1947 the United States' secretary of state, George Marshall, proclaimed America's readiness to offer large grants and loans to ensure the recovery of Europe. Between 1948 and 1953, the Marshall Plan poured $9.4 billion into Western Europe; France received $2.9 billion of this amount.[3] Approximately half of the investment in transportation, electrical, cement, coal, and steel came from the United States. The Monnet and Marshall plans were such a success that by 1958 planning shifted to the consumer sector, until then the neglected sector of the French economy.

At the same time, Monnet and MRP deputy Robert Schumann set up a system of joint management with West Germany to run the coal and steel industries that each had on either side of the Rhine. Rather than annex (as France had tried unsuccessfully to do following World War I) the idea was to form a cooperative venture that would prevent future conflict. This was a first step toward the creation of a European Common Market.

De Gaulle decreed all Vichy legislation null and void. Then, going against the wishes of the Consultative Assembly, he decided that a referendum on France's government should be part of the general elections of October 21, 1945. In this referendum the population voted overwhelmingly (96 percent) for the elected assembly to draw up a new constitution. Moreover, 62 percent voted that the assembly's powers should be limited to a seven-month period and that the constitution should be also put to a referendum.[4] De Gaulle had gone directly to the people over the heads of the politicians.

When the parties wished to limit his power, however, de Gaulle grew restive, fearing the return of the parliamentary system he believed was in part responsible for recent debacles. To everyone's surprise, he did not quickly return to political power. Indeed, he wandered in the political wilderness for twelve years.

Following his departure, the assembly drew up a constitution for a Fourth Republic. With the specter of Vichy and the Third Republic before them, the politicians were wary of establishing a strong executive and senate. Consequently, the new constitution of the Fourth Republic, adopted in April, gave full authority to a unicameral legislature: the president was a figurehead. The Communist party strongly supported the new draft and de Gaulle, as expected, denounced it. In the May 5, 1946, election, 53 percent of the voters turned down the proposed constitution, and the discredited assembly dissolved itself.

In the June 2, 1946, election for a new assembly, the MRP emerged as the top vote getter with 22.6 percent of the vote, followed by the Communists (20.8 percent) and the Socialists (SFIO) (a mere 16.1 percent).[5] Leadership passed to the MRP and Résistance hero Georges Bidault. Their new constitution returned to a bicameral legislature. In the new constitution, the president, elected for a seven-year term, held most of his earlier power but had no right to dissolve the National Assembly. The Fourth Republic's constitution also set up a new relationship between France and its colonies, the French Union. African leaders such as Leopolde Senghor and Félix Houphouet-Boigny hoped the union would helped speed the attainment of legal equality and economic and cultural development. However, no serious efforts were made to this end until the mid-1950s. In the October 13, 1946, election (in which one-third of the eligible voters did not even bother to go to the ballot box), this pale imitation of the Third Republic's constitution was unenthusiastically accepted by 53 percent of the voters.

Ministerial instability was even greater than it had been under the Third Republic: 24 governments took office between December 1946 and

May 1958. Results from the first National Assembly elections of November 10, 1946, had the Communists again gaining the most votes (28.8 percent)[6] and MRP deputies taking second place (26.3 percent). The big loser, again, was the SFIO which lost 24 seats. The Radicals and moderates made only a small dent in the new chamber with a gain of six seats (Radicals) and a loss of two (moderates), but they would later prove vital in government coalitions.[7] Ironically, the SFIO gained in influence what it lost in direct power; as the party in the middle, it emerged as kingmaker, indispensable in forming the coalition governments of the Fourth Republic. From the Socialist ranks came the first president, Vincent Auriol, and the first premier, Paul Ramadier, of the Fourth Republic.

By 1947 to 1949, all the key economic indicators were back at 1929 prewar highs. Between 1950 and 1958, France sustained an 80 percent increase in output and an annual growth rate of 5 percent. As industry boomed, so did agriculture. The number of tractors in use jumped from 50,000 in 1945 to 500,000 in 1958 and over a million by 1966. Thanks in part to the "tractor revolution," agricultural productivity soared. Adding to this confidence was the booming economy of French cities which provided jobs for the excess farm population, rendered redundant by increasing agricultural productivity. In consequence, the rural population, about 45 percent of the population before 1945, fell to less than 10 percent by 1975.[8]

In 1947 political tensions, stemming from the Cold War (the ideological and political—but not military—struggle between the capitalist United States of America and the Communist Soviet Union) ended the experiment in tripartite government. It had become increasingly clear, once France had accepted the Marshall Plan, that the country would not declare its neutrality between the Soviet and American camps. When the Communist party voted against the government in a debate on economic and social policy, Premier Ramadier expelled the Communists from the government. In retaliation, the Communists used their control of the labor unions of the General Confederation of Labor (CGT) to unleash a series of major strikes in 1947 and 1948, bringing public services to a standstill. Opposing the strikes, the Socialists withdrew from the CGT and formed a rival union Workers' Force (Force ouvrier). Schoolteachers also set up an independent union, the National Federation of Education (Fédération de l'Education national).

While the Communists challenged the new Republic from the left, de Gaulle did likewise from the right. The general returned to politics with a new political movement. At Strasbourg on April 7, 1947, he announced the creation of the Rally for the French People (Rassemblement du peuple française, or RPF). This popular coalition was dedicated to rising above the petty political infighting of the parties. In municipal elections that October, RPF candidates secured 40 percent of the votes, and then, in the legislative elections of June 1951, the RPF placed 106 of its members in the National Assembly. Four other parties—Communist, SFIO, Radical, and Independent Peasant—received about the same number of seats, making government coalitions ever more complex.[9] Within two years, these RPF deputies had become so well assimilated into parliamentary life that de Gaulle dissolved the RPF in May 1953. The remaining RPF deputies then called themselves Social Republicans.

In March 1952 the SFIO entered the opposition, a move that increased the chances of a centrist Radical party politician becoming premier. Two significant (if short-term) Radical premiers were Antoine Pinay and Pierre Mendès-France. Pinay (March 6 to December 23, 1952) helped bring stability to French finances by the successful floating of a loan that decreased inflation. When the decrease in inflation was accompanied by a rise in unemployment, Pinay was removed from office.

Pierre Mendès-France (June 18, 1954 to February 6, 1955) extracted France from its colonial quagmire in Vietnam. France had lost control over Indochina following the Japanese conquest in 1941 and had never really been able to reassert its rule after the war because Communist Vietminh guerrillas under Ho Chi Minh controlled most of the countryside. Ho traveled to France in 1946 to try to gain at least independence under the rubric of the French Union, but talks stalled when France decided to split Indochina into four countries: Laos, Cambodia, and a northern and southern Vietnam.

Reaching no final agreement with France, Ho returned home in September. Subsequently, the French High Commissioner of Vietnam, Thierry d'Argenlieu, seized control of the country and forced the Vietminh again to become guerrilla fighters. Bao Dai, a "puppet emperor" first installed by the Japanese in World War II, was then reinstalled as leader to appease nationalist sentiment.[10] In 1948 France agreed to reunify Vietnam under his rule and within the French Union. France, however, retained all the real power in the new Vietnam as in the two other Indochinese states. Their control, however, was based in the cities; the Vietminh controlled the countryside.

The struggle took on a new level of intensity after the Communist takeover in China and the Soviet Union recognized the Vietminh. The French then turned to the United States. America, wishing to find a middle path between communism and colonialism, backed Bao Dai. The outbreak of the Korean War in June 1950 convinced America, on French prodding, that Vietnam was the southern flank of an Asian-wide Communist offensive. America stepped up its aid in the face of French reverses and applauded when the famous World War II hero General Jean de Lattre de Tassigny was appointed both commander and high commissioner at the end of 1950. By this point France had sent 200,000 troops to Indochina, of whom 90,000 were French; the rest were volunteers and legionnaires. French governments realized that this unpopular war would become even more so if large numbers of conscripts were sent. De Lattre persuaded the United States to increase its aid through his program of creating a loyal Vietnamese army. His plans were cut short, however, when he contracted cancer and died in January 1952. The U.S. government subsequently spent close to a billion dollars annually (80 percent of the war's cost) and pressed the French to prosecute the war vigorously.

Under General Henri Navarre, French forces launched an offensive in the north and tried to force the Vietnamese army to fight in the south, in a program of "pacification." The French army, however, soon found that rather than trapping the Vietminh, it had itself been encircled. At the northern fortress of Dien Bien Phu, Vietnamese General Giap surrounded and then routed the French army. The fortress fell on May 7, 1954, and the French government of Laniel fell shortly thereafter.

Pierre Mendès-France, a maverick and visionary member of the Radical Party since the 1930s, became premier as a result of the French defeat at Dien Bien Phu. Within a month, at a Geneva conference, he achieved a negotiated settlement. While North Vietnam gained its independence, under the rule of Ho Chi Minh, Laos and Cambodia became sovereign nations under noncommunist governments. In South Vietnam France continued to have some influence under the rule of Ngo Dinh Diem, a staunch Catholic and polyglot politician—part courtier, part Mandarin pending elections (that, it turned out, were never held) in 1956.

To prevent nationalist revolutions in North Africa, Mendès-France offered autonomy to Tunisia and to Morocco. These colonies became independent two years later (1956). In divesting France of some of its colonies he alienated the colonial lobby and especially the army. The debacle of Dien Bien Phu had humiliated and enraged the French army, and they were determined not to lose another colonial conflict.

During his premiership Mendès-France brought a hardheaded approach to France's domestic problems. His plan to rationalize the retail sector, by encouraging supermarkets and chain stores by an elimination of tax subsidies for small shops, met with fierce opposition from small-town and rural shopkeepers and artisans, who feared he meant to destroy their livelihoods, and the Radical party, whose most faithful supporters came from these occupational groups. The last symbolic straw for many petty bourgeois came when Mendès-France advocated an antialcohol measure: the French should drink milk rather than wine.

By early 1955 Mendès-France had accumulated too many enemies to remain in power. After flirting with his brand of fearless reform, the Radical party was back under the control of the conservatives: nevertheless, many young reformers generated a fervent following around Mendès-France and his ideas. One of his protégés among Fourth Republic ministers was François Mitterrand.

The last elections of the Fourth Republic, held in 1956, found the Radicals and the MRP shaken by the revolt of the shopkeepers and artisans during the last months of Mendès-France. The leader of this revolt, Pierre Poujade, created a party that won 11.6 percent of the vote and 531 seats in the new assembly. The MRP fell back to a weak 10.6 percent of the vote.[11] At this point, the Socialists rejoined the government now led by Guy Mollet, an admirer of Robespierre in whose hometown, Arras, he was mayor. Although elected head of the SFIO in 1946 as a Marxist, Mollet had jettisoned any radicalism by the time he became premier. This government would prove to be the longest lived, 16 months, of the Fourth Republic.

Under Mollet, France was one of the primary architects of and first entrants into the European Common Market (later known as the European Economic Community). The other countries joining Germany and France in the new Common Market included Italy, Belgium, Holland, and Luxembourg. In essence, the treaties signed in Rome on March 25, 1957, aimed to make member nations a single market with no internal tariffs among them. It was hoped that a common tariff policy would lead to further economic cooperation. At the same time, the six members pledged to develop peaceful uses for atomic energy. French negotiators bargained hard to ensure that French agriculture would continue to thrive and won concessions with the creation of a Common Agricultural Policy in 1962 that provided subsidies to farmers. Nevertheless, French farmers, due to the unprecedented agricultural expansion of the era, accepted a degree of economic competition unthinkable before 1945.

Mollet's government also passed some social welfare measures, but his tenure eventually became engulfed in the problem of Algeria. As with the Third Republic, a left-wing government moved steadily to the right under the pressure of events. Even the decolonizer Mendès-France asserted in the National Assembly that Algeria was part of France. This sentiment was widely shared because Algeria had been a French colony for over 120 years, it was home to a million European settlers (approximately one-tenth of the population), and it had seats in the National Assembly. For many French, including the young minister François Mitterrand, it was inconceivable that this part of France, a few hundred miles off the Mediterranean coast, could be split from the mainland. Over a century of deprivation, neglect, and discrimination of the indigenous Muslim majority had nevertheless bred a fervent nationalism.

The Algerian war for independence started on All Saints Day, November 1, 1954, when a string of bombings announced the presence of the National Liberation Front (Front de Libération Nationale, or FLN). By the end of 1955, the war was in full swing; only this time, France received no help from the United States, which regarded the conflict in colonial rather than Cold War terms. Despite the military force of 500,000 French soldiers (most of them conscripts), the use of torture, and the summary executions, the uprising could not be crushed. The military's determination not to lose another war added further stimulus to the ill-conceived and quickly aborted attempt to retake, along with Great Britain, the Suez Canal in late 1956. The French believed that the Egyptian nationalist leader General Gamal Abdel Nasser had not only illegally seized the canal but had also given ideological and material aid to the Algerian revolution. The quick retreat that France and England had to execute shortly after taking the Suez Canal did not increase the military's confidence in the civilian leadership.

When Mollet's government fell in May 1957 he was succeeded by two short-lived governments; in April 1958, after the fall of yet another premier, more than a month was needed for the various factions to form another administration. Rumors swept the military in Algeria that the new prime minister, the MRP's Pierre Pflimlin, was in favor of negotiation with the Algerian revolutionaries (FLN). When he was scheduled to present his cabinet in Paris on May 13, extremist colonists in Algiers organized a mammoth street demonstration to intimidate Parisian parliamentarians. The demonstration turned into a riot, and the main government building in Algiers was invaded and sacked. A Committee of Public Safety was then proclaimed.

With Algeria in revolt, mainland France also moved toward upheaval. Into the breech stepped de Gaulle, the most deft of all the manipulators.

On May 15 he proclaimed he was ready to serve but not under conditions of violent force nor parliamentary deliberation. Without a firm commitment from any one group, he was able to appeal to all sides and appeared to be above all factions (always his preferred position). He seemed to many to be the only person who could save France from either a new Popular Front or a military dictatorship. De Gaulle was supported in his maneuvers by the fact that President René Coty believed that the Fourth Republic's constitution needed revising anyway. On May 28 Pflimlin resigned, and on the following day Coty called upon "that most illustrious of Frenchmen" to form a new government. On May 31 the SFIO came out in favor of de Gaulle and on June 1–2, the National Assembly voted 329 to 224 to accept his government. He was to have full powers for six months in order to draft a new constitution.

De Gaulle's first action was to go to Algeria (June 4–7) to bring the army back in line. Amidst a large crowd of Arabs and Europeans, de Gaulle seemed once again to satisfy all factions. He did not make any firm commitments, however, but rather surveyed the situation and kept his options open.

When De Gaulle returned to Paris he set to work with a committee chaired by the Gaullist Michel Debré to draft a new constitution. Having a committee rather than a parliament write the constitution broke with French Republican tradition, but it was well in line with de Gaulle's distrust of parliaments. On September 4, 1958, the anniversary of the proclamation of the Third Republic, at the Place de la République in Paris, de Gaulle announced the constitution of his Fifth Republic. It was very much the type of constitution he had been advocating since 1946. The president, elected by an electoral college, similar to the one in the United States, to a seven-year term, held paramount power above the turmoil of parliament. The president had the authority (1) to dissolve the National Assembly, (2) to appeal directly to the French people by referendum, and (3) to assume full powers. The critical areas reserved especially for the office of president were those of foreign policy and defense. The new constitution did not fully elaborate upon the duties of the president and prime minister, however, which left much room for potential conflict. Nevertheless, the president clearly was to set the priorities and the prime minister was to implement the policies. To obviate conflict, a nine-member constitutional council supervised the institutional relations among the various branches of government. Finally, the constitution created an economic and social council with purely advisory functions.

The prime minister and parliament, while still vital, had clearly been demoted. The prime minister, no longer called a premier, was to be chosen by the president. Though the prime minister actually chose the members of his cabinet, the president officially appointed them. The constitution retained two legislative houses, but the Senate continued without veto power over the National Assembly. The power of the National Assembly was likewise limited. Parliamentarians could no longer be ministers at the same time. In addition, the parliament could sit for only six months a year, and its power to overturn a cabinet was drastically diminished. The prime minister and the parliament nevertheless retained power to mold and run the government.

Parliamentary elections would be conducted in single-member districts in two rounds. De Gaulle believed that proportional representation by departments had been too favorable to the proliferation of maverick parties and was trying to ensure that only two main parties would face each other on the second round. He also believed that single-member districts would ensure that "notables" of each department had the best shot at victory.

Much of the left, including Mendès-France and former minister Mitterrand, believed that de Gaulle's constitution ensured that the left would never gain power; however, through the efforts of Mollet, de Gaulle was able to win over most of the Socialists.

Although much of the left was in opposition, as well as such famous existentialist intellectuals as Jean-Paul Sartre and Simone de Beauvoir, the Gaullist constitutional referendum was passed by over 79 percent of the electorate. Only 15 percent of the voters abstained, the lowest figure since the Popular Front elections of 1936. Voter approval for de Gaulle was reinforced in the November 1958 parliamentary elections when the newly revived Gaullist party (now the Union for the New Republic, Union pour la Nouvelle Republique, or UNR) won 26 percent of the final vote and 198 seats. The worst fears of the left came true when the Communist party was able to garner 18.9 percent of the vote but only 10 seats; the party created by Mendès-France and Mitterrand (the Union of Democratic Forces—UFD) gained no seats at all. The electoral college chose de Gaulle as president with 78.5 percent of the vote against two leftist candidates, and de Gaulle named Debré as prime minister.[12]

One of the first moves of the new Gaullist government was to shore up the economy: the expansion that had continued since 1945 had taken a recent dip. Antoine Pinay, now finance minister, cut the budget deficit by reducing government subsidies to nationalized industries, agriculture, and consumers. He also raised indirect taxes, issued a new "heavy franc" (worth 100 old francs), terminated some currency exchange controls, and opened up the French market by lowering tariff barriers.

Along with the new political stability and the first fruits of membership in the Common Market, Pinay's economic stimulus resulted in rising French growth rates, which ultimately remained higher than the growth rates of all other Western industrialized countries for the next fifteen years. In 1963 inflation returned, but only temporarily, and the boom continued. In short, de Gaulle had a favorable economic wind in his sails as he turned to decolonization and the seemingly intractable problem of Algeria.

In October 1958 de Gaulle undertook a two-pronged approach: continuing the war and also conducting negotiations with the FLN. By the summer of 1960 French public opinion, led by union leaders and intellectuals such as Jean-Paul Sartre and Simone de Beauvoir, had publicized the policy of torture, terror, and mass detentions typical of the French army's attempt to "pacify" Algeria. Noting the growing public distaste for the Algerian war, de Gaulle called for a referendum on self-determination for Algeria. On January 8, 1961, more than 75 percent approved of freedom for Algeria. The following April, de Gaulle proclaimed that Algerians should be independent if they wished. The FLN accepted, but the right-wing general in Algeria formed the Secret Army Organization (Organization Armée Secrète, or OAS) dedicated to keeping Algeria French by any means necessary. The OAS tried to seize power in Algeria, but de Gaulle, using the emergency powers of the Fifth Republic, remained in power after three grueling days of standoff. The OAS was not finished: the organization tried twice to assassinate de Gaulle, once in September 1961 and once in August 1962.

De Gaulle's secret negotiations with the Provisional Government of Algeria (GPRA), the governmental wing of the FLN, yielded results in March 1962. The resulting Evian Accords led to a referendum in France in April 1962 in which 91 percent of the French voters approved of independence for Algeria. The OAS stepped up terrorism both in France and in Algeria, resulting in the flight of almost all Europeans out of Algeria by the end of 1962. On July 1, 1962, 99.7 percent of the Algerian voters approved the Evian Accords. De Gaulle had lost many long-term supporters, but he had pulled France out of its messiest colonial intervention.

At the end of this brutal war, France turned not only politically but also economically away from its former colony. By the end of the war,

France had lost 17,456 soldiers and over 10,000 European settlers had been killed (many at the hands of settler extremists in the OAS). Muslim casualties, civilian and combatant, were much higher. The conservative estimate is 300,000; the Algerian government claims over one million. Franco-Algerian trade declined dramatically after 1962. At its summit, 1958, France shipped virtually 20 percent of its exports across the Mediterranean, and Algeria, in turn, received over 80 percent of its goods from the hexagon. By the 1990s, while Algeria accounted for only 3 percent of French exports, France remained Algeria's primary source of imports: over 20 percent.[13]

Decolonization of the rest of the French empire went much more smoothly. In 1958 the constitution established a "French Community," which de Gaulle at first hoped would satisfy the desire for greater autonomy. But when de Gaulle realized that almost all the colonies wished for full independence, he granted it and still allowed them to stay within the French community. In 1960, preempting further problems, de Gaulle let all the colonies in sub-Sahara Africa declare their independence. Aside from a few remaining outposts, in the Caribbean and the South Pacific, the French colonial empire was dissolved. French influence in these regions, however, continued to be strong and pervasive through the mid-1990s.[14]

The assassination attempts convinced de Gaulle that the president should be elected by direct vote rather than by an electoral college, and the issue was put to a referendum in September 1962. The resulting storm of protest was one of the first constitutional crises of the Fifth Republic. Parliament protested vigorously, but de Gaulle dissolved the parliament and called for the referendum.

This referendum led to another triumph for him. The electorate in October 1962 approved the measure with 62 percent of the vote. In the November parliamentary elections, de Gaulle's UNR gained 85 seats for a total of 233, just short of a majority. Prime Minister Debré was replaced by Georges Pompidou, a former chief of staff, former lycée teacher and Rothschild banker, but new to parliament.

Besides the referendum, another of the tools the general used to speak directly to the French people was the new technology of the consumer age—television. It is appropriate that de Gaulle used the epitome of the new consumer durable goods revolution which was fully and finally coming to France under his regime.

In the mid-1950s, French economic planning and production shifted increasingly from infrastructure and production to consumption. The average French person, in short, was finally beginning to feel the effects of the economic boom of the "30 glorious years."

What ignited the consumer durables revolution of the 1960s was the fact that per capita income almost doubled between 1960 and 1975.[15] In 1850 the average French person spent 65 percent of his income on food; a century later, this percentage had shrunk to 38 percent and by 1993 amounted to a mere 14.7 percent. As a result, French consumers could spend a higher percentage of their budget on health, convenience, leisure, and entertainment items.[16] The new technology spawned the age of television, which served not only as entertainment but also as a means of direct communication between politicians and their constituents.

The rise in the number of consumer durables is impressive: only about 7.5 and 8.4 percent of families, respectively, had a refrigerator and a washing machine in 1954; by 1977 these percentages were, respectively, 92.9 and 75 percent.[17] The percentage of the French population owning cars and televisions also jumped dramatically: cars, from just 30 percent in 1960 to 50 percent by 1966, and televisions, from 26 percent in 1962 to 50 percent by 1966. The total number of cars rose from 5 million in 1958 to 15 million in 1973, and the number of televisions in the same period from 1 million to 11 million.[18] Sales of dishwashers, freezers, and bathtubs increased more slowly. Telephone sales lagged even more; in 1968, a mere 15 percent of the population had one in their homes.[19] Buying on credit, diffusion of supermarkets and hypermarkets (negligible in 1957 but more than 1,000 by 1970), and other forms of mass distribution accounted for many of these changes.[20]

Longer weekends, new types of tourism, and the emergence of the second home facilitated the growth of leisure activities. The Popular Front's two-week paid vacation was increased to three weeks in 1956 and to four weeks in 1963. In unprecedented numbers, the French traveled abroad or to second homes in the countryside; the number of these weekend or vacation homes increased more than fivefold between 1954 and 1975, from 330,000 to 1.7 million.

As befitting a leader who constantly stressed France's need to achieve grandeur to remain fully true to its heritage, de Gaulle wished for more than mere economic prosperity. He wished to make France a world leader in such high-technology fields as aerospace, automobiles, electronics, and chemicals. In promoting such growth industries (*industries de pointe*), de Gaulle not only poured huge amounts of capital into research and development but also created new industrial and technological centers around the country. Thus in 1963 a new administrative bureau, the Delegation for the Arrangement of Territory and Regional Action (the acronym in French is DATAR), was set up to distribute industries and technological expertise across the regions of France. For example, Toulouse, once a provincial backwater on the southwestern border with Spain, became the home of scientific institutes once centered in Paris; its aerospace manufacture was greatly expanded, and various electronics industries moved there. De Gaulle also oversaw an extensive transformation of the Paris region. To relieve congestion in the old central city, five new satellite cities, to house between 200,000 and 300,000, were laid out as well as a new commercial and financial complex, La Défense, west of the Arc de Triomphe and on the other side of the Seine.

De Gaulle's striving for economic grandeur produced mixed results. While industrial concentration and consolidation did produce some large conglomerations—such as Peugeot in automobiles and transportation; Thomson, electronics; Sacilor, steel; Rhône-Poulenc, chemicals; BSN, food products; and the multifaceted Bouygues, everything from energy products to tourist facilities—these companies were still dwarfed in size by American multinationals. Moreover, some of the high-profile projects, such as the supersonic passenger plane, the Concorde, failed to live up to its promise. This vast and expensive joint project with Britain, built in France and having a French e at the end of its name, ultimately resulted in the production of a mere 16 planes for commercial airlines (as opposed to the 80 or more planes that had been projected for sales).

Such prosperity and grand economic vision, one would think, should have made de Gaulle and his government extremely popular. This was not the case, however, for a variety of reasons. Intellectuals lamented what they perceived as crass commercialism and feared that France was losing its identity and becoming Americanized. Ironically, the average French person, judging by opinion polls, did not feel affluent, but instead felt less than satisfied or optimistic about economic progress. In 1969, the last year of de Gaulle's presidency, only 5 percent of the French citizenry believed that under his rule their standard of living had risen; 41 percent believed that it had remained stable, and 49 percent thought it had declined.[21]

Artisans, shopkeepers, and members of the working classes from the traditionally poorer regions of the south and west had more reason to feel this way, especially in terms of housing. After more than a century of chronic housing shortage, the post-1945 government engaged in a massive housing campaign: After only 1.7 million residential structures had been built between 1915 and 1948, 3.1 million were constructed between 1949 and 1974 and 4,338,100 additional housing between 1970 and 1978.[22] Much of this housing construction was subsidized government housing (housing of moderate rents—Habitation de loyer modere, HLM) and was large, impersonal, and poorly built. Within a generation, much of it had become dilapidated slums. Due in large part of the systematic exclusion of cafés (a measure intended to fight alcoholism) and other types of informal public settings, the new housing lacked the sociability and community of earlier working-class neighborhoods. Workers were also much less likely to get out of these dreary sites for vacations: only 40 percent of them took a holiday outside their homes, in contrast to 90 percent of the middle class.[23]

François Mitterrand exploited these sources of discontent in the 1965 presidential elections. As the candidate of a united left, he forced de Gaulle into a humiliating second-round election. Although he lost to the legend, Mitterrand gained greatly in stature by running against the founder of the Fifth Republic and by utilizing, for the first time in a presidential election, extensive television exposure. De Gaulle's margin of victory, 54.6 percent to 45.4 percent, was not large enough to preclude hope of an eventual left-wing success in future presidential elections.[24]

With the Algerian crisis resolved and his reelection campaign behind him, de Gaulle turned to completing his new conception of French diplomacy. His goal was to resurrect French glory and prestige on the world stage by gaining room to maneuver between the two superpowers, the Soviet Union and the United States. Although de Gaulle staunchly supported the United States and Western Europe in the crises over Berlin and Cuba in the early 1960s, he gradually pulled French forces out of the North American Treaty Organization (NATO), and by 1966 all NATO forces had left France. Believing that France needed nuclear weapons in order to be a credible world power, he created an independent nuclear strike deterrent (*force de frappe*). The first French atomic test was made in the Sahara in 1960: later testing took place in the French colonies of the South Pacific. Subsequently, de Gaulle refused to take part in the Geneva disarmament conference in 1963 and did not agree with the Soviet Union and the United States to suspend above-ground nuclear tests.

At the same time, de Gaulle focused on achieving closer ties with West Germany. Realizing that France, in terms of both geography and population, simply could not be a world power on its own, he sought a "European Europe" with a Franco-German alliance at its core. Toward this end, he forged a strong relationship with West German Chancellor Konrad Adenauer during the early 1960s. Subsequent French and German leaders have maintained this close relationship, which has been at the heart of the success of the European Community over the past 40 years. De Gaulle twice vetoed Great Britain's entry into the European Community on the grounds that the British were still not sufficiently "European" and would be the United States' "Trojan horse," permitting American cultural and economic influence to enter Europe by stealth.

After 1963 de Gaulle's diplomacy constantly gained world headlines. In January 1964 he recognized the People's Republic of China. In 1966 he went to Moscow and talked vaguely, but provocatively, about his idea of Europe from the Atlantic Ocean to the Ural Mountains. As the American war in Vietnam dragged on, he became an unsparing critic and later hosted the peace talks in Paris. During the Arab-Israeli war of 1967, de Gaulle had sharp (some felt anti-Semitic) words for Israel. In the same year, he journeyed to Quebec, Canada, and talked in general terms about *Québec Libre* (that is, the possibility that Quebec might become an independent nation) without fully elaborating on his position.

Overall, de Gaulle's foreign policy was built upon the idea of the permanence of nations and the transience of ideologies. He hoped that France could provide a model for national independence in a world still in thrall to the Cold War, and he wanted France to be a benefactor of Third World development as well as another pole of attraction in what he envisioned as a multipolar world. De Gaulle's unique brand of diplomacy has been substantially followed by his successors.

De Gaulle's New Year's Day message in 1968 smugly pontificated: "Amidst so many countries which are being shaken by so many upheavals, our own country will continue to offer an example of effectiveness in the conduct of her affairs."[25] Initially this prophecy seemed to come true as France was swept up in the Winter Olympics held at Grenoble and proudly united by the exploits of the French triple-gold-medal winner skier Jean-Claude Killy. The economy continued to hum along despite a mild rise in inflation and unemployment, and de Gaulle and Pompidou arranged an ambitious agenda of foreign travel for the spring.

At the end of March, however, frustrated by overcrowded facilities and what seemed like medieval rules and picayune restrictions, university students erupted in revolt. The biggest outbreak occurred at the satellite campus of the University of Paris in suburban Nanterre. Specific student demands expanded and blended with protests against the American war in Vietnam and international capitalism and sympathy for Third World revolutionaries in Asia (Mao Tse-tung in China) and Latin America (Che Guevara in Cuba and Bolivia). The French students were inspired by militant students in the United States, as well as students in

Italy and Mexico, who had also been actively fighting for justice and liberation. Finally, many were additionally inspired by the Situationists, a new group of activist artists and social theorists who wanted both personal liberation and social revolution. When the Nanterre campus was closed on May 2, the militant leadership moved their protest to the Sorbonne in Paris. On May 3 university authorities in Paris ordered the police to arrest the "agitators" and close the Sorbonne, one of France's premier universities. At this point, the university lecturers—often poorly paid, temporary teachers, pressed into duty because of surging enrollments—declared a strike in solidarity with the militant students. Demonstrations soon engulfed the Latin Quarter and led to frequent running battles with the police. The night of Friday–Saturday, May 10–11, became known as the "night of the barricades" when students overturned cars, uprooted trees, and tore out cobblestones in their fight with the police, who countered with tear gas, water hoses, and nightsticks.

The government vacillated, but finally Prime Minister Georges Pompidou's policy of conciliation prevailed over de Gaulle's desire to send in the army. Pompidou allowed the Sorbonne to reopen, and its courtyard, along with the nearby Odéon Théâtre, quickly became the scene of a spontaneous and continuous teach-in where all aspects of society were questioned and challenged.

As student protests were televised and broadcast around France, the Communist party and the CGT refused to condemn this activity as "ultra-leftist adventurism" but tried to channel it. The CGT called a one-day strike on Monday, May 13, that turned into a general workers' strike. In Paris 800,000 marchers yelled, "Ten years is enough," referring to de Gaulle's tenure. The following day, de Gaulle flew off for a state visit to Romania. Spontaneous, wildcat strikes spread during the week, until finally 10 million workers were on strike and had effectively shut down the economy.

De Gaulle returned on May 19 and tried to restore order with a television speech. His charisma deserted him, however, for he came across as old and irrelevant when he proposed holding a referendum on workers' participation in industry. Pompidou stepped into the vacuum and negotiated with union leaders at his office on Grenelle Street in the vain hope that higher wages and better conditions would bring France back to work. The young leaders were not impressed with these "Grenelle agreements" of May 27 and so the strikes continued. Responding to the growing paralysis, prominent left-wing politicians Pierre Mendès-France and Mitterrand offered to head a provisional government.

De Gaulle disappeared on May 29. In retrospect, many saw his actions as a master stroke of Machiavellian cunning, but while traveling east by helicopter to visit French troops in Germany, de Gaulle was not exactly sure himself what he wished to do. The next day, after getting encouragement from the French generals and a renewed sense of purpose, de Gaulle returned and spoke to the nation on radio. In essence he said, as he had said in 1940, 1944, and 1958, that France had two choices: himself or chaos. Accusing the Communists of scheming to take power, he dissolved the National Assembly and called for the support of all good French people. Over the following days the students, the strikers, and the left proved unable to formulate a viable alternative to de Gaulle. A demonstration of the "well-dressed," half a million strong, marched down the elegant Champs Élysées in support of the general.

The elections of June proved to be de Gaulle's last great triumph. On June 23 and again on June 30, the electorate swung massively to the right. De Gaulle's political party, the UDR (the UNR—Union for the New Republic—had been transformed into the UDR—Union for the Defense of the Republic—in response to the political crisis) won 294 seats, an absolute majority, and votes for the left fell to 41 percent.[26] In a fit of anger and jealousy, de Gaulle dismissed Pompidou, who had shown more stamina than himself throughout most of the crisis, and replaced Pompidou with the loyal Maurice Couve de Murville. Ever astute, de Gaulle then appointed a minister of education to initiate a whole-scale reform of education.

The strikes of May 1968 were caused not only by continuing inequalities, anxieties, and discontent, but also by the postwar baby-boom generation's coming of age, creating a French version of the American counterculture. Unlike America, where the unrest of the 1960s unfolded over the span of six or seven years, the French youth exploded in one dramatic moment. The baby boom of the 1940s and early 1950s was reaching adulthood by 1968 but had not yet achieved a defining self-expression. The crisis in the French university system was the cause around which that self-awareness emerged. By the late 1960s, a veritable flood of youth had reached college age—a larger college cohort than ever before because educational reforms permitted 30 percent of eighteen-year-olds to go to college as opposed to 4 or 5 percent during the prewar period and just 10 percent during the late 1950s. In 1958 France had 175,000 college students; by May of 1968 the number had almost tripled to 500,000.[27] No wonder this overwhelming number were underhoused in their dorms and understaffed in their classrooms.

The cramped conditions and restrictive policies of the French university came as a shock to a generation whose expectations had been raised extremely high by a consumer culture that had catered to their whims and desires. The consumer culture had generated a youth subculture of rock and roll—to wit, the American and English bands and French counterparts such as singers Johnny Hallyday and Sylvie Vartan—which glorified freedom, spontaneity, and self-awareness. Although the grand liberation movement of 1968 may have fizzled, the ears of the young had been opened to other voices. Once marginal or novel subcultures—feminists, gays and lesbians, prisoners, the mentally ill, immigrant groups, and the new ecology movements—all found a new means of expression in a new media age which dramatizes cultural creativity. These movements would all play a major role in French society in the subsequent decades.

Edgar Faure, de Gaulle's new education minister, made an earnest attempt to solve the problems spawned by the archaic educational structures. Eventually his reforms did address most of the worst problems, particularly overcrowding, but the upheaval continued for several years and spread to the elite high schools (*lycées*).

De Gaulle remained in power, but it was clear as the months passed that he had lost much of his former verve. He presided over the bickering that accompanied the educational reform, the continued rise in inflation and unemployment, and the controversies over the nature of public order. To reenergize his presidency and to implement some of the reforms that he had advocated in May 1968, de Gaulle submitted another referendum to the French people. He wished to augment the power of local government and to make the Senate a body that would represent not just the old notables but social and economic groups as well in a form of corporatism. In this fashion he hoped to find a middle way between capitalism and communism. One last time he put his prestige on the line, stating that if this referendum (scheduled for April 27, 1969) failed, he would resign. The situation in France, however, was no longer a matter of stark contrast between de Gaulle and disorder: Georges Pompidou let it be known that if the referendum failed he would run for president. On April 27, the referendum was, indeed, voted down, by a margin of approximately 53 to 47 percent.[28] De Gaulle delivered a terse speech stating that he would resign by noon of the following day. "Without music or fanfare," de Gaulle departed the next day for his home in the village Colombey-les-Deux-Églises and spent the last two and one-half years of his life writing his memoirs. At his death in November 1970, he became the first French head of state to have both a public and a private funeral. In this matter, as well, he remained innovative.

From our perspective at the end of the twentieth century, de Gaulle's achievement remains extremely impressive. The Fifth Republic was more durable and more flexible than even his admirers would have thought possible. The sharp battles between the left and the right, which he detested, have largely receded. He seemed able to fuse, much more effectively than any previous French ruler, the monarchal and republican strains in the French body politic.

NOTES

1. Maurice Agulhon, *The French Republic, 1879–1992* trans. Antonia Nevill (Oxford: Blackwell, 1993), p. 326.

2. Jean-Pierre Rioux, *The Fourth Republic, 1944–1958*, trans. Godfrey Rodgers (Cambridge and Paris: Cambridge University Press and Editions de la Maison des Sciences de l'Homme, 1987), p. 59.

3. William I. Hitchcock, *France Restored: Cold War Diplomacy and the Quest for Leadership in Europe, 1944–1954* (Chapel Hill: University of North Carolina Press, 1998), p. 207.

4. G. de Bertier de Sauvigny and David H. Pinkney, *History of France*, Revised and Enlarged Edition, French text trans. Jams Friguglietti (Arlington Heights, IL: Forum Press, 1983), pp. 368–369.

5. Ibid., p. 369.

6. Ibid., pp. 369–370.

7. Jean-Pierre Rioux, *The Fourth Republic, 1944–1958*, p. 110.

8. de Sauvigny and Pinkney, *History of France*, p. 373.

9. Jean Lacouture, *De Gaulle, The Ruler, 1945–1970*, trans. Alan Sheridan (New York: W. W. Norton, 1993), p. 143, and Rioux, *The Fourth Republic, 1944–1958*, p. 166.

10. M. Wall, "Indochina, Relations With," in *Historical Dictionary of the French Fourth and Fifth Republic, 1946–1991*, Wayne Northcutt, ed. (Westport, CT: Greenwood Press, 1992), p. 230.

11. Rioux, *The Fourth Republic, 1944–1958*, p. 259.

12. Lacouture, *De Gaulle, The Ruler, 1945–1970*, pp. 221–222 and 226 and Roger Price, *A Concise History of France* (Cambridge: Cambridge University Press, 1997), p. 321.

13. Alistair Horne, *A Savage War of Peace: Algeria, 1954–1962* (Harmondsworth, Middlesex, England: Penguin Books, 1965), p. 538.

14. R. A. Jonas, "Algeria, Relations With," in *Historical Dictionary of the French Fourth and Fifth Republics*, pp. 8–9.

15. Price, *A Concise History of France*, p. 282.

16. Patricia Prestwich, "Food and Drink in France," in *The Transformation of Modern France*, William B. Cohen, ed. (Boston: Houghton Mifflin, 1997), p. 166.

17. de Sauvigny and Pinkney, *History of France*, p. 387.

18. Colin Jones, *The Cambridge Illustrated History of France* (Cambridge: Cambridge University Press, 1994), p. 290.

19. Price, *A Concise History of France*, p. 292.

20. John Ardagh, *France in the New Century: Portrait of a Changing Society* (London: Viking, 1999), p. 634.

21. Richard F. Kuisel, *Seducing the French: The Dilemma of Americanization* (Berkeley: University of California Press, 1993), p. 152.

22. Gérard Mermet, *Francoscopie: Les Français: qui son-ils? Où vont-ils?* (Paris: Larousse, 1989), p. 181, section Logement, en vrac. My thanks to Professor William B. Cohen for this source.

23. Jones, *The Cambridge Illustrated History of France*, p. 292.

24. de Sauvigny and Pinkney, *History of France*, p. 385 and Jeremy D. Popkin, *A History of Modern France* (Englewood Cliffs, NJ: Prentice Hall, 1994), p. 326.

25. Daniel Singer, *Prelude to Revolution: France in May 1968* (New York: Hill and Wang, 1970), p. 37.

26. de Sauvigny and Pinkney, *History of France*, p. 390.

27. Ted Neather, "Education and Training," in *Modern France: Society in Transition*, Malcolm Cook and Grace Davie, eds. (London: Routledge, 1999), p. 179, and Singer, *Prelude to Revolution*, pp. 44–45.

28. Lacouture, *De Gaulle, The Ruler, 1945–1970*, p. 575.

11

After de Gaulle: Experimentation and Consolidation (1969–1988)

After the shock of the strikes and student revolt of May 1968 and the retirement of Charles de Gaulle, could any Gaullist politician, much less a politician from any other party, prove that the Fifth Republic was not simply the general's own personal creation, one that was destined to die with him? Over the course of the following two decades, despite a persistent economic crisis after 1974 and three different presidents from three different political parties, the answer proved to be a resounding yes. Under the successive presidencies of the Gaullist Georges Pompidou (1969–1974), the liberal Valéry Giscard d'Estaing (1974–1981), and the Socialist François Mitterrand (1981–1995), the Fifth Republic was revised in three different ideological fashions. By the end of Mitterrand's first term in 1988, the economic crisis had not been solved (but then again no nation had been able to do that), but the Fifth Republic had become fully stabilized.

De Gaulle's abrupt departure in 1969 forced a new presidential election three years ahead of schedule. His former prime minister, Georges Pompidou, emerged immediately as the front runner in the race even though the interim president, Alain Poher, also chose to run. A man of diverse talents and tastes, Pompidou had served on de Gaulle's staff during and after World War II and then as director of the Rothschild bank, before finally returning to government service. A bon vivant, a lover of modern art, and more approachable than de Gaulle, Pompidou promised to carry on the general's work. Poher, a Catholic moderate-liberal candidate, represented a center-right alternative to Gaullism. Having failed in their bid to form a provisional government in May–June 1968, neither Pierre Mendès-France nor Mitterrand ran. The plethora of left-wing candidates—four of them—indicated an initial fragmentation of the left.

Using the new supersonic Concorde plane as his campaign symbol, Pompidou won easily. With the left unable to place a candidate into the second round, Poher outpolled the Communist candidate Jacques Duclos by 5,200,000 to 4,800,000, revealing the depth of the left's disarray.[1] De Gaulle did not intervene in any way; he merely approved of Pompidou's victory after the fact.

Once at the Élysée Palace (the French equivalent of the White House), Pompidou proved to be more pragmatic than his mentor in politics and economics and less strident in foreign affairs. He did not engage in grand gestures on the world stage. For example, he supported Great Britain's entry into the European Economic Community. In domestic affairs, he displayed both caution and daring. As one might expect of a former banker, he followed the classic laissez-faire liberal approach in economics. On questions of urban renovation and artistic innovation, however, this lover of modern art proved more daring. In Paris Pompidou oversaw extensive urban renovation and the creation of a museum of modern and contemporary art that eventually bore his name.

Pompidou selected a Gaullist prime minister "baron" (who had served with de Gaulle in London during the war), the flexible Chaban-Delmas. Under Chaban, parliament played an enhanced role. He envisaged a "new society" based upon cooperation, tolerance, and greater flexibility—in short, he attempted to resolve the alienation that had spawned the May 1968 events. When his initiatives seemed to take an overly statist turn—envisioning an extensive expansion of government programs—Pompidou replaced him in July 1972 with a more reliably conservative, law-and-order politician, Pierre Messmer. Pompidou's government showed that the Gaullists did not need de Gaulle in order to rule. Indeed, under the capable hands of Pompidou, the Gaullist movement became an even more formidable political machine now that it had to function without the general's personal charisma.

Conservatism in economic issues served Pompidou well. The economic expansion of the "Thirty Glorious Years" (*trente glorieuses*) continued to hum along. Indeed, French growth rates in the late 1960s and early 1970s were so impressive (ahead of all other European nations) that some American forecasters believed France's economy would eventually outstrip Germany's. Under Pompidou the French telephone industry finally started to meet the needs of its citizens: only about 14 percent of homes had a phone in 1968; 75 percent, by 1982.[2]

Pompidou also made his most memorable mark (or blight, depending on one's perspective) on Paris by pushing through more expressways for cars (along the Right Bank of the Seine, the expressway bears his name). He also transferred the central market (Les Halles) to suburban Rungis and transformed the old market area into a shopping mall. A nearby area was converted into an avant-garde art museum and cultural center that carries his name. In addition, American-style skyscrapers appeared in Paris at Montparnasse and Bercy, on the Left Bank, and at a new office complex just across the Seine at La Défense (on the western axis from the Arc de Triomphe). These works, along with slum clearance that had been going on since the late 1950s, made Paris a cleaner, healthier, and more "modern" city. Although Pompidou conjoined Paris and the automobile, he did so at the cost of more congestion, more pollution, and the loss of much of the ambiance that had attracted expatriates from the 1920s through the 1950s.

Despite continued economic expansion, the stresses and strains that had led to May 1968 were still not resolved. Adopting some of the issues espoused by the Left, Pompidou continued the educational reforms of de Gaulle's last year and granted more power and regional autonomy. Under Pompidou, for the first time since their creation in the 1790s, the departments lost power to new regional assemblies. At the same time, economic modernization in the chronically underdeveloped south became more significant. The aerospace industry centered around Toulouse, oil refining around Marseilles, and new tourist complexes on the coast of Languedoc. To lessen the perception of the presidency as an aloof and authoritarian institution, Pompidou tried to get a referendum to reduce the presidential term from seven to five years, but his measure did not make it out of parliament.

A new problem, not central to May 1968, also began to emerge. In the mid-1960s the nature of immigration into France had started to change. The flow of European immigrants declined, and the flow from Africa and Asia even increased. As a result, racial tensions began to rise. In response to a growing number of attacks against non-European immigrants, Pompidou's government enacted a law (in July 1972) against racism and increased (but only to a small degree) social welfare benefits for immigrants.

Pompidou's liberal measures could not stop the reemergence of the left. Though the 1968 elections had been a debacle, the energy of the streets was percolating through society, not only on the issues of feminism, ecology, gay liberation, and rights of prisoners and patients, but also in the reorganization of the noncommunist left. Following 1968 Mitterrand redoubled his efforts at party building. His goal was to create a strong noncommunist left from the remnants of the old Socialist party (or SFIO), the followers of Mendès-France, and various political clubs. In June 1971, at the Epinay Congress, Mitterrand became first secretary, strategist, and leader of the new Socialist party. This move did, indeed, quickly tap the energies of the noncommunist left.

Although the Communists and Socialists were extremely wary of each other, they were able to forge a common program for the 1973 parliamentary elections. Joined by the left part of the old Radical party (MRG), their alliance made for a close race in the popular vote: 46.9 percent to 45.5 percent; however, with the two-tier single-seat voting system, the Gaullist UDR retained power by picking up 278 of 490 seats in the National Assembly.[3] The news was especially good for the new Socialist party: they had polled as many votes as the Communists.

Pompidou and Messmer now altered the government's composition. Another old Gaullist, Michel Debré, was dropped. Pompidou also helped maneuver education reformer Edgar Faure past his rival Chaban-Delmas into the post of president of the National Assembly. The old Gaullists, in short, were on the way out. Increasingly, the two most influential ministers around Pompidou were Giscard d'Estaing at the Ministry of Finance and Raymond Marcellin at the Ministry of the Interior. Giscard proved to be photogenic on television. News shots of him with his accordion or on the soccer field promoted him as a "man of the people."

In the fall of 1973, the Pompidou government and France suddenly confronted a dramatic change in the world economy. The Arab-Israeli conflict led to an Arab oil embargo that increased the price of a barrel of oil by 400 percent.[4] Since France had based much of its post-1945 economic prosperity on cheap oil (and used more oil than either Great Britain or Germany), this dramatic jump hit the French economy with special severity. France, like the rest of the world, faced an era of economic crisis. Unemployment shot up, production plummeted, and inflation soared.[5] After averaging a yearly increase of 3.8 percent between 1963 and 1969, and then 5.9 percent between 1970 and 1973, prices would register an annual increase of 10.7 percent between 1974 and 1980. The result was an unprecedented, and seemingly impossible, economic condition: simultaneous recession and inflation. Economists soon termed this novel situation "stagflation."

Pompidou's government proved no more adept than any other in the West in dealing with the crisis. One measure taken in 1974 to counter growing unemployment was to restrict immigration. Henceforth the only immigration permitted would be to reunite family members of immigrants already in the country. As a result, the various ethnic communities became more permanent. As it turned out, however, Pompidou's tenure as president came to an end much faster than anyone could have anticipated. After his doctors told him that he had cancer, Pompidou kept his condition a closely guarded secret and plunged back into work. Before he made his condition public or designated a successor, he died on April 2, 1974. Amidst economic turbulence, France found itself faced with presidential elections.

When Prime Minister Pierre Messmer declined to run, the Gaullist UDR selected Chaban-Delmas as a candidate. This choice did not garner unanimous assent. A portion of the party, led by Jacques Chirac, split away and supported Giscard d'Estaing, head of the Independent Republicans—a party Chirac had founded—believing that Giscard had a better chance of victory. Honing his pleasant television personality and brandishing his slogan, "Change with continuity," Giscard gained the votes of the non-Gaullist centrists and the liberals.

Chaban, Giscard, and a dozen other candidates faced a united left who once again ran François Mitterrand. Television played an expanded role and seemed to favor Giscard who projected a vigorous personality. The first round found Mitterrand with a higher percentage of votes (43.4 percent) than Giscard (33 percent).[6] As during the 1965 and 1969 presidential elections, a second round of elections was needed because no candidate had won more than 50 percent of the vote. During the second round, Giscard was able to eke out a razor-thin victory, 50.8 to 49.2 percent.[7]

Giscard moved into the Élysée Palace and promised to reshape France into "an advanced liberal society."[8] The continuing world economic downturn limited Giscard's initiatives in the economic sphere, but in the political and social spheres new laws did bring about significant changes. In particular, he targeted the rising feminist movement.

Although the new feminist action and consciousness were being developed in neighborhoods, universities, and workplaces, prominent public events also publicized women's oppression and aspirations. In 1970 some activitists placed a wreath at the Tomb of the Unknown Soldier, not for the soldier but for someone they asserted was even less known: his wife. In 1973 a manifesto calling for free, legal abortion appeared in the liberal magazine *Le Nouvel observateur*; 343 women, including prominent intellectuals and feminists such as Simone de Beauvoir, novelist Françoise Sagan, and actress Catherine Deneuve—signed the manifesto.

To appeal to women, Giscard named two women to cabinet posts: politician Simone Veil for the Department of Health and journalist Françoise Giroud as secretary of state for the condition of women. These women helped pass laws long desired by millions of women: a 1974 law liberalized the dissemination and sale of contraceptives (first permitted in 1967); and a 1975 law made abortion both available and more accessible. Another law in 1975 made divorce more easily obtainable.

To appeal to the youth, Giscard lowered the voting age from 21 to 18 and tried, by expanding the secondary school curriculum, to provide greater opportunities for the children of the working classes to go to college. He also addressed another of the 1968 complaints by loosening government control over radio and television. He also continued to cultivate the image of a young, dynamic, informal leader in touch with the people by dropping in unexpectedly on ordinary families at dinner time.

On the economic front, however, Giscard policies met with little initial success or subsequent popular support. In 1974 Prime Minister Chirac tried to end the recession by the Keynesian methods used since 1945 by almost all industrial nations (pumping money into the economy to stimulate purchasing power). In this changed economic environment, however, the result was a swollen budget deficit and a roaring 15.2 percent inflation.[9] The left capitalized on this poor economic performance and continued to gain in the opinion polls. Increasingly, too, Chirac quarreled with Giscard over the best means of blunting the rising influence of the left. At the end of August 1976, Chirac resigned and was replaced by Raymond Barre, minister of foreign trade and a liberal economist. Barre followed the new economic policy of monetarism, which argued that the best way to fight inflation was to raise interest rates and cut social spending.

Chirac then embarked on his own fateful political agenda. He refashioned the UDR into the RPR (Rassemblement pour la République) modernizing the party, pushing old Gaullists still farther into the background, and preparing for a future run at the presidency. Young militants and parliamentarians became the nucleus of the RPR. In early

1977, when Giscard restored the position of mayor of Paris (abolished after the Paris Commune), Chirac ran against Giscard's hand-picked choice, Michel d'Ornano. In the March 1977 municipal elections, Chirac won in Paris, and the left made strong gains, especially in the west. Chirac's party and presence at the Paris city hall forced Giscard to moderate his liberalism to preserve his center-right coalition.

On top of these political setbacks, the anti-inflationary policies that Barre adopted to fight inflation, although stabilizing the economy, led to increasing unemployment, a little over 4.0 percent in 1976 to around 6.3 in 1980.[10] Labor costs played a part in inflation, along with the steep increase in the price of oil. Indeed, French labor costs had become much higher than those of its industrial competitors. During the 1970s, too, social security payments increased faster in France than in all the rest of the European Community and North America except Sweden and the Netherlands. During these same years, French business lagged in its investments in new machines and factories.

Political infighting between Giscard and Chirac over the faltering economy thus gave the left a reason to expect victory in the 1978 parliamentary elections, but, in September 1977, with the elections only eight months away, the Communists and Socialists dissolved their alliance.

In essence, the Communists feared that their once dominant status on the left was being endangered by the steady growth of the Socialists. But the Communists' problems were as much sociological as political. The factory workers and their closely knit neighborhoods were declining in importance due to technological change and urban renewal. In 1968 the number of workers reached a peak of 39 percent and then started to decline: 37.6 percent in 1975, 32.3 percent in 1985, and 25.4 in 1996.[11] Even more dramatic was the decrease in the number of union members, a two-thirds drop between 1974 and 1993.[12] At the same time, the number of white-collar workers rose from 52 percent in 1975 to 59.4 percent in 1985 and virtually 70 percent in 1996.[13] The Socialist party did well with white-collar workers, especially teachers. After 1981 one-third of Mitterrand's ministers and Socialist party parliamentary deputies were teachers. In short, the Communist base was in decline and the Socialist base was on the ascent.

Although the right won the 1978 elections, Giscard's troubles did not end. The split in the left did ensure that Giscard retained a friendly parliament after the March elections, though with only 50.5 percent of the vote.[14] The following year, 1979, brought more problems for Giscard. A second oil crisis caused by the Iranian revolution doubled the price of oil and made Barre's austerity program even more austere, cutting government programs and freezing wages and prices. On top of these jolts, scandal surfaced. The satirical daily *Le Canard enchaine* ("the Manacled duck") broke the news in October of a gift of diamonds to Giscard by the corrupt, despotic African ruler who called himself "Emperor Bokassa." In addition, unfortunately, over the previous few years, Giscard had become a more remote, isolated, and regal president, even to the extent of demanding a more somber rendition of the national anthem, the "Marseillaise" Nevertheless, opinion polls still showed him ahead of Mitterrand (often by as much as 20 percent) for the 1981 elections. Even so, growing tensions between Giscard and Chirac's RPR in parliament indicated that the election might not go smoothly. By the spring of 1980, the left union, sensing victory, was back on track.

In the presidential elections of 1981, four major candidates faced off in the first round, Giscard and Chirac on the right and Mitterrand and Georges Marchais, the head of the Communists, on the left. In this election, Mitterrand seemed to have mastered the modern marketing techniques of political candidates. His theme *"la force tranquille"* (the tranquil force) showed a reassured Mitterrand against the backdrop of a rural church.[15] In television debates, now reaching 90 percent of French homes instead of 70 percent in 1970, with Giscard, Mitterrand came across as the more relaxed and self-possessed candidate.[16] Giscard, in contrast, seemed gaunt, imperious, and older than Mitterrand though actually fifteen years younger. Nevertheless, on the first round, Giscard obtained 28.31 percent of the vote; Mitterrand, 25.84 percent; Chirac, 18.00 percent; and Marchais, 15.34 percent.[17] In the second round, Marchais instructed the Communists to vote for Mitterrand; Chirac, in a decisive move, told his voters to do what they pleased. The result was a small but highly significant victory for Mitterrand: 51.75 to 48.24 percent.[18] The "eternal loser" (Giscard's phrase for Mitterrand) had proven his own prediction wrong: the left could win under de Gaulle's Fifth Republic. The left's victory was greeted with a joy and anticipation not seen since 1936, but without the same level of hope, anxiety, and action. After all, France had become an "affluent society" in which the welfare state cushioned the worst of the economic downturn. Labor would not, therefore, occupy factories or go out on strike as they had during previous times of leftist ascension to power.

After his victory Mitterrand—doing what he had previously criticized de Gaulle for doing—called for new parliamentary elections to extend his mandate. The results of these two rounds of parliamentary elections

were even better than the Socialists anticipated: an absolute Socialist parliamentary majority. The Socialists now had 285 deputies, the Communists 44, and the center-right only 152. The French populace seemed to
have given Mitterrand and the Socialists a clear mandate.

What would a left-wing French government mean in the context of
the economically troubled 1980s? The answer, in large part, can be found
in the character of Mitterrand himself. One of the best short sketches of
Mitterrand has been penned by French historian Maurice Agulhon: "authority and charm, eloquence and skillfulness, a refined culture and
Machiavellian savoir-faire, the society allure of the town and the rustic
allure of the country-side."[19] Mitterrand had campaigned on the platform
that his "French style of socialism" would deliver a real break with capitalism and be more radical than Western Social Democracy while at the
same time more libertarian than the Soviet Union's version of socialism.
What would this mean in practice?

Mitterrand initiated his presidency with a series of symbolic acts
meant to place the Socialist victory within the context of the history of
left-wing republicanism. He visited the Panthéon—the memorial resting
place on the Left Bank for national heroes—and placed a red rose—the
Socialist party's symbol—on the tombs of antislavery advocate Victor
Schoelcher, turn-of-the-century socialist leader Jean Jaurès, and resistance
hero and leader Jean Moulin. Mitterrand also held a special reception at
the Élysée Palace for Mendès-France, who had been his patron during
the Fourth Republic. He also visited the Tomb of the Unknown Soldier
under the Arc de Triomphe on May 21. Finally, Mitterrand restored the
tempo of the "Marseillaise" to a military march. By these actions, he
united the cult of national defense and the cult of the revolution and
paid his respects to the Fourth Republic. Mitterrand was inclusive in his
cabinet appointments; he selected six women and four Communists. The
Communists filled such minor positions as health and transportation—
not, as the right feared, to show how far left Mitterrand was willing to
go, but to ensure that the Communists could not snipe at him from a
position outside of the government (as they had in 1936). The women
ministers assumed more crucial positions, for example, in agriculture
and the environment. Mitterrand also upgraded the Office of Women's
Affairs to the Ministry of Women's Rights.

Mitterrand also addressed the issues of human rights and freedom of
speech and expression. The government quickly issued an amnesty for
149,000 illegal immigrants. The death penalty was abolished in 1981, and
the political powers of the courts were either curbed or, in the case of

courts dealing strictly with political crimes, abolished. Local radio stations were freed of government regulation in 1981, and in 1982 an independent broadcasting agency, free of government control, was established.

To spark a renaissance in public participation at the local level, Mitterrand enacted a comprehensive program of administrative decentralization and placed it in the hands of Gaston Defferre, the long-standing mayor of Marseilles. His reform, carried out between 1982 and 1986, was one of the most radical and durable measures of Mitterrandist socialism. In 1982 local representative bodies (especially at the departmental but also at the regional level) gained greater control over spending. Departmental prefects could now only monitor, rather than supervise and ratify, the budgets of the presidents of the new departmental councils and the 22 regional councils. The budgetary powers of mayors and municipal councils were also augmented. In addition, starting in 1986, departmental councils became elective. Although these measures did, indeed, produce more local control and flexibility in economic development, they also led to corruption.

To spark a cultural renewal in Paris, Mitterrand embarked upon an extensive architectural enhancement of Paris and other major French cities. His work in Paris has justly drawn the most extensive amount of attention. Not since the time of Napoleon III and Baron Georges Haussmann had any president or his administration created so many new public monuments. Mitterrand drew upon a wide array of French and foreign architects. After arriving in office, he expanded a project to turn the former slaughterhouse on the northeast of Paris, La Villette, into a science museum. The initial design of French architect Adrien Fainsilber was expanded to include music and cinema facilities too. Mitterrand then initiated the following projects: American architect I. M. Pei's glass pyramid at the Louvre museum; Danish architect Otto von Spreckelsen's great arch at the La Défense business complex directly west of the Arc de Triomphe on the Champs Élysées; French architect Jean Nouvel's Institute of the Arab World south of Notre Dame cathedral on the Left Bank; Canadian architect Carloss Ott's opera house on the Place de la Bastille on the east side of Paris; and, finally, French architect Dominique Perrault's new grand national library at Tolbiac on the Left Bank of the Seine at the city's edge. Although many of these projects have drawn much criticism, they have already transformed Parisian cultural life.

Mitterrand chose an old-fashioned Socialist militant politician, Pierre Mauroy, as the prime minister to enact his "break with capitalism." As mayor of the large, northern textile city of Lille, Mauroy embodied the socialism of traditional factory workers. The new Socialist government set about to reverse Barre's austerity program with an ambitious program to expand the economy through Keynesian stimulation, which Chirac had done in 1974, combined with nationalization and a generous increase in welfare payments and services. Mitterrand and Mauroy were convinced that this program would jump-start the French economy and provide a model to the rest of the world. Pumping money into the economy, they postulated, would spur economic expansion and reduce unemployment. To be able to direct the economic expansion into the most efficient and productive avenues, the government would nationalize the remaining private financial institutions as well as some of the most important sectors of the economy. Rather than the usual Social Democratic strategy of nationalizing only companies in trouble (often called "lemon socialism"), Mitterrand proposed to bring under state control some of the most advanced high-technology companies in electronics. The government could then help spur technological innovation. By the end of 1982, 13 of France's 20 largest companies were nationalized, and the percentage of the labor force employed by nationalized companies rose to 20 percent. In addition, to further reduce unemployment, 140,000 jobs were created in the public sector.[20]

At the same time, the Socialists rewrote employment legislation (the 1981 Auroux laws) to favor workers rather than employers. The minimum wage was raised by 10 percent; family allowances, housing subsidies, old-age pensions, and medical benefits were increased by from 25 to 50 percent. In addition, the 40-hour workweek was cut back by one hour with no loss in pay, and a fifth week of paid vacation was added.[21] To pay for these benefits, Mitterrand increased employer taxes and introduced a wealth tax on the biggest fortunes in France.

Within a year, this brave and comprehensive experiment in social transformation was in trouble. Mitterrand and his government found that one nation could not adopt an inflationary economic program when the other major Western leaders (Helmut Schmidt, then Helmut Kohl in Germany, Margaret Thatcher in England, and Ronald Reagan in the United States) had adopted the deflationary policies of monetarism (the economic theory that the best way to fight inflation is to raise interest rates to restrict the circulation of money). Imported goods, rather than French products, were the beneficiaries of the program of economic stimulus; unemployment increased, and French capital flew out of the country (into countries with higher interest rates). The disparity between low

French and high international interest rates forced Mitterrand's government to devalue the franc three times between 1981 and 1983. Moreover,
between 1981 and 1984, the French economy grew at a weak 1.5 percent
per annum, and unemployment rose to over 2 million after November
1981.[22]

After losses in the March 1983 municipal elections, the Socialists took
a dramatic U-turn. The government developed an austerity program and
adopted the deflationary strategy that had been earlier shunned. The
proposed Savary law on education, giving the government tighter control over Catholic schools, was withdrawn in the summer of 1984 following a massive protest staged in Paris. Freedom from government control
rather than Catholicism was the great issue for the one million middle-
class marchers, who did not wish the educational options of their children to be narrowed.

Elections for the European Parliament, which had occurred just before
this demonstration, registered dissatisfaction with the Socialist experiment in new and ominous ways. The major surprise was neither the
Socialist plunge to only 21 percent of the vote nor the continued decline
of the Communists, but the sudden emergence of a new hard-right party,
the National Front, which won 11 percent of the vote.[23] In 1981, when
the National Front's leader, Jean-Marie Le Pen, had tried to run for the
presidency, he could not even obtain signatures of the 500 political "notables" necessary to be put on the ballot. Instead he called for his supports to vote for Joan of Arc. During the legislative elections of the same
year, his party had polled less than 1 percent of the vote.[24]

Le Pen's career encapsulates much of the history of the French extreme
right since 1945. Born into a conservative middle-class family in Brittany,
Le Pen attended a Jesuit high school, then the conservative Paris Law
Faculty. While in law school he developed his abilities as a debater,
brawler, and organizer. In addition he handled the security needs of the
right-wing politician Jacques Isorni. Before obtaining his law degree, Le
Pen enlisted in a French Foreign Legion paratroop division where he
served first in Indochina, then at Suez, then in Algeria. In between these
military stints, he became associated with the small shopkeeper movement of Pierre Poujade and won election to the parliament in his party.
After breaking with Poujade, he drifted into circles close to the extremists
who were determined to keep Algeria French at all costs. Between the
fall of Algeria (1962) and the founding of the National Front (1972), Le
Pen ran an advertising firm, sold recordings of Nazi songs, and associ-

ated himself with a wide variety of extremist politicians and intellectuals. Le Pen calls these years his years of "crossing the desert."[25]

The growing unemployment and economic downturn of the late 1970s and early 1980s set the stage for the National Front's rise. At first, the question of immigration was marginal to the National Front's cult of French racism, the cult of Le Pen as leader, and the notion, similar to that of Nazism, of the "new man." Not until the late 1970s did the National Front declare that the cause of unemployment was the immigrants taking the jobs of "real French people." By the 1981 presidential election, Giscard d'Estaing was making the same link between unemployment and immigration, and even some Communist mayors were blaming immigrants for a variety of problems. By the mid-1980s, according to opinion polls, 60 percent of the French people opposed the Socialist proposal to give immigrants the vote in local elections.[26] The Socialists dropped the proposal.

In 1984 Le Pen's party did especially well among disaffected bourgeois voters, who wished to register their sharp disapproval with the failure of the traditional Right, as well as among the young and the unemployed, who focused their anxieties on immigrants. Ironically, the National Front had its greatest success often not in areas of high immigrant concentration but in areas (such as in the eastern department of Alsace) where few immigrants lived. Their vote was obviously motivated more from fear than experience. By the end of the 1980s, however, the National Front had established a broader and deeper appeal in the French electorate, having made especially large inroads into the working class (but not in areas where the Communists retained a strong grassroots presence). Research found that the National Front had hardened into as solid and as loyal a block of voters as could be found in France.[27]

The National Front's party structure and expertise in organizing and mobilizing at the local level permitted this ongoing success. Until 1998 Le Pen held a tight reign on his hierarchy with its central committee at the top and its party militants on the street. In addition, the Front benefited from a think tank—the watch club (*club de l'horloge*)—in which it could develop its ideology and a network of newspapers. Despite periodic anti-Semitic and pro-Hitler statements, Le Pen and his followers have tried to shed the image of racist extremists. Instead of talking about race, they refer to culture; instead of asserting the supremacy of French and the inferiority of non-European culture, they stress their right to cultural difference and assert that French culture will be destroyed by globalization. This effort to make the Front's ideas appear moderate and commonsensical has achieved a measure of success. By the 1990s a third of the French public, according to opinion polls, agreed with some of his ideas, usually on immigration—that there are too many immigrants in France and that they pose a threat to the national identity.[28]

Le Pen and his party put squarely on the national agenda during the 1980s and the 1990s the questions of immigration, French identity in an increasingly multicultural world, and the nature of citizenship.

To counter Le Pen's growing popularity, the Socialists and others on the French Left launched an antiracist movement entitled SOS-Racisme in 1984. Its leaders, appropriately, included a Socialist party member, Julien Dray of Algerian Jewish origins, and Harlem Désir, born in Guiana, whose father originally came from the French Caribbean island of Martinique. Dray and Désir proved expert at catching media attention with a striking yellow hand symbol emblazoned with the slogan, "Keep your hands off my pal" and by sponsoring rock concerts and by granting television interviews. Although its connections to the Socialist party subsequently alienated some immigrant groups, who felt they were being used, Désir was right to note, "We have forced a part of French society to look at what it really is; sick from old age and fear. . . . This kind of racism is the expression of a retreat, a reflex of fear in face of others and of a style of living . . . that is different."[29]

During the mid-1980s Mitterrand and the Socialists embraced another aspect of cultural mixing: Francophonie. This concept, referring to areas of the world where French is spoken and advocating closer cultural if not also economic and political contact, was first championed by the poet and later president of Senegal, Léopold Sédar Senghor as well as by French Canadian nationalists. It took a few decades following decolonization, however, for a French president to promote this idea. Mitterrand did this in 1982 and held the first of several international summits of Francophone nations four years later, in 1986. He asserted, "We are carriers of a culture that can have the ambition of being universal."[30]

Despite Mitterrand's energetic innovations across the economic, political, and cultural landscape, the rise of the National Front revealed deep discontent with the new Socialist government. The continuing rise of unemployment meant that the Socialists might lose the 1986 parliamentary elections. In preparation for these elections, Mitterrand replaced Pierre Mauroy in 1984 and appointed a dynamic, young technocrat from the National Administrators College (ENA), Laurent Fabius, as prime minister. At this point, the Communists, whose popularity was plummeting, left the government.

With the dream of a Socialist France in tatters, the party turned increasingly to energizing the institutions of the European Community. The Socialists hoped that France could turn Europe into a strong and unified economic entity, and that they, as Europe's new leaders, could have more freedom and effectiveness over economic decisions. Toward this end, French Finance Minister Jacques Delors became president of the European Commission, the advisory board of the European Union, which contained the germ of an idea for a single European market and currency. But the sharp rightward turn the Socialists had taken disillusioned many supporters, especially as Fabius sounded more and more like Giscard's finance minister, Raymond Barre.

Fabius's program emphasized cutting inflation and promoting productivity. The hope was that these measures would restore business confidence, increase productivity and profitability, and result in the hiring of more workers. Public spending declined, and further wage restraints and tax incentives began to restore business confidence. By the 1986 elections, inflation was down to 5 percent, economic growth had picked up, and exports had increased. Unemployment had risen to over 10 percent, but job creation and early retirement prevented further increases.[31] Fabius turned to neo-liberal ideas to "relaunch" the economy: business-friendly policies curbing taxes, wages, and government spending.[32] The economy, though somewhat improved, was not at all in the shape that the Socialists had promised after the 1981 elections. Therefore, to stem potential losses, a compliant parliament in 1985 passed Mitterrand's electoral law restoring a degree of proportional representation in the departments. Many observers believed that Mitterrand took this step to enhance the chances of the National Front's winning seats in parliament, thereby preventing the mainstream right from either winning the elections or forcing a coalition government.

The 1986 parliamentary elections showed the electorate's frustration with the Socialists. Jacques Chirac led a center-right coalition—including Giscard's and Barre's supporters—to victory: 286 seats to the Socialist party's 212.[33] The proportional representation helped the National Front gain more seats than any other right-wing movement had won since Poujade in 1956. In fact, the National Front gained as many seats as the Communist party (35). In this election, the National Front picked up much working-class support among former Communist voters who feared immigrants.

The first Socialist experiment in governance came to an end. Despite his loss, however, Mitterrand would show that a leftist government could survive in the Fifth Republic and not have its power slowly drained away by increasingly conservative coalitions, as had happened in the Third and Fourth Republics.

After the elections, Mitterrand and Chirac were forced to become constitutional innovators. Mitterrand refused to resign and was forced to choose a prime minister and approve a cabinet from the opposition parties. From these circumstances came the term "cohabitation," meaning that one party held the presidency and another the parliament. A division of labor was worked out which allowed the government to function smoothly: Chirac ran internal affairs, and Mitterrand concentrated on foreign affairs and defense. This distribution of power worked largely because Chirac and Mitterrand shared essentially the same vision of French foreign policy and even, to some extent, domestic policy. Although Chirac talked favorably about Thatcher's program in England and Reagan's in the United States, neither he nor his coalition was prepared to attack or dismantle the French welfare state as his conservative counterparts across the English Channel and the Atlantic Ocean wished to do.

Chirac promised to promote a Reagan-style supply-side prosperity and, looking to win votes from the National Front, to be tough on immigrants and crime. Once in power his finance minister, Alain Madelin, tried to implement the supply-side theory, which called for removing or curtailing government regulation and control on businesses so they could maximize their profits and, in theory, make society more prosperous. Madelin started to denationalize the industry brought under state control by the Socialists. Much of the rest of the Socialist program was also revised: wage and price controls were abolished, bosses regained broad latitude to fire workers, the wealth tax was abolished, and income-tax rates were cut at the upper levels. Decentralization and the liberalization of television and radio, not surprisingly, remained in place. To satisfy the growing strength of the National Front, Chirac passed a law in 1986 restricting immigration, which had already been drastically cut, and tightening residence requirements for immigrants already in France.

Unable to guide internal affairs, Mitterrand posed as a leader above politics, concerned only with the national interest, much as de Gaulle had wished the president to do. Mitterrand's Olympian detachment, however, did not preclude criticizing Chirac as heartless for the right's austerity program, which had cut welfare benefits, restricted workers' rights, and tightened an already restrictive immigration policy. When Chirac's education minister tried to give greater autonomy to universities over admissions, the students took to the streets in numbers not seen since 1968 in an effort to protect the right of all students with baccalaureats to go to college. Again in imitation of 1968, a series of spontaneous strikes erupted in protest over stagnant wages. Chirac's popularity fell when he failed to deliver on his two primary promises: restoring prosperity and standing tough on crime. In the summer of 1986, a string of terrorist bombings by various Arab groups in the Middle East hit Paris; in late 1987, the privatization program suffered a setback when stock markets around the world crashed. While such crimes tarnished Chirac's image, Mitterrand's luster grew, according to opinion polls. Economic growth rose from an average of 1.5 percent per year (between 1980 and 1986) to over 3 percent in 1988 and 1989, but this spurt did not help Chirac electorally.[34]

From the moment he became prime minister, it was clear that Chirac would run for president in 1988. Mitterrand, however, kept silent about his own plans until an advantageous moment. With public opinion polls showing much dissatisfaction with Chirac, Mitterrand now declared that he would run for reelection. In the electoral campaign he portrayed himself as the epitome of France, the one candidate who stood above all factions. Chirac, by contrast, who had to battle with Barre for the conservative vote, seemed to be a candidate beholden to narrow interests, considering his attacks on immigration and welfare. In the first round of the presidential elections, the great surprise was Le Pen's ability to gain 14.4 percent of the vote, running especially strong among workers, small shopkeepers, and petty entrepreneurs. Barre achieved only 16.5 percent of the vote and failed to displace Chirac, at 19.9 percent, as the conservative candidate. In the second round, Mitterrand easily beat Chirac, 54 to 46 percent.[35]

Ironically, the politician who had once called the Fifth Republic "a permanent coup d' état" had in his first presidential term stabilized de Gaulle's system.[36] Mitterrand proved not only that the Republic could function under a Socialist government but also that one party could control the presidency (Mitterrand) and another the parliament (Chirac's coalition). By 1988 Mitterrand had abandoned his attempt to "break with capitalism," and he reduced the French Communist party to a mere appendage to his Socialist party.[37] Under his resourceful (many said Machiavellian) presidency, Mitterrand proved that the left could win and hold power, an unprecedented development. Neither the revolutionary republicans after the 1848 revolution nor the various left-wing governments of the Third Republic, for example the *Cartel des Gauches* and the Popular Front, had been able to do so.

Economically, however, Mitterrand's first term continued the uneven economic performance of the Giscard era. Over the course of the first decade of Mitterrand's presidency, France's economy had averaged a growth rate of 2.2 annually, a bit better than Germany and Britain but a bit worse than Italy, the United States, and Japan.[38] In short, none of the economic programs—Mitterrand's statism or his shift to monetarism or Chirac's privatization—had either dramatically improved or worsened France's economic performance vis-à-vis the other industrialized nations.

As a result, Mitterrand had been unable to lift the poor out of poverty or incorporate immigrants more fully within the French society. At the start of his second term, the major questions looming were, with the Socialist model abandoned, how could the economy be revived and the poor and the marginal incorporated into society?

NOTES

1. Maurice Agulhon, *The French Republic, 1879–1992*, trans. Antonia Nevill (Oxford: Blackwell, 1993), p. 430.

2. Roger Price, *A Concise History of France* (Cambridge: Cambridge University Press, 1997), p. 292.

3. G. de Bertier de Sauvigny and David H. Pinkney, *History of France*, Revised and Enlarged Edition, French text trans. Jams Friguglietti (Arlington Heights, IL: Forum Press, 1983), p. 391.

4. Colin Jones, *The Cambridge Illustrated History of France* (Cambridge: Cambridge University Press, 1994), p. 303.

5. "La Rechute: bilan économique et social 1980. Supplément aux dossiers et documents," *Le Monde*, January 1981, p. 118.

6. de Sauvigny and Pinkney, *History of France*, p. 392.

7. Jones, *The Cambridge Illustrated History of France*, p. 302.

8. Ibid., p. 303.

9. Ibid.

10. "La Rechute," p. 17.

11. Jeremy D. Popkin, *A History of Modern France* (Englewood Cliffs, NJ: Prentice Hall, 1994), p. 345, and Michel Freyssenet, "Empoli et Travail," in *L'État de la France 1998–1999* (Paris: Editions la Decouverte, 1999), 114.

12. B. H. Moss, "Trade Union Movement," in *Historical Dictionary of the French Fourth and Fifth Republics, 1946–1991*, Wayne Northcutt, ed. (Westport, CT: Greenwood Press, 1992), p. 450, and Susan Milner, "Trade

Unions," in *Modern France: Society in Transition*, Malcolm Cook and Grace Davie, eds. (London: Routledge, 1999), p. 132.

13. Freyssenet, "Empoli et Travail," p. 114.

14. de Sauvigny and Pinkney, *History of France*, p. 393.

15. Price, *A Concise History of France*, p. 343.

16. John Ardagh, *France in the New Century: Portrait of a Changing Society* (London: Viking, 1999), p. 620.

17. James F. McMillan, *Twentieth-Century France: Politics and Society, 1898–1991* (London: Edward Arnold, 1992), p. 203.

18. Maurice Larkin, *France Since the Popular Front: Government and People, 1936–1986* (Oxford: Oxford University Press, 1988), p. 355.

19. Agulhon, *The French Republic, 1879–1992*, p. 452.

20. Jones, *The Cambridge Illustrated History of France*, p. 312.

21. Ibid.

22. McMillan, *Twentieth-Century France*, pp. 208–209 and J. N. Tuppen, "Economic Trends," p. 151 and J. R. Pitts, "Unemployment," in *Historical Dictionary of the Fourth and Fifth Republic*, p. 457.

23. Jones, *The Cambridge Illustrated History of France*, p. 313.

24. Harvey G. Simmons, *The French National Front: The Extremist Challenge to Democracy* (Boulder, CO: Westview Press, 1996), p. 17 and Jones, *The Cambridge Illustrated History of France*, p. 313.

25. Simmons, *The French National Front*, pp. 46–48.

26. Ibid., p. 159.

27. Ibid., p. 183.

28. Edward G. DeClair, *Politics and the Fringe: The People, Policies, and Organization of the French National Front* (Durham: Duke University Press, 1999), p. 117.

29. Ardagh, *France in the New Century: Portrait of a Changing Society*, p. 236.

30. Mort Rosenblum, *Mission to Civilize: The French Way* (New York: Anchor Press, Doubleday, 1988), p. 13.

31. Jones, *The Cambridge Illustrated History of France*, p. 313.

32. McMillan, *Twentieth-Century France*, p. 211.

33. Gordon Wright, *France in Modern Times*, 5th ed. (New York: W. W. Norton, 1995), p. 429.

34. Tuppen, "Economic Trends," in *Historical Dictionary of the Fourth and Fifth Republic*, p. 151.

35. Price, *A Concise History of France*, p. 356.

36. Ibid., p. 360.

37. Alistair Cole, *François Mitterrand: A Study in Political Leadership* 2nd ed. (London: Routledge, 1997), p. 32.

38. Robert Gildea, *France Since 1945* (Oxford: Oxford University Press, 1997), p. 96.

12

France at the End of the Twentieth Century (1988–1999): Crisis and Renewal

The last twelve years of the twentieth century began negatively but have ended positively. François Mitterrand's second presidential term contained none of the creativity of his first. A deteriorating economy, inept diplomacy, and political scandals produced a conservative landslide in the 1993 parliamentary elections. The Right, although also victorious in the 1995 presidential elections, in which Jacques Chirac was elected president, suffered a major reversal. In the spring of 1997, President Chirac called a snap parliamentary election to ensure continued parliamentary power for the rest of his term. The Socialist party, however, headed by Mitterrand's education minister Lionel Jospin, scored an unexpected victory. The French economy's sudden and strong upturn helped Jospin implement his economic and social policies and has given him high approval ratings. France has been successful in sports (winning soccer's world cup in 1998), in economics (entering the common European currency in 1999), and in war (joining the 1999 coalition to stop Serbian ethnic cleansing in Kosovo). Nevertheless, as France enters the twenty-first century and a new millennium, profound challenges await the hexagon.

Upon his reelection in 1988, Mitterrand again dissolved the National Assembly but received only a small majority in the ensuing election. He selected his great rival for leadership in the Socialist party, Michel Rocard, to head the new government. Rocard led a much more cautious and sober Socialist party. In parliament, Rocard looked to the center rather than to the left for allies, but his attempt to rule from the center quickly failed.

On economic and social matters, Rocard strove to temper rather than transform capitalism. Toward this end, he tried to fill some gaps in France's welfare system. In 1988 his government established a guaranteed monthly income (*revenue minimum d'insertion*, or RMI) for those not covered by unemployment compensation. At roughly half the minimum wage, these payments alleviated poverty but did not end marginality. Few were able to use these payments to find jobs. Two years later (1990), a law strengthening the rights of families to find and stay in adequate housing passed the Socialist-led parliament.

Rocard also strove to integrate immigrants more fully into French society. In 1990 a Consultative Commission was established to track racism, and a High Counsel on Integration was established to document racial segregation. The following year (1991), another law prohibited local officials from directing immigrants to only certain units in government housing. In short, the law aimed to prevent the rise of American-style ghettos. Rocard's administration tried to speed the integration of immigrants into French society; however, it too was worried about the continuing influx of new immigrants into France. The Socialists then tightened border controls and restricted the number of immigrants granted asylum.

Although Rocard pulled away from many of the free market schemes of the previous Chirac government (1986–1988), austerity was still the order of the day. Pierre Bérégovoy, again finance minister as he had been under Laurent Fabius, succeeded in keeping inflation in check. Rocard also did not try to renationalize the companies the right had privatized. In short, nationalization had lost its luster for the Socialists.

Rocard's government foundered on the world economic downturn of the early 1990s. Unemployment, after having declined in the late 1980s, was again on the rise, going from 9 percent in 1990 to 11.9 percent in 1993.[1] Strikes erupted but did not cause major disruptions as they had under Chirac's tenure. When the economy slowed down following the Gulf War of 1991, in which France joined the Americans in fighting Saddam Hussein, Mitterrand replaced Rocard with France's first female prime minister, Edith Cresson.

Cresson's short term in office was marked not only by anemic economic growth (less than 1 percent in 1991 and only 1.4 percent in 1992) but also by her own controversial statements on such questions as the evils of international economic competition.[2] At the same time, Mitterrand lost his deft touch in foreign affairs. He was caught off guard by the fall of the Berlin Wall and the attempted coup in Moscow against Mikhail Gorbachev in August 1991, and he was wary about German unification. France thus reacted to more than participated in the momentous events that reshaped Europe between 1989 and 1991.

When Cresson failed to deliver a Socialist victory in the regional elections of 1992, Mitterrand replaced her with his loyal finance minister, Pierre Bérégovoy. He was a model of upward mobility, whose father had been a café owner and an immigrant from the Ukraine, presided over a period of financial scandals, rising unemployment, and the outbreak of the Bosnian conflict in the Balkans. Perhaps the most shocking of the scandals for the French public concerned the National Center for Blood Transfusion allowing HIV-contaminated blood products to be used in transfusions for hemophiliacs out of concern for cost and nationalism. (American technologies that detected HIV were judged too costly and an infringement on French medical technology.) By 1993 Bérégovoy himself was accused of insider manipulations with financiers.

To recoup some of his declining prestige, Mitterrand decided to put ratification of the 1992 Maastricht Treaty—which would create the single European market—into the hands of the electorate in 1992. The referendum quickly became as much a question of Mitterrand's popularity as the suitability of closer European integration. The measure passed by a much closer margin than expected: 51 percent in favor to 49 against.[3] In general, wealthy and educated urbanites voted for Europe, and poor, uneducated, rural voters opposed further integration. As in the United States, the growing globalization of the economy was perceived as a positive development by those whose education and finances allowed them to thrive; those who were unemployed or felt threatened by layoffs believed the new international order would leave them in the margins of society.

The following year, 1993, brought more bad economic news. The economy contracted by almost a percentage point, and the number of unemployed reached 3.4 million.[4] A 1993 survey found that almost 50 percent of the French males of working age (18–65) had experienced at least one period of unemployment in the previous 10 years.[5]

The low point of Mitterrand's presidency occurred during the 1993 parliamentary elections. The right—Chirac's RPR (Rassemblement pour la République, or Rally for the Republic) and Giscard's UDF (Union pour la démocratie française, or Union for French Democracy) won by the largest landslide in modern French electoral history. The Socialists and their allies, in contrast, lost over 200 seats. The RPR now had 242 seats and the UDF 206, compared to 67 for the Socialists and 25 for the Communists. Although the National Front tallied 12.7 percent of the first-round vote, it augmented its total of votes by 700,000 compared to its total in the 1988 legislative elections. Including independent conservatives, the National Assembly was now over 80 percent conservative.[6] In addition, conservatives won control of most of the regional and municipal councils. Mitterrand would now have to cope with another period of cohabitation government. Within a few days of resigning as prime minister, after defeat, scandal, and Mitterrand's personal rebuff, Bérégovoy committed suicide.

In this second cohabitation government, Chirac declined the position of prime minister, and Mitterrand, instead, appointed Chirac's longtime colleague Édouard Balladur. Chirac would play Mitterrand's game, remaining in the wings to prepare his campaign while someone else took the heat of day-to-day government operations. Initially, this seemed to be a mistake on Chirac's part. Balladur gained much popularity by making a realistic assessment of the crisis facing France, his desire to be flexible, and his promise of "no easy answers." Moreover, the economy picked up after Balladur assumed power, growing by 3 percent in 1994 and 2 percent in 1995.[7] He adopted the Right's now familiar austerity program and focused on increasing business confidence through reduced taxes.

Trying to reduce unemployment, especially among the young, Balladur suggested that employers pay youth only 80 percent of the minimum wage. This seeming compromise (to the unemployed it promised jobs; to employers it promised cheaper labor) united students, teachers, and the unions in outrage; after a series of demonstrations were held in Paris, Balladur withdrew his recommendation. The conservative National Assembly offered another proposal to provide unprecedented amounts of public funds for private schools. This idea also united the left, especially the teachers, and Balladur retreated on this issue, too. Balladur's popularity was further shaken when his attempt to restrict admissions to universities brought new, large demonstrations.

Balladur and his conservative parliamentary majority were much more successful in revising French immigration and nationality law. Charles Pasqua, who had been minister of the interior under the 1986–1988

Chirac government, became minister again in 1993. During his second tenure, Pasqua achieved much of what he and his allies on the right desired: new restrictive measures on immigration, including rigorous identity controls at the borders and by police within France and a reform of the nationality code. After his reforms of the national code, French citizenship was no longer automatically granted to any child born in France. Now teenagers had to declare which nationality they wished to have before the age of twenty-one. Pasqua's toughness was evident when the number of legal immigrants entering dropped from 93,000 in 1993 to 45,000 in 1996.[8] Most now entered to reunite with their families already living in France.

These measures, however, did not achieve his unrealistic, but politically expedient, goal of zero immigration or the wooing of National Front voters over to the moderate Right. Despite Pasqua's harsh set of regulations, he nevertheless had come to accept the permanent presence of non-whites and non-Christians in France. He implicitly recognized France's growing multiculturalism when he established the Representative Consul of French Muslims (Conseil représentatif des musulmans de France) and when, at the opening of a new mosque in Lyon in 1994, he called for the creation of an independent French Islam.

In the meantime, the prospects of the Socialists seemed only to worsen. After another poor showing by the party in the 1994 European elections (obtaining a mere 14.5 percent of the vote), Michel Rocard resigned as party secretary.[9] In September the full extent of Mitterrand's participation in Right-wing movements during the 1930s and later with Vichy during the early years of the Occupation delivered another severe jolt to the party. Seemingly sealing the party's doom, their strongest candidate for the presidency, Jacques Delors, the recent president of the European Commission (that oversaw the functioning of the European Union), bowed out. Eventually the Socialists chose the former head of the party and education minister Lionel Jospin. With little support from Mitterrand, Jospin's chances seemed slim at best; over the months leading up to the election, however, he turned his outsider status to his advantage by arguing that he represented a "new Left."

Through January 1995 Balladur was the front runner of the right for the presidency. Despite some of his ministers being forced to resign due to financial irregularities, Balladur had the support of former President Valéry Giscard d'Estaing and Giscard's party, the UDF, and several of the smaller rightist and centrist parties, as well. But the cumulative effect of ineffectual policies (unemployment continued to rise), his haughty behavior, scandals within his government, and his poor performance on the campaign trail, was a drop in his approval ratings. Once on the campaign trail, Chirac's outgoing personality and energy won over increasing numbers of voters.

As the 1995 presidential elections approached, the electorate was undecided. Indeed, with two weeks to go, 20 percent of the voters had still not made up their minds. Their indecision was not surprising, given that all three major candidates had essentially the same agenda: cutting unemployment, increasing European integration, improving the lot of the poor, and expanding the role of parliament. Although the parties still aligned themselves on a right/left axis, their rhetoric had less and less relevance. Chirac's campaign slogan, "France for everyone," was virtually interchangeable with Jospin's, "A more just France."

Voter indecision and alienation continued through the first round of voting. The National Front, with Le Pen once more their candidate, received 15 percent. Other small parties also did well, with a combined total of 40 percent of the vote. This was the highest percentage of votes ever for peripheral parties in the Fifth Republic. Jospin, to everyone's surprise, received the most votes. Chirac's 20.84 percent put him into the second round ahead of Balladur with 18.58 percent. Voter alienation continued into the second round with an abstention rate of 20 percent (the highest since 1969), but Chirac emerged as the victor by a 52.63 to 47.37 percent margin. By the end of the campaign, Chirac promised to make the reduction of unemployment his "priority of priorities." His prime minister, Alain Juppé, was prepared to put his reputation on the line to lower this scourge that affected over 3.5 million workers.

Chirac's presidency got off to a rocky start. One of his first acts, his decision to resume nuclear testing in the Pacific, evoked strong protests around the world and alienated Germany, France's key ally in Europe. Even in France public opinion was divided on the wisdom of these tests. His major miscalculation, however, occurred over his choice of priorities. Instead of fulfilling his electoral campaign concerning unemployment, he switched his attention to lowering France's budget deficit in order to meet the criteria for joining the new European single-currency scheme set to begin in January 1999. In order to lower the budget deficit from 4.6 percent to the required 3.0 percent, his prime minister Juppé proposed, with virtually no public discussion, an austerity program that included reductions in health, education, retirement, and other benefits. Although he did propose new funds to create jobs, the public perceived

Juppé's budget as putting fiscal austerity before the fight against un-employment.

This sharp U-turn from Chirac's and Juppé's election promises precip-itated the most extensive strike wave since 1968. As in 1968, unrest first started among the students then spread to the unionized workers in the transportation sector (trains and urban subways, such as the Paris metro) and to government employees' unions. For much of November and De-cember 1995, France ground to a halt. On December 7, over a million people took to the streets in a monster demonstration to express their anger. Unlike May 1968 these demonstrators did not wish to overturn society but simply ensure that the benefits they had already won, as students or workers, were not removed. An undercurrent of fear was also evident in regard to France's further integration into Europe and into the global economy.

Juppé, facing criticism not only from the Left but also from the con-servative deputies still loyal to Balladur in parliament, was forced to make concessions. Although he preserved his chief goal, to cut the health care deficit, he compromised regarding the trimming of the education budget and reducing union pensions. Despite these compromises, Juppé's belt-tightening had lowered the budget deficit from 5.6 percent in 1994 to 4.2 percent in 1996 and lowered inflation to 1.1 percent, its lowest point since 1945.[10] However, his popularity as well as Chirac's plummeted as the unemployment rate took yet another jump: to 12.8 percent. Even more ominous for the new president was the decline in economic expansion: from 2 percent in 1995 to 1.3 percent in 1996.[11] No wonder Juppé's poll numbers fell through the floor! Two-thirds of the respondents answered that they had "little confidence" in the prime min-ister, and three-quarters answered, "dislike the way the country is being governed."[12]

Struggles over the budget deflected attention from some decisive mea-sures passed by the center-right-dominated parliament between 1995 and 1997. The most important measures concerned parliament's own powers and flexibility in the workplace. In August 1995, parliament created a single yearly parliamentary session. As a result, parliament gained in-creased time to debate and amend bills, and thus increased control over the government's agenda. Some commentators believe that this change is perhaps the single most important constitutional reform since 1962 because it makes parliament more coequal to the president in power. (Nevertheless, the president, in the same law, augmented his powers to call a referendum.) During the same year and over the following two, a series of laws and agreements created greater flexibility in French working hours. An August 1995 pact between bosses and unions permitted working hours to be calculated either by the week, the traditional method, or by the year. Thus employers can tailor the workloads of individual workers to the demands of the market. In 1996 the De Robien law provided financial incentives to businesses reducing working hours to save or create jobs. Finally, in 1997, Juppé rescinded a decree dating from the Popular Front permitting banks to be open no more than five days a week. Now banks could do what they had lobbied for: be open for business on Saturdays.

In early 1997 Chirac and Juppé made the fateful decision to call for new parliamentary elections. They calculated that further economic restructuring—to get the budget deficit under 3 percent as required to join the emerging European Monetary Union—would bring further strikes and demonstrations and that it would be best to renew the right's parliamentary majority while the left was still in disarray from the parliamentary election debacle of 1993 and the loss of the presidency in 1995. The polls indicated that their plan would work. Moreover, though still dismal, Juppé's approval ratings were rising. Proclaiming that the country needed new energy, Chirac dissolved the parliament and called for new elections. His move was unprecedented in the Fifth Republic. Four times previously the president had dissolved the parliament, twice under de Gaulle and twice under Mitterrand, in order to resolve issues involving the president and the people (1962 and 1968) or to provide the president with a like-minded parliament (1981 and 1988). No president had ever dissolved parliament in order to renew his mandate on economic matters.

To counter Chirac and Juppé, Jospin formed an alliance with the Communists and the Ecology party. Although these parties could not agree on a common program, as they had in the early 1970s, they did issue a "joint declaration." Unemployment was their central concern. Jospin pledged to add 700,000 new jobs (half in the public sector and half in the private) for out-of-work youth and to cut the workweek from 39 to 35 hours without loss of pay (a measure designed to create jobs). He also promised to increase the wealth tax, to rescind the rigid immigration laws, and to end the privatization of public companies (such as the French telephone company and national airlines). Finally, Jospin accepted the advice of feminist groups, Choose (choisir) and Club Parity 2000 (Club Parité 2000), and established a quota system to ensure that the Socialists fielded more women candidates. He also pledged to improve the legal status of gays and lesbians. Perhaps, most compelling in the light of the wave of scandals and broken political promises, Jospin promised to "say what I do and do what I say."

Once again, the French electorate demonstrated their capriciousness. Although no poll had predicted it, the Socialists and the left staged a dramatic recovery and regained control of the National Assembly. The National Front continued to show its power by achieving 15 percent of the first-round vote, and, with 133 candidates running for seats, made it into the second round. In addition, the National Front abandoned the Right on the second round and either abstained or voted for the Left. The Left benefited from a close alliance among the Socialist, Ecologist, and Communist parties. Sensing the magnitude of his defeat, Juppé resigned after the first round, precipitating a scramble between the RPR and the UDF. After the second round, the Socialists and their allies held 283 seats to the Communists' 36; the UDF dropped to 113 seats and the RPR to 140 in 1997. In short, Chirac's dissolution *tactique* turned into a dissolution *tragique*.

France thus had its third cohabitation government in 11 years. This time, however, a left-wing National Assembly shared power with a conservative president. As the new prime minister, Jospin had a clear, if not resounding, mandate. He quickly established a good rapport with the French media and improved his public image (achieving and holding an approval rating around 66 percent).[13] Certainly this solitary introvert did not have the cohort of camp followers that had caused so many scandals among other politicians.

Jospin quickly tried to fulfill his campaign promises. To reward the Communists, he gave them three ministries and raised the wealth tax. For the Ecologists, he provided a crucial ministry, that of the environment, and raised the tax on diesel fuel. Jospin also fulfilled, in large part, his promises toward immigrants and gays and lesbians. As far as immigrants, he immediately legalized the status of 80,000 immigrants and greatly diminished the police checks. In addition, he established a commission on immigration law which called for more care for human rights, but he has not rolled back Pasqua's laws. Many critics believe that Jospin's efforts to improve the status of immigrants have been insufficient. As for gays and lesbians, couples were legally recognized for insurance purposes. In 1998 and 1999 the National Assembly and then the Senate passed what is known as the Civil Solidarity Pact, which provides gay couples with rights but does not (yet) allow real marriage or the right to adopt children. Despite its moderation, the parliamentary debates have placed the question of gay rights at the center of French politics in an unprecedented fashion.

Overall, however, Jospin, this graduate of the elite National School of Administration (ENA), has proved to be less of an ideologue than his program had promised. He shelved, temporarily, full implementation of the 35-hour-workweek proposal. When the first installment of the 35-hour law passed in March 1998 it applied only to private-sector workers, not the substantial public-sector workforce too. Rather than resenting the law, employers have reinterpreted the law to suit their own needs. They have fused the 35-hour law with the earlier Juppé measure granting them more flexibility in determining work schedules. As a result, employers can adjust their employees' schedules to meet their own needs. As so many previous prime ministers have done, Jospin has essentially continued the monetarist policies of the last fifteen years.

Although he had campaigned against further privatization, his government sold more state companies in the first 18 months than the previous conservative government had done in two years. Jospin tried to reconcile privatization with socialism by ensuring that the employees of state-owned companies would receive much of the stock. He displayed a dogged commitment to getting France into the single European currency by 1999. Indeed he was able to achieve this goal (by bringing the budget deficit down to 3 percent), and without the draconian austerity Juppé had desired, largely because the French economy grew at a much stronger rate than expected in 1998: 3.2 percent.[14] As a result, the economy added more jobs and had a foreign trade surplus of FF173 billion, double the 1996 statistic.[15]

As of the summer of 1999, Jospin's ideological flexibility, combined with a rising economy, a falling unemployment rate, and the new Euro currency functioning smoothly, has made him the most powerful political force in the country. Even foreign affairs and defense, which had been the president's preserve, are a "shared domain." But Jospin's encroachment has not led to a major conflict, for he has continued Chirac's reduction and rationalization of the armed forces (including ending conscription).

Jospin's success has thrown the Right into disarray. Several factions have emerged and developed their own prescription for French renewal in an increasingly Europeanized and globalized marketplace. Chirac's party, the RPR, has been especially affected by this fracture. Charles Pasqua has broken away and formed what he believes is a restored Gaullist party. In this bid to return to the "original" message of the great leader, Pasqua has returned to the original name: Rally for France (RPF) of de Gaulle's movement. Not only has Pasqua resurrected the original name, he has also retrieved the original logo. His message is also a throwback to the general focus on a Europe of nations, rather than one of an integrated federation, and on France first rather than simply pro free enterprise. Pasqua has positioned himself to the right of Chirac's RPR, which remains pro-European and free market. Meanwhile the UDF and its leader, François Bayrou, have come to occupy a pro-European integration center position. The Right was therefore unprepared to launch an effective campaign either for the regional elections of March 1998 or the European Parliament elections of June 1999. But this was not the end of the Right's splintering.

The March 1998 elections brought the National Front its greatest success to date. Although the left, center-right, and National Front essentially won the same percentage of the vote as in the previous elections (37, 36, and 15 percent, respectively, with 40 percent abstaining), the proportional system of awarding seats on the councils resulted in only two regions being controlled outright by a single party.[16] As a result, the rest of the councils contained no absolute majorities, a situation that allowed the National Front to emerge as a power broker. Although the parties of the center-right, the RPR and the UDF, and President Chirac demanded that their members not make any deals, five regional council presidents disregarded the injunction. In three other regions, the presidents stepped down after having been reelected with the help of the National Front. To prevent controversy and to appear moderate, the National Front did not make great demands for their support.

The most portentous fallout from the 1998 elections was former Prime Minister Edouard Balladur's call, in the following June, for an independent governmental commission to study the National Front's idea of "national preferences." This notion, developed by the National Front's chief theoretician Bruno Mégret, demanded that native-born white French be given first crack at jobs and social services over foreigners (particularly those from outside Europe). By this move, Balladur hoped to draw a clear distinction between the Right and the Left and the 30 percent of French voters who agreed with the National Front's position. Clearly, the distinction between the Center Right and the far Right was starting to blur.

Just when the National Front seemed poised to make major inroads into French politics, however, a schism developed between the younger

Mégret (aged 49) and the senior Le Pen (aged 70). The younger man felt it was time to end his apprenticeship and take control of the movement he had done so much to shape. Le Pen wished to remain a powerful but peripheral force in French politics; Mégret wished to enter the mainstream. This fissure widened in December 1998. In January 1999, at a conference held at Marignane, the split became official. Mégret obtained the support of half the party's elected officials, the young brain trust, including Le Pen's chief of staff. The rest of the movement remained loyal to Le Pen. The June 1999 European parliamentary elections showed the negative effect of the split on the Far-Right's electoral support.[17] Suddenly, the greatest asset of the National Front, its unity in the midst of the divisiveness of French politics, had been lost.

While the National Front has undergone a schism, the external economic climate in France has continued to improve and has created jobs, thus cutting into the unemployment rate that helped fuel the National Front's rise. The economic expansion has brought down the unemployment rate from 12.6 percent in 1997, when Jospin became prime minister, to 11.4 percent by April 1999.[18] Increasing numbers of employers are viewing the Socialist-led drive to enact into law the 35-hour workweek not as an impediment to profitability but as a spur to increasing labor market flexibility. To the dismay of labor union leaders, employers are not taking the government grants for hiring new workers or taking 35 hours as a weekly norm. Instead, bosses are computing the total number of hours that can be worked in a year and then dividing that figure by the number of weeks in a year. They are then apportioning work schedules based upon their peak periods of business. In addition, they are paying overtime rather than hiring more workers. Finally, recent collective wage increases in France have been lower than in Germany and have made the French labor market less rigid than its neighbor across the Rhine.

France's growing confidence in its economy may have contributed to its strong support of NATO's decision in the spring of 1999 to bomb Yugoslavia. The French showed strong and sustained support for the NATO air strikes when diplomatic efforts had failed to end Slobodan Milosevic's ethnic cleansing of the overwhelmingly Muslim province of Kosovo. Both Chirac and Jospin fully backed this effort to stop ethnic conflict in the Balkans, the scene of the outbreak of World War I. In fact, the French air force contributed more fighter/bombers than any other European country. Moreover, the press and public were uncommonly resolute. Nevertheless, the French also became increasingly anti-

American as this American-led war continued: from public opinion polls to graffiti on the metro to the comments of such diverse politicians as Bruno Mégret, on the far right; Charles Pasqua, on the center right; and Jean-Pierre Chevenement, on the left. Public opinion polls found majorities of 60 percent and over anxious about what they perceived as American domination in the cultural, economic, and military spheres of European life. The traditional Gaullist distrust of American power remains a potent force in French politics and culture. Polls in no other European nation found such distrust of the United States or so much support for a European military force separate from America's.[19]

Soon after the end of the Kosovo conflict, in June 1999, the elections to the European Parliament arrived. Although these elections had a low rate of participation (47 percent) and a high rate of blank ballots (6 percent) among those who went to the polling booths, voters indicated the popularity of Jospin, the political weakness of Chirac, and disorganization on the right as well as the crumbling of the far right National Front.

The left alliance (Socialists, Communists, and Greens) slipped slightly, gaining about 39 percent of the vote. Even so, the left outpolled the right by 3 percentage points and, more important, showed unity in the face of further fracturing on the right.[20] The big surprise on the left was the vigorous rise of the Greens, under the lead of Daniel Cohen-Bendit, a student revolutionary in 1968. The ecologists saw their vote tripled from the previous European elections; the Greens garnered 10 percent of the total. By contrast, the Communists saw their vote fall to 7 percent, the second lowest since 1945.

The shifting strengths of the Communists and Greens could mean trouble for Jospin's coalition in the future. The Greens might wish to obtain more ministries in the coalition government, and the Communists might become more recalcitrant. The Communist hard-liners might blame party leader Hue's liberalization for the falling fortunes of the party. The problems of the Left, however, are minimal compared to those of the Right.

Chirac's party not only failed to outpoll the Socialists, it was also beaten by Pasqua's revived RPF. Thus behind the Socialists' 22 percent and the RPF's 13 percent came Chirac's RPR at 12 percent.[21] This was the lowest total ever for the RPR. A major factor for the collapse of the RPR was that its leader, Philippe Séguin, resigned in the middle of the election. Shortly after the results were announced, the RPR's new leader, Nicolas Sarkozy, also resigned. The UDF held its own at 9 percent of the vote and thus has little reason to wish to merge with any other party on the right. Thus Chirac's hope that he could create a president's party before the 2002 presidential and parliamentary elections appeared doomed. Finally, an additional fragment emerged on the Right when a party supporting hunter's rights, the Nature party, gained 6 percent of the vote. The group is now considering forming a permanent party organization.

The far Right National Front came out of the elections in even worse shape than the center right. The two splinter groups were able to poll only a combined 9 percent (down more than 6 percentage points from their vote in the regional elections held the previous year). Le Pen's faction, which achieved 6 percent of the vote, did better than Mégret's, which garnered a mere 3 percent.[22] Failure prompted neither leader to call for reconciliation and so the National Front seems to be irretrievably split for the foreseeable future. The weakness of the far right has prompted one of the former UDF municipal counselors, Charles Millon, ousted for making a deal with the National Front in 1998, to form his own party.

Although France enters the twenty-first century with greater confidence and unity than one would have expected a few years ago, pressing problems and substantial social and economic evolution will pose dramatic challenges to French identity in the new millennium. In February 1999, Prime Minister Lionel Jospin summed up the country's dilemma, "France cannot live without having its own identity.... The People of France cannot live as a people whose destiny will be forged among others."[23] A large part of the answer to the way in which France preserves its identity will revolve around the questions of France's response to continued European integration, an aging population, and immigration.

Although France achieved entry into the new European monetary union in 1999 with little problem, but after much hand-wringing, its role within Europe may be changing. A unified Germany of 82 million people, its capital once again in Berlin and the problems of economic development in former East Germany more resolved, may very well be less closely allied to France than it was during the Cold War when the German nation was divided. Recent commentary in France already sees a fundamental change occurring in Franco-German relations. Does this mean that France will lose its traditionally innovative role in European integration?

The continuing issue of unemployment will be aggravated by the graying of the French population. All advanced industrialized nations face this problem, but the French situation has some unique characteristics.

Most nations have considered raising the age of retirement as one so-lution, but much support has built in France for lowering this ceiling. Recently, the General Confederation of Labor (CGT) has called for re-tirement to start at 55 (the Socialists in 1982 had already lowered the age to 60), and polls indicate that two-thirds of the public support this po-sition.[24] It is difficult to conceive how one could lower the age of retire-ment in the early twenty-first century when a quarter of the French population will be over the age of 60 by 2015.

The solution to this demographic and welfare quandary will probably be immigration. One authoritative study expects France will absorb be-tween 16 and 20 million young immigrants by the year 2050. Their labor can provide the only solution, aside from another baby boom, to the travails of the social security system.

How will French society handle increased immigration and the atten-dant problems of assimilation and accommodation? Most of the discus-sion and research have focused on how French people of European descent perceive non-European immigrants, but it is equally important to evaluate how immigrants from Third World countries who have set-tled in France view their own situation. Here, some individual examples can provide illumination. Fatouma Gassama, a 19-year-old resident in the suburb of Corbeil-Essons in the Paris region, observes, "I can't change my Africanness. But if you ask me if I am a Malienne, what can I tell you? I was born in France. I've never set foot in Mali." When one of her neighbors, Hatouma Doucoure, traveled to their native Mali, she felt "like a tourist." Taking a field trip with her classmates to the Eiffel Tower, however, was equally strange. It made her "wonder if such things will ever have the same meaning for me that they seem to have for French kids."[25] Some second- or third-generation Algerians, such as the writer Sakinna Boukhedenna, feel alienated from both France and Algeria and dream of creating a country in the middle of the Mediter-ranean where children of North African immigrants, such as herself, can feel at home.[26]

Despite such feelings of dislocation, assimilation is proceeding at a rapid pace. Surveys conducted in the mid to late 1990s show that 70 percent of second-generation North Africans have a greater attachment to France than the culture of their parents' homeland, and 90 percent wish to be integrated into French society.[27] Even Boukhedenna has cho-sen France over Algeria as the more palatable alternative. An important measure of assimilation is the fact that non-European immigrants are adopting the French demographic model of two children (1.7 in the most recent data) per family. For example, the Algerian birthrate has fallen from 8.5 children per mother in the early 1960s to 4.2 children in the early 1980s, to 3.2 children (and falling) in the 1990s.[28] The birthrate of sub-Saharan Africans, although still close to 5 children per mother, is also falling and is much lower than in the home countries. The fertility decline arises from another important measure of assimilation: non-European women are marrying later in life like their European French counterparts.

The immigrant children also tend to abandon the religion of their parents. This is true even of Muslim immigrants. Polls and studies have found that between 20 and 35 percent of the children of Muslim families say they do not follow their parents' faith, and a sizable number state that their adherence to such Muslim holidays as Ramadan is weak.[29] Moreover, a high percentage of immigrants have internalized the French concept of laïcité: the concept that religious symbols and practices should be a personal and private affair and not publicly propagated. This commitment was clear when a nationwide controversy erupted in October 1989 over the actions of a school principal in Creil (30 miles north of Paris) who expelled two girls for wearing head scarves because their scarves allegedly were a too conspicuous display of Islam. Opinion polls conducted among the French Muslim population in the heat of the controversy and again in 1994 reveal that only about a quarter of those polled approved of the wearing of the head scarf; between 44 and 45 percent disapproved.[30]

An important factor facilitating assimilation has been the lack of dense, poverty-stricken ghettos, which are found in the United States. France's welfare system, more comprehensive than that found in the United States, ensures that the rate of poverty, misery, and crime is much lower than in urban ghettos in the United States.

Will the government be able to promote the equality and social mobility that will assure that France will not experience a racial problem similar to that in the United States? Certainly the popularity of the National Front, supported by public opinion polls that consistently show the French being the second most prejudiced people in Europe (just behind the Belgians), points to the difficulties that may lie ahead. This prejudice, however, does not seem to be deeply rooted. While two-thirds of those polled say France has too many immigrants, virtually the same percentage admit that they have never had any extended or meaningful encounters with immigrants.[31]

Hopeful signs of a vital and dynamic multicultural future can already be glimpsed in music and sport. French rap has a major white component among both performers and audience. Rap artists such as MC Solar and the group IAM have album sales of between 500,000 and 900,000. Moreover, rap and hip-hop have become part of French advertising. This development is significant because advertisements generally convey positive and festive images; the use of music created by immigrant groups in ads thus purveys positive images of Third World cultures on television and counters the dominant trend of portraying immigrants as causing problems.

The most dramatic instance of multiculturalism in sports is the fashion in which the French rallied around their World Champion soccer team after it won the World Cup on the home turf of Paris in the summer of 1998. That team was a microcosm of contemporary France: of the 22 team members, 8 were of African, Arab, or Asian origin; 1 was a Basque, and 1 was a Breton. Perhaps the lesson learned from watching the victory and the fraternal crowd that gathered in Paris afterward (the largest since the liberation of Paris in 1944) can be carried over not only to the playing field (which now sees 13.3 million French actively participating in athletic clubs), but also into the rest of society. France's influential newspaper, *Le Monde*, believed the victory could be a milestone, "something which could symbolize a change in epoch."[32]

Even if the World Cup victory and attendant celebration does not prove to be a watershed, France's continued dynamism ensures that it will remain one of the world's most vital nations. The infusion of immigrants, the growing educational level of its population, the creativity of its entrepreneurs, and the activism of its government are all forces that make France a stable, balanced, and caring society.

NOTES

1. Robert Gildea, *France Since 1945* (Oxford: Oxford University Press, 1997), p. 97.

2. Ibid., p. 96.

3. Ibid., p. 215.

4. Ibid., p. 97.

5. Howard Davis, "Class and Status," in *Modern France: Society in Transition,* Malcolm Cook and Grace Davie, eds. (London: Routledge, 1999), p. 31.

6. Roger Price, *A Concise History of France* (Cambridge: Cambridge University Press, 1997), p. 359. Edward G. DeClair, *Politics and the Fringe: The People, Policies, and Organization of the French National Front* (Durham, NC: Duke University Press, 1999), p. 94.

7. "France," in *Political Handbook of the World, 1997*, Arthur S. Brooks,

Alan Day, and Thomas C. Muller, eds. (Binghamton, NY: CUNY Publications, 1998), p. 282.

8. Patrick Harismendy, "Age: The Life Course," in *Modern France: Society in Transition*, Malcolm Cook and Grace Davie, eds. (London: Routledge, 1999), p. 74.

9. William Safran, *The French Polity*, 5th ed. (New York: Longman, 1998), p. 103.

10. "Lionel Jospin's Soggy Programme," *The Economist*, June 21, 1997, p. 53, and "The French Election: Chirac and Juppé Hope for Change," *The Economist*, May 24, 1997, p. 22.

11. "Crossed Fingers in France," *The Economist*, April 26, 1997, pp. 45–46.

12. "The French Election: France's Once and Future Man," *The Economist*, May 3, 1997, p. 41.

13. "Funny Weather over France," *The Economist*, July 11, 1998, p. 51.

14. Ibid., p. 52, and "Survey France: The Grand Illusion," *The Economist*, June 5, 1999, p. 5.

15. "Daffodilly," *The Economist*, March 7, 1998, p. 56.

16. "France's Right-Wing in Disarray," *The Economist*, March 28, 1998, p. 46.

17. "Bruno Mégret, France's Far Right Schemer," Charlemagne, *The Economist* January 30, 1999, p. 50.

18. "France's Shorter Week: Unintended Results," *The Economist*, April 3, 1999, p. 44.

19. "France Survey: The Grand Illusion," *The Economist*, June 5, 1999, p. 15.

20. "Europe's Voters Stay at Home," *The Economist*, June 19, 1999, pp. 51–52.

21. Ibid., and "France: Right Old Mess," *The Economist*, June 19, 1999, p. 52.

22. "Europe's Voters Stay at Home," pp. 51–52.

23. Frank Viviano, "Europe Suddenly Doesn't Even Recognize Itself," Dispatch from Europe Number 4, *San Francisco Chronicle*, Friday, March 5, 199, p. A10.

24. "Retire Early, Bust the State," *The Economist*, February 15, 1997, p. 47.

25. Viviano, "Europe Suddenly Doesn't Even Recognize Itself," p. A10.

26. Alec G. Hargreaves, "Resistance at the Margins: Writers of Maghrebi Immigrant Origin in France," in *Post-Colonial Cultures in France*, Alex G. Hargreaves and Mark McKinney, eds. (London: Routledge, 1997), p. 236.

27. Alec G. Hargreaves, *Immigration, "Race," and Ethnicity in Contemporary France* (London: Routledge, 1995), p. 148.

28. Ibid., p. 109.

29. Ibid., pp. 120–121.

30. Ibid., pp. 127–128.

31. "How Racist Is France?" *The Economist*, July 18, 1998, p. 43, and Hargreaves, *Immigration, "Race," and Ethnicity in Contemporary France*, p. 158.

32. John Ardagh, *France in the New Century: Portrait of a Changing Society* (London: Viking, 1999), p. 326.

Notable People in the History of France

Simone de Beauvoir (1908–1986). Philosopher, novelist, and feminist. Long-standing companion of Jean-Paul Sartre, she helped formulate the philosophy of existentialism. Although *The Mandarins* won the prestigious Gouncourt literary prize (1954), her most important work was *The Second Sex* (1949), which delineates women's oppression and, along with her multivolume autobiography, has played a decisive role in the rise of contemporary feminism.

Leon Blum (1872–1950). Socialist politician and writer. Blum broke with the emergent French Communist party at the Congress of Tours (1920) because he opposed the Communist concept of proletarian dictatorship in the name of republican legality. Leader of the Socialist party (SFIO), prime minister during the Popular Front (1936–1937), he was jailed and prosecuted during World War II. He advocated strong ties with the United States after 1945.

Louis Napoleon Bonaparte (1808–1873). Nephew of Napoleon Bonaparte and creator of the Second Empire (1851–1870). A failed conspirator in his youth, after the 1848 Revolution he was elected, on the basis of the Napoleonic myth, president. He staged a coup d'état in December 1851 and proclaimed himself emperor. During his reign, he promoted rapid industrialization and urbanization. A military debacle in the Franco Prussian War (1870) resulted in his abdication. He died in exile.

Napoleon Bonaparte (1769–1821). Revolutionary general, head of the Consulate government (1799–1804), and emperor (1804–1814). The military master of Europe, he also created the modern French legal and administrative system and spread it to the rest of Europe. His most famous military victory was Austerlitz in 1805; his downfall occurred after the Russian campaign (1812); the last battle he fought was at Waterloo in 1815. He ended his life as an exile on the Atlantic island of Saint Helena.

John Calvin (1509–1564). Chief theologian of the Protestant Reformation in the French language. Born and educated in France, he moved to Geneva, Switzerland (1541) to escape Catholic persecution. Here he established a model Protestant community and wrote *Institutes of the Christian Religion*. His doctrine, known as Calvinism, which spread throughout much of France, England, the British Isles, and Holland, emphasized the notion of predestination.

Hugh Capet (941–996). Founder of the Capetian Dynasty in 986. A duke of France later proclaimed king, he made Paris his capital. A weak king vis-à-vis his vassals, nevertheless he established an important precedent: he crowned his successor during his own lifetime thus preventing a succession struggle upon his death. This custom was continued by his successors.

Jacques Cartier (1491–1557). Leading French navigator in the age of European exploration and expansion. He claimed much of Canada for Francis I between 1534 and 1541.

Charlemagne (742–814). King of the Francs, emperor of the west (800–814). The son of Pépin the Short, he conquered much of present-day Germany and Eastern Europe in the name of Christianity. He also restored administrative centralization and promoted education and scholarship. Crowned emperor by pope in Rome. The empire lasted during the lifetime of his son (Louis the Pious, ruled 814–840) but was divided among Louis's three sons after 840.

Jacques Chirac (1932–   ). Prime minister, mayor of Paris, and president of France (1995–   ). A de Gaulle aide in late 1960s, he backed Valéry

Giscard d'Estaing in the 1974 presidential election. He was named prime minister (1974–1976) but resigned and became mayor of Paris (1977–1995). He served as prime minister (1986–1988) and was victorious in the presidential elections of 1995. His dissolving of parliament in 1997 led to the defeat of his party and a new cohabitation government.

Georges Clemenceau (1841–1929). Politician, journalist, prime minister. From a Republican family, he trained as a doctor but became a politician. He served as mayor of Paris in the district of Montmartre, parliamentary deputy, head of the left radicals, journalist champion of Alfred Dreyfus, and prime minister (1906–1909). As prime minister at the end of World War I, he led France and the Allies to victory. His dogged determination earned him the nickname of "Tiger."

Charles de Gaulle (1890–1970). Soldier, resistance leader, president, military theorist, and writer. The leading French statesman of the twentieth century, he served as an officer in World War I, advocated mechanized warfare, and organized the resistance government in 1940. He was the president of the provisional government from 1944 to 1946. He left political life until 1958 when he returned in the wake of the Algerian crisis to form the Fifth Republic. He served as president from 1958 to 1969.

Alfred Dreyfus (1859–1935). French army officer. Condemned in 1894 for espionage. His wrongful prosecution and imprisonment led to one of the great political battles of modern history. Pitting free-thinkers, liberals, socialists, and anticlericals (most prominently Émile Zola) against Catholics, Monarchists, and anti-Semites, the affair ended in Dreyfus's pardon (1899) and rehabilitation (1906).

Jules Ferry (1832–1893). Republican politician most famous for his work in educational and colonial issues. The reforms bearing his name (1882–1884) while minister of education made a free secular education available to all French children and helped root the Republic in French hearts and minds. He was also a vigorous advocate of colonialism; as foreign affairs minister, he expanded the empire into Tunisia, the Congo, and Indochina.

Francis I (1494–1547). King at the height of the French Renaissance (1515–1548). This powerfully built warrior led France into the Italian peninsula in 1494 and brought the Renaissance style in architecture and painting to France. He fought the Hapsburgs for hegemony in Europe, substituted French for Latin in the administration, and augmented the royal army.

Saint Francis de Sales (1567–1622). Bishop of Geneva. He is famous for his devotional works typifying the Catholic Counter-Reformation: *Introduction to the Devout Life* (1609) and *Treatise of Divine Love* (1616). He reconverted many Protestants and inspired devout women, such as Jeanne de Chantal, who created the Congregation of the Visitation to aid women in the quest for the spiritual life.

Valéry Giscard d'Estaing (1926–   ). Politician and president of France (1974–1981). A graduate of the elite National School of Administration (ENA), he served as finance minister in both Charles de Gaulle's and Georges Pompidou's administrations. Elected president, his goal of liberalizing society foundered on the economic problems of the 1970s, and he lost to François Mitterrand in 1981. He has remained active but not prominent in politics.

Henry IV (1553–1610). King of France (1589–1610). He renounced Protestantism to become king, and he reestablished order after the age of Religious Wars. He issued the Edict of Nantes (1598), which granted religious toleration to Protestants. An astute administrator, he appointed brilliant ministers, balanced the budget, cut taxes, and expanded French colonization in Canada. Before he could begin his campaign against the Hapsburgs, he was assassinated by a Catholic zealot.

Jean Jaurès (1859–1914). Politician, philosopher, historian. A parliamentary deputy from the working-class district in Southern France of Carmaux, he rallied the Socialist movement to the defense of Alfred Dreyfus. Using eloquence and charisma, he unified the fractious Socialist movement (SFIO) in 1905 and also founded the Socialist, later Communist, newspaper *L'Humanité*. He was an advocate of civilian defense. He was assassinated at the start of World War I.

Joan of Arc (1412–1431). Peasant girl who became a warrior and inspired Charles VII and the kingdom to defeat England in Hundred Years' War. Born in the Lorraine village of Domremy, she heard the voices of Mary and Jesus telling her to save France. She liberated Orléans from the English in 1429. While laying siege to Paris, she was captured by the

English and tried and burned at the stake as a heretic. She was declared a saint in 1920; her national festival day is May 8.

Jean-Marie Le Pen (1928–   ). Leader of the Right-wing National Front. A life-long Rightist, he was a law student in Paris, a paratrooper in the colonial wars in Indochina and Algeria, and a member of parliament in Pierre Poujade's party (1956). He became president of the National Front in 1972, but had little success until the early 1980s. Tapping on anti-immigrant xenophobia, his party garnered 15 percent of the electorate by 1997. In January 1998 a split in the party caused a significant setback.

Louis IX (1214–1276). King of France (1226–1270). Pious crusader, law giver, innovative administrator, and skilled warrior, he was canonized as Saint Louis in 1927. He created the Parlement of Paris (high court of justice) and gained the provinces of Anjou, Poitou, and Maine from England, and, after a crusade against Albigensian heretics, the southern province of Languedoc. He failed, however, to wrest the Holy Land from Muslims in last crusade.

Louis XIV (1638–1715). King of France (1643–1715). Known as the Sun King, and as Louis the Great, he dominated European politics and warfare. Coming of age after the *Fronde* revolt, he was determined to maintain order and expand the kingdom. The first 12 years of his reign were devoted to cultural and internal development; he spent the following 40 years in a quest for glory. He failed in his bid to dominate Europe, but he created the greatest age of French monarchical power.

Louis XV (1710–1774). King of France (1715–1774). The great grandson of Louis XIV, he was crowned king at five. During his regency, the monarchy lost power and parlements regained veto of royal acts. As an adult, Louis was devoted to hunting and women, especially Madame de Pompadour. During his reign, the crown lost dynamism and the allegiance of writers. At the end of his life, he abolished the parlements, but he died before any meaningful reforms could be enacted.

Louis XVI (1754–1793). King of France (1774–1792). He tried to be an enlightened monarch and appointed reform-minded ministers, but he always dismissed them as soon as any opposition emerged at court. From 1788 to 1789, he faced political, economic, and social crises. His indecision made the French Revolution more radical. In the fall of 1791, he tried to flee France but was caught at Varennes, near the border, put on trial (1792), and executed (1793).

Louis XVIII (1755–1824). King of France (1814–1824). Brother of Louis XVI, he took the title Louis XVIII in honor of Louis XVI's son who died in prison. An exile during Revolutionary and Napoleonic eras, he knew the fragility of royal power and instituted a Charter as a compromise between divine right monarchy and revolutionary constitutionalism to restrain ultraroyalists. His caution ensured that he died on the throne.

Louis-Philippe (1773–1850). Duke of Valois, duc de Chartres, king of France (1830–1848). He fought in the Revolutionary wars but went into exile during the Reign of Terror. Chosen "citizen king" after the 1830 Revolution that toppled his cousin Charles X, he started as a liberal but became increasingly conservative although he was responsible for much economic progress. He was caricatured as a "pear" and toppled at the start of the 1848 Revolution.

Jules Mazarin (1602–1661). Cardinal and head of the government under the regency of Anne of Austria (1644–1661) for Louis XIV. An Italian-born prelate, he was the protégé of Cardinal Armand Richelieu. After Richelieu's death in 1644, he successfully consolidated the French gains in the Thirty Years' War (1618–1648) but faced a nationwide revolt (*Fronde*, 1648–1652). He ended the revolt by playing one faction off against another and led France until his death.

François Mitterrand (1916–1996). Founder of contemporary French Socialist party (1972) and president of the Republic (1981–1995). Of middle-class provincial origins, he flirted with Right-wing movements in his youth (1930–1942) but then became part of the resistance (1942–1944) and of Pierre Mendès-France's reformist government (1954). As a two-term president of experimental but moderate government, he demonstrated that the left-wing party can govern without turmoil.

Guy Mollet (1905–1975). Socialist politician and prime minister during the Fourth Republic (1956–1957). From 1946 to 1969, he served as secretary general of the Socialist party (SFIO). His tenure as prime minister was marked by France's ill-fated attempt to retake the Suez Canal (along with Great Britain) in 1956 and the attempt to keep Algeria French. His support was crucial in Charles de Gaulle's establishing the Fifth Republic (1958–1959).

Jean Monnet (1888–1979). Economist and advocate of European integration. The son of brandy distillers in Cognac, he was inspired by the size and efficiency of America during World War II and became an advocate of French economic planning and intra-European economic cooperation after 1945. The first head of the French Planning Commission, he oversaw the creation of the National College of Administration (ENA). He was one of the architects of the European Community.

Philippe Pétain (1856–1951). World War I general, minister of military, and head of the Vichy state under Nazi domination in World War II. As a general he advocated defensive warfare and halted the German advance at Verdun in 1916. He was brought into the government when France fell in 1940, believing that the Republic was responsible for France's defeat. He advocated collaboration with the Nazis but was more of a figurehead than a strong leader due to his advanced age.

Philip IV (1268–1314). King of France (1285–1314). One of the most ambitious and infamous of the French monarchs, Philip the Fair tried and failed to conquer Flanders. Under his reign, France experienced the rise of bureaucratic government and the French representative assembly, the Estates General. Philip struggled with the papacy and installed the pope at Avignon in the south of France.

Raymond Poincaré (1860–1934). Lawyer and politician. President of the Republic during World War I (1913–1920) and prime minister both before and after (1912, 1922–1924, 1926–1929), he was a fervent nationalist who prepared France for war and after war sent troops to occupy the Rhine when Germany would not pay reparations. He returned to service to restore the currency in 1926 and stayed in power until poor health forced him to retire in 1929.

Georges Pompidou (1911–1974). Teacher, banker, prime minister (1962–1968), president (1969–1974). The son of poor schoolteachers, he excelled in school, graduated from elite technical schools, and served in the army. He joined the staff of Charles de Gaulle in 1946 and played a vital role as advisor through May 1968. As president of the Fifth Republic, he proved that the country could be run by someone other than de Gaulle and maintain prosperity. He died at the onset of the 1970s economic crisis.

Pierre Poujade (1920–). Small shopkeeper and right-wing politician. He established the Union for the Defense of Shopkeepers and Artisans (UDCA in French) in 1953. He led the revolt against taxation and then turned the movement into a political party and won 11 percent of the vote and 52 seats in the National Assembly in 1956. His lack of administrative skill and the rise of Charles de Gaulle led to a rapid decline of the movement. Poujade helped launch the career of Jean-Marie Le Pen.

Armand Richelieu (1585–1642). Cardinal and prime minister (1624–1642) under Louis XIII. He consolidated the crown's power over nobles, cities, and Protestants and increased taxation and the power and efficiency of the government and army. His immediate goal was to increase French power during the Thirty Years' War. He laid the foundation of royal absolutism that flowered in age of Louis XIV.

Maximilian Robespierre (1758–1794). Lawyer and leader during French Revolution. He was a member of the Estates General, the Constituent Assembly (1789–1791), the National Convention (1792–1799), and the Jacobin Club. During the Reign of Terror, he was head of the Committee of Public Safety (1793–1794). He fell from power in the summer of 1794 and was executed by guillotine. He is still a very controversial figure.

Charles Maurice de Tallyrand-Périgord (1754–1838). Prelate and diplomat during the French Revolution. He served as Bishop of Autun in 1788, was a member of the Estates General (1789) and the Constituent Assembly, and head of the Constitutional Clergy (which favored the Revolution). While Napoleon's minister of foreign affairs (1799–1807), he was dismissed for conspiracy. At the Congress of Vienna (1814–1815), he ensured that France would not suffer dismemberment.

Adolph Thiers (1797–1877). Politician, journalist, historian, newspaper editor. He served as prime minister (1836–1840) and a member of the National Assembly (1848–1851), but was banished by Napoleon III. He later returned to parliament (1863). After the fall of the Second Empire (1870), as president, he concluded a peace treaty with Prussia and crushed the Paris Commune (1871). He resisted monarchal restoration, a decisive moment in the establishment of the Third Republic.

Maurice Thorez (1900–1964). Leader of French Communist party (1932–1964). He guided the rapid expansion of the Popular Front (1934–1938) and reaped the benefits of Communist resistance in World War II. By 1946 the party had gained 28 percent of the vote. In the 1950s and early 1960s, however, unimaginative leadership, in an era of unprecedented economic prosperity, resulted in the party's stagnation. He was liberal on culture and open to an alliance with the Socialists.

Pope Urban II (1042–1099). Pope (1088–1099). As pope, he launched the First Crusade against the Muslims in Jerusalem. Born in eastern France, Urban announced the crusade at the Council of Clermont (1095). His call to arms was received especially enthusiastically in France.

Vercingetorix (72–46 B.C.E.). Gallic chief and general. As head of the Arvernian tribe in what is today the Auvergne region of the Massif Central in south central France, he was decisively defeated by Julius Caesar at Alesia (in modern Burgundy) in 51 B.C.E. Put in chains and displayed as a trophy in Rome he was subsequently strangled. He became a cultural hero in the nineteenth century.

Saint Vincent de Paul (c. 1580–1660). Last great saint of the Catholic Counter-Reformation. Inspired, in part, by Saint Francis de Sales, he devoted his life to training priests and undertaking charitable work. He created the Ladies of Charity (1617) and the Congregation of the Mission (1625) to alleviate suffering and poverty. Both of these institutions established numerous chapters in France and later throughout the world.

Pierre Waldeck-Rousseau (1846–1904). Politician and lawyer. As the longest running prime minister during the Third Republic (1899–1904), he headed a government of Republican defense during the Dreyfus affair. A new law on associations (1901) expanded freedoms for lay associations, especially those for the working class, but limited those for Catholics, a prelude to separation of Church and state (1906).

Émile Zola (1840–1902). Late nineteenth-century novelist. The developer and champion of the "naturalist novel," he was dedicated to the scientific study of human conditions. He championed Alfred Dreyfus, the French officer of Jewish heritage accused of spying for the Germans. Zola's article, "I Accuse" (*J'accuse*, 1898) helped ensure Dreyfus's eventual liberation from prison on Devil's Island, his retrial, and eventual exoneration.

Bibliographic Essay

The list of histories of France is almost endless, but the books discussed below provide a diverse and profitable elaboration on the themes outlined in this book. Colin Jones, *The Cambridge Illustrated of France* (London: Cambridge University Press, 1994), has a superb narrative and excellent illustrations; John Ardagh, with Colin Jones, *Cultural Atlas of France* (New York: Facts on File, 1991), is good on regions; G. Bertier de Sauvigny and David Pinkney, *History of France*, rev. and enl. ed. (Arlington Heights, Ill.: Forum Press, 1983), is strong on French history before 1789; Gordon Wright, *France in Modern Times: From the Enlightenment to the Present* (New York: W. W. Norton, 1995), is a classic; Jeremy D. Popkin, *A History of Modern France* (Englewood Cliffs, N.J.: Prentice Hall, 1994, new ed. 2000), provides the best recent survey; Maurice Agulhon, *The French Republic, 1879–1992*, trans. Antonia Nevill (Oxford: Blackwell, 1993), is a perceptive overview by one of the best contemporary historians in France.

Personal but very stimulating interpretations of French history include the two-volume studies written by Fernand Braudel, *The Identity of France*, trans. Siân Reynolds (New York: Harper & Row, 1988 and New York: Harper-Collins, 1990) and Theodore Zeldin, *France 1848–1945*, vol.

1, *Ambition, Love and Politics*, and vol. 2, *Intellect, Taste and Anxiety* (Oxford: Clarendon Press, 1973, 1977).

Two of the best concise short histories, respectively, of the French Revolution and Napoleon are Jeremy D. Popkin, *A Short History of the French Revolution*, 2d ed. (Upper Saddle River, N.J.: Prentice Hall, 1998), and David C. Chandler, *The Illustrated Napoleon* (New York: Henry Holt, 1990). Both also contain good bibliographies for further reading.

As far as French history, politics, and society since World War II, Robert Gildea's *France Since 1945* (Oxford: Oxford University Press, 1997) is informative. For contemporary Paris, see Daniel Noin and Paul White, *Paris* (Chichester, N.Y.: John Wiley & Sons, 1997); for an up-to-date analysis and exposition of French politics, see William Safran, *The French Polity*, 5th ed. (New York: Longman, 1998), Nick Hewlett, *Modern French Politics: Analysing Conflict and Consensus Since 1945* (Cambridge: Polity Press, 1998), and Vincent Wright, *The Government and Politics of France* (London: Routledge, 1989).

The study of gender has recently become a prime topic in French history. Three exemplary studies are Robert A. Nye, *Masculinity and Male Codes of Honor in Modern France* (New York: Oxford University Press, 1993), Mary Louis Roberts, *Civilization Without Sexes: Reconstructing Gender in Postwar France, 1917–1927* (Chicago: University of Chicago Press, 1994), and Jeffrey Merrick and Bryant T. Ragan Jr., eds., *Homosexuality in Modern France* (New York: Oxford University Press, 1996).

Readers wishing concise overviews of all aspects of French history since the French Revolution should consult the multiple volumes of the Historical Dictionaries of French History series published by Greenwood Press, including the following:

Historical Dictionary of the French Revolution, 1789–1799, ed. Samuel F. Scott and Barry Rothaus

Historical Dictionary of Napoleonic France, 1799–1815, ed. Owen Connelly

Historical Dictionary of France from the 1815 Restoration to the Second Empire, ed. Edgar Leon Newman

Historical Dictionary of the French Second Empire, 1852–1870, ed. William E. Echard

Historical Dictionary of the Third French Republic, 1870–1940, ed. Patrick H. Hutton

Historical Dictionary of World War II France: The Occupation, Vichy, and the Resistance, 1938–1946, ed. Bertram M. Gordon

Historical Dictionary of the French Fourth and Fifth Republics, 1946–1991, ed. Wayne Northcutt.

The best source for books, articles, and doctoral dissertations on all aspects of French history is the journal *French Historical Studies*. At the back of each issue is a detailed bibliography covering each of these areas.

Finally, French history and society—both in English and in French—can now be accessed easily on hundreds of sites on the Internet and the World Wide Web. Below is a list of English language web sites of interest to historians of France compiled and annotated by Bertram M. Gordon, the former moderator of the listserv group of French historians, H-France. Although primarily in English, these web sites may have material in French or direct students to French language web sites.

1. H-France: http://h-net2.msu.edu/~france/welcome.html. H-France is an electronic/Internet newsletter for those interested in all periods of French culture and history. It is part of a larger network, H-Net, which includes some 70 lists in various specialties of history and culture (see http://www.h-net.msu.edu/lists/). One of the H-Net lists, H-Français, focuses on history and geography and is in French. H-France publishes book reviews which are archived on its web site. Its web site is also linked to additional resources that focus on French culture and history.

2. The History of France: Web Resources:http://www.hnet.msu.edu/~france/history.html. Written by Ran Raider, The History of France: Web Resources is now linked to H-France. It links to some 40 additional sites on a wide variety of topics related to French history and culture. Most are in English, but some are in French. Examples include "History of Paris," "Hundred Years' War," and "Directory of Royal Genealogical Data." Several sites are devoted to the 1789 Revolution, Napoleon, and the two world wars of the twentieth century. Caution: not all the sites are operational.

3. Histoire de France: http://instruct1.cit.cornell.edu/Courses/french _history/. Although the title is in French, the site uses both English and French. It was developed and is maintained by Jacques Béreaud and Jeremy Paquette. Béreaud is a professor of French in the Department of Romance Studies at Cornell University. Paquette is currently a French Area Studies major. Histoire de France has links to a large number of

web sites, arranged by chronological periods, beginning with the Middle Ages and extending to the present. There are also sections on "générM-ités" and "cinema."

4. Netscape Special Collections: The Siege and Commune of Paris: http://www.library.nwu.edu/spec/siege/. This highly specialized web site, using materials from the Special Collections of the Deering Library at Northwestern University (Evanston, Illinois), contains links to more than 1,200 digitized photographs and images from the Siege and Commune of Paris of 1870 and 1871. The collection also holds some 1,500 caricatures, 68 newspapers in hard-copy and film, hundreds of books and pamphlets, and about 1,000 posters. The illustrations are especially useful for presentations to students.

5. A History of the Condé and the Conti Families:http://www.ping.be/~pin12133/conde/english.htm. This web site, created by Denis Van den Broeck (pin12133@ping.be), is in English and French. It is lavishly illustrated with pictures of prominent members of the Condé and Conti families. It is linked to short biographies of each of these figures. These biographies are helpful in offering the basic facts for beginning students and for the pictures, which show something of aristocratic life in early modern France.

6. The World War I Document Archive: http://www.lib.byu.edu/~rdh/wwi/. This is an excellent source for World War I. Although most of its contents relate to countries other than France, there is considerable material of interest about France in the official papers, documents (arranged by year), memorials, personal reminiscences, biographical dictionary, and special topics. The World War I Document Archive also has links to other sites. Parts of it are still in preparation. This site is organized by the Great War Primary Document Archive, a nonprofit organization dedicated to the encouragement of the collection, preservation, and development in electronic form of materials relating to World War I.

7. *New York Times*: http://www.nytimes.com/. Coverage of current events in France is probably more thorough in the *New York Times* than in any other mass-circulation American newspaper. One may also search the archives of the newspaper.

8. Napoleon Series, http://www.historyserver.org/napoleon.series/. This web site covers Napoleon's life, career, and reputation.

Index

About the Author

W. SCOTT HAINE is a resident scholar of Holy Names College, Oakland, California.